change wars

Solution Tree

Cover Design by Grannan Design, Ltd.

Printed in the United States of America

ISBN: 978-1-934009-31-4

Acknowledgments

We extend our gratitude to our 11 colleagues who joined us in this volume, all of whom made it a priority to craft their current change theories-in-action for inclusion here. The result is a powerful array of many of the best active and applied practical theories and strategies to achieve large-scale education reform available in the world. All of these theories are grounded in the realities of the educational change wars taking place across the globe.

We also pay tribute to Solution Tree, its president Jeff Jones, and his staff. Our experience was high quality from beginning to end as the staff worked under tight timelines turning complexity into virtue. A special thanks to Gretchen Knapp and Suzanne Kraszewski who worked with us virtually every day.

—Andy Hargreaves and Michael Fullan

Table of Contents

About the Editors

Andy Hargreaves and Michael Fullan

 Andy Hargreaves, Ph.D., is the Thomas More Brennan Chair in Education in the Lynch School of Education at Boston College. Previously, he was the founder and codirector of the International Centre for Educational Change at the Ontario Institute for Studies in Education at the University of Toronto. Until he moved to North America in 1987, Dr. Hargreaves taught primary school and lectured in several English universities, including Oxford. He has held visiting professorships and fellowships in England, Australia, Sweden, Spain, the United States, Hong Kong, and Japan. He was awarded the Canadian Education Association/ Whitworth 2000 Award for outstanding contributions to educational research in Canada. His book *Teaching in the Knowledge Society: Education in the Age of Insecurity* (2003) received outstanding writing awards from the American Educational Research Association and the American Library Association. Dr. Hargreaves initiated and coordinated the editing of the *International Handbook of Educational Change* (1998). His most recent books are *Sustainable Leadership* (2006) with Dean Fink and *The Fourth Way* (ASCD,

2009) with Dennis Shirley. He is founding editor-in-chief of the *Journal of Educational Change.* Dr. Hargreaves' work has been translated extensively into more than a dozen languages. His current research interests include the emotions of teaching and leading and the sustainability of change and leadership in education, business, sport, and health.

Michael Fullan, Ph.D., is professor emeritus at the Ontario Institute for Studies in Education at the University of Toronto and special adviser on education to Dalton McGuinty, the Premier of Ontario. He served as dean of the Faculty of Education at the University of Toronto from 1988 to 2003, leading two major organizational transformations including a merger of two large schools of education. He is currently working as adviser-consultant on several major education reform initiatives around the world.

Michael Fullan bases his work on the moral purpose of education as it is applied in schools and school systems to bring about major improvements. He has written several best sellers that have been translated into many languages. His latest books include *The New Meaning of Educational Change* (4th edition, 2007) and *The Six Secrets of Change: What the Best Leaders Do to Help Their Organizations Survive and Thrive* (2008).

Introduction

Change Wars: A Hopeful Struggle

Andy Hargreaves and Michael Fullan

Anyone who tries to change something in the world, their colleagues, or themselves has a theory of how to bring about that change. This theory may be implicit or explicit, reflectively aware or blindly willful, but it is a theory of change-in-action that is driven by knowledge, experience, beliefs, and assumptions concerning how and why people change, and what can motivate or support them to do so.

Our popular television culture thrives on sensationalizing particular theories of change-in-action. Soccer-player-turned-celebrity-chef Gordon Ramsay revitalizes failing restaurants by performing an initial evaluation, stipulating the changes that are needed, publicly humiliating the staff (whom he blames for poor performance), coaching them in new culinary or hospitality skills, then berating them once more when they backslide. England's Supernanny uses a similar blend of support wrapped up in exaggerated strictness to transform misbehaving children and their misdirected parents through straight talking, structured routines, consistent enforcement, and the occasional use of the "naughty chair." American talk show host Dr. Phil, meanwhile, expresses more explicit empathy, but he still retains enough no-nonsense confrontation with his guests to keep viewers tuning in.

In reality, few people really change unless, at some point, they see the need to do so. It is by no means clear whether the strict and spectacular turnaround strategies of reality television are endorsed by their subjects because they feel they have reached the far end with their own obvious failures, or because of the fortune or fame that televised humiliation will bring them. In other walks of life far away from the media spotlight, fear or force may bring temporary lifts in performance, but it rarely secures deep or lasting change.

Theories of change-in-action abound in education. In the innovation era, it was thought that large and impressive projects in math, science, or social science would change teachers' practice with the benefit of some good materials, well-written teachers' guides, and an orientating workshop or two, but too much emphasis was placed on the material being used rather than on the characteristics and understandings of those using the material. Schools that manage to break the mold and turn around dramatically are often driven by charismatic leaders, and their success cannot be sustained once the leaders leave. Pilot projects are often meant to go further and develop promising practices while ironing out wrinkles, but schools rarely succeed in securing ongoing resources or support, so pilot programs are usually taken to scale long before the results of the evaluation are in.

In schools, teachers might start an exciting new project with a few equally energetic colleagues, but they get stuck when trying to convert those who are more skeptical. The same problems arise when trying to spread innovative practices from a few beginners to a network of wider peers. Impatient principals might try changing the structure of the school by shrinking the number of departments or knocking down walls, but unpersuaded teachers retreat to their comfortable identities and make new walls out of shelves and cupboards. Many leaders emphasize trust and relationships as the foundation of change, but building them takes time that often runs out as leaders get noticed, promoted, or transferred elsewhere.

These examples by no means exhaust the theories of action with which teachers, leaders, and others operate in their schools and systems. All, however, have their limitations. Their effects are temporary, they do not spread, they benefit some at the expense of others, or they do not take into consideration the deep aspects of learning and teaching.

The problem is even greater in today's era of educational change where reforms proliferate, initiatives abound, legal responsibilities are constantly expanding, and both teachers and leaders complain constantly of overload. The challenge here is no longer just how to have a theory of action that can implement particular changes, but how to develop one that can choose between changes, prioritize them, and create coherence among all of them. This is as much a challenge for the teacher in the classroom, the principal in the office, and the policymaker in government. How do we do the right things well, not get distracted by the wrong things, involve and include everyone who is affected, keep the momentum and the impact going, and prevent burnout by ensuring the change agenda is manageable and coherent?

For some theorists of change-in-action, this is a question of brilliant design at the top so all the parts of change fit together in reform initiatives. For others, it is about designing cultures and systems so they can initiate, manage, and monitor worthwhile change themselves.

Working separately and sometimes together, we (the editors) have three quarters of a century of experience of studying, initiating, implementing, and evaluating educational change from the classroom frontier to the frameworks of policy. Over this period, our experiences of change and our understanding of the growing body of change knowledge have led us to develop and shift our own theories-in-action of educational change. Many of our insights and forms of knowledge of change are shared in common—the power of a compelling moral purpose, the importance of trust and relationships, the indispensability of teachers and leaders, and the need for progressive forms of assessment, to mention just a few. Some are areas of current difference and disagreement that we believe are necessary to discuss and debate on a continuing basis, for in the end, we each care about the moral purpose of high-quality and inclusive public education and the importance of struggling as best we can to improve it.

We sometimes differ about what the content of change should be, about the importance of achievement targets and whether they should be shared or imposed, about the relative distribution of top-down or bottom-up control, about the particular expression of lateral change strategies, and about whether school leadership should appear early or late in change designs. Despite our differences, we are part of the same change family and its compelling narrative of improvement and justice—supporting each other when we can and challenging each other when we must. This book is an extension and externalization of this debate.

The Leading Edge™ series unites education authorities from around the globe and asks them to confront the important issues that affect teachers and administrators. The first book in the series, *On Common Ground*, brought together leading educators and researchers to address the imperative of professional learning communities. The second book in the series, *Ahead of the Curve*, brought thinkers, researchers, teachers, and writers together to wrestle with assessment issues. *Change Wars'* theory-in-action is to bring some of the leading thinkers and change agents together from across the world, to articulate, develop, and make explicit their own theories-in-action of educational change—the changes they want, why they want them, and how they believe they can be brought about and sustained. We agree with much of what follows in these pages, and we also disagree with aspects of the same material, and that is the point: for these highly influential change analysts and advocates to make clear the foundations on which their work rests.

In the end, our purpose is not to have merely a menu or a medley of change options, but to use these articulations of change theory-in-action to stimulate your own thoughts and reflections about the change strategies that underpin your efforts to improve the educational world. In the end, we may not get and should not get one universal change theory that transcends all people, situations, time, and space. But we will start to understand better how and why we approach change in the way we do, and even to find some areas of broad agreement that can bring us together while we continue to debate the differences.

Education is entirely about change—about drawing things out of people and creating the generations of the future. And effective change is inalienably about learning—figuring out the best way forward for the greatest good. In the past, competing theories of change-in-action—top-down or bottom-up, prescriptive or self-developed, politically or professionally driven—have divided people and set them against each other in wars over how to change the world and for what purpose. This book is designed not to intensify or prolong these wars, but to move beyond them by bringing the different arguments together in a common forum of stimulating and respectful debate. Change does not come passively or always peaceably. Sometimes positive change has to be something for which we fight together—not in a war against each other, but in a hopeful struggle against the odds of drift, despair, and despondency. Changing the world begins with a change in ourselves, and then with changes in one another. This book brings to the surface the theories of practice about how to do that. For in the end, there is nothing as practical as a good theory.

Chapter Overviews

In chapter 1, Andy Hargreaves describes the three stages of change in education, and then proposes The Fourth Way—an alternative path of change-in-action that can move education into an age of inspiration and sustainability with five pillars of purpose and partnership, three principles of professionalism, and four catalysts of coherence.

In chapter 2, Linda Darling-Hammond describes four approaches to school management and change: a bureaucratic approach, a professional approach, a market approach, and a democratic approach. She argues that the purposeful pursuit of a democratic and professional approach to change is essential for the kinds of goals that now confront education systems. She provides recommendations for how a democratic, professional vision for educational systems can be pursued in the service of schools that empower learners with deep knowledge and the ability to problem-solve, invent, and guide their own learning in ways that support greater equity and social justice for democratic societies.

In chapter 3, Sir Michael Barber describes three paradigms of public service reform—what he calls "21st-century solutions"—and gives examples of system improvement from around the world. He extends his argument with an analysis of the relationship between government and professions, a central issue in all education reform. He then draws conclusions both for government and for leaders of the teaching profession.

In chapter 4, Andreas Schleicher examines the merits of international comparative benchmarks as drivers for educational change. He begins by setting out a rationale and theory of action and then illustrates the role and functioning of international benchmarks with the example of the Programme for International Student Assessment (PISA), which the Organisation for Economic Co-operation and Development (OECD) launched in 2000 to monitor learning outcomes on a regular basis in the principal industrialized countries. Within less than a decade, international benchmarks such as PISA have established themselves as indispensable for reform in the field of education, which thus far has been conceived of as essentially domestic.

In chapter 5, Marc Tucker describes his experiences with industrial benchmarking to examine what makes education systems successful in countries across the world. He points out that there is great variation among nations in the ability of their students to do well on international assessments of student achievement, but surprisingly little of the variance in results can be explained by per capita education spending, gross domestic product per capita, or differences in instructional methods. Rather, a substantial amount of the variance can be explained by the design of education systems. He explores some examples of the differences in system design that account for the variations in national education performance and how researchers from the National Center on Education and the Economy find these variations through a seven-step process.

In chapter 6, Dennis Shirley discusses why American educators have turned against recent reforms, and he contends that to correct course, multiple strands of educational change need to be interwoven. He highlights the strands of change most important for long-term, sustainable learning: developing a focus on learning, signature practices, and a network of strategies merging bottom-up community organizing with top-down antipoverty programs. He then describes how the strands need to be embedded by multiple social sectors if they are to attain a truly systemic level of impact.

In chapter 7, Pedro Noguera describes the challenges immigrant students face and offers strategies for addressing the needs of these students in our school systems. He contends that educational theories that presume to be color-blind, theories of school change that are devoid of reference to immigration or race, and theories that are oblivious to cultural and transnational differences create barriers to achievement in schools. This chapter provides concrete recommendations to educational leaders about what they can do to play a positive and supportive role in helping their schools and the larger society adjust to inevitable demographic change.

In chapter 8, Jonathan Jansen, the first black dean of education at the former all-white University of Pretoria, uses examples from post-apartheid South Africa to underscore the complexity and contours of change and the roles of leaders within racially polarized institutions. He gives a brief overview of the change literature on emotion and explores the link between emotion and educational change. He then examines the challenges for leadership in divided societies and looks at how emotions configure within leadership that operates in a racial minefield. He offers seven platforms for thinking about a new politics of emotion in pursuing educational change in divided societies.

In chapter 9, James Spillane argues that in order to make a substantial contribution, research and development efforts must focus on the day-to-day *practice* of leadership and management, a focus that has been largely neglected in the field of school administration. He claims that if leadership and management research and development are to make a substantial difference in further educational reform, then school leaders must be central players in the work. Efforts to understand and develop practice must involve the twin processes of diagnosis and design, and a distributed perspective offers a rich framing for these processes.

In chapter 10, Richard Elmore examines the relationship between research and practice. He uses the example of his work in an urban school district characterized by all the issues of instructional quality and student performance that plague most urban school systems. He explores the deep disconnect between research and practice embedded in the culture of American schooling. He then explores the pathologies of "nested" systems and relates them to his own research and practice in an urban setting.

In chapter 11, Douglas Reeves discusses what we know but too rarely admit: Traditional change strategies are failing. First, he considers the elements of change: direction, speed, and scope. He then considers the essential balance between hierarchy and networks. Next, he presents the five levels of networks, giving examples of each level. Finally, he explores multidisciplinary examples of dynamic level-five change networks in action to learn what a school system, a global multibillion-dollar organization, and remarkable public health systems all have in common.

In chapter 12, Ben Levin discusses the shortcomings of large-scale reform efforts that are done to the system and why they do not have the desired effects. He then poses an alternative approach to generate real improvement in schools, to the benefit of students, that also creates greater energy and motivation among educators and support for students, parents, and the broader community. The strategy he describes has been implemented in Ontario, Canada, and has four key elements.

In chapter 13, Michael Fullan presents a theory of action for whole system improvement in education. The Theory of Action for System Change (TASC) has six components: direction and sector engagement, capacity-building linked to results, supportive infrastructure and leadership, managing the distractors, continuous evaluation and inquiry, and two-way communication. He describes the elements and underlying thinking of each component, and then he describes the framework's use since 2003 in the public school system of Ontario, Canada.

Andy Hargreaves

Dr. Andy Hargreaves is the Thomas More Brennan Chair in Education in the Lynch School of Education at Boston College. Previously, he was the founder and codirector of the International Centre for Educational Change at the Ontario Institute for Studies in Education at the University of Toronto. Until he moved to North America in 1987, Dr. Hargreaves taught primary school and lectured in several English universities, including Oxford. He has held visiting professorships and fellowships in England, Australia, Sweden, Spain, the United States, Hong Kong, and Japan. He was awarded the Canadian Education Association/Whitworth 2000 Award for outstanding contributions to educational research in Canada. His book *Teaching in the Knowledge Society: Education in the Age of Insecurity* (2003) received outstanding writing awards from the American Educational Research Association and the American Library Association. Dr. Hargreaves initiated and coordinated the editing of the *International Handbook of Educational Change* (1998). His most recent books are *Sustainable Leadership* (2006) with Dean Fink and *The Fourth Way* (ASCD, 2009) with Dennis Shirley. He is founding editor-in-chief of the *Journal of Educational Change*. Dr. Hargreaves' work has been translated extensively into more than a dozen languages. His current research interests include the emotions of teaching and leading and the sustainability of change and leadership in education, business, sport, and health.

In this chapter, the author describes the three stages of change in education, and then proposes The Fourth Way—an alternative path of change-in-action that can move education into an age of inspiration and sustainability. This theory-in-action consists of five pillars of purpose and partnership, three principles of professionalism, and four catalysts of coherence.

To learn more about Dr. Andy Hargreaves and his work, visit www.andyhargreaves.com. He can be reached at hargrean@bc.edu.

Chapter 1

The Fourth Way of Change: Towards an Age of Inspiration and Sustainability

Andy Hargreaves

At the end of the 20th century, Anthony Giddens wrote an influential book—*The Third Way: The Renewal of Social Democracy* (1999)—that challenged prevailing thinking and inspired a shift in direction in social policy. *The Third Way* proposed extensive state investment in the welfare, medicine, transportation, and energy resources, housing, municipal services, pensions, and education that had characterized the 3 decades following World War II. It called for full or partial privatization of these services along with market competition for and among clients and providers. Giddens argued that despite providing social services and opportunities for everyone, the social state had expanded far beyond what its creators had first envisaged. It had become unsustainably expensive and fostered long-term dependency and even irresponsibility among hard-core recipients. The market, meanwhile, had promoted individual initiative and responsibility, but also made social safety nets unacceptably threadbare and created self-centered cultures of individualism and divisiveness.

Giddens describes how professions once had great freedom and autonomy (The First Way), and then became more subject to government interference and market forces (The Second Way). In order to further the goals of economic prosperity and an inclusive social democracy, he argued, The Third Way promised a more creative combination of public, private, and voluntary solutions—top-down leadership with bottom-up support and professional engagement that did not extend to unrestricted license.

In practice, much of what has passed for The Third Way has been a new kind of autocratic and all-seeing state that has used technological and data-driven self-surveillance along with lateral professional interactions to deliver unchanging government goals. The result has been a shift from a theory-in-action of change as represented in Figure 1 (The Second Way) to a modified orthodoxy of change (or Third Way) in Figure 2. This signifies progress, but there has also been missed opportunity to develop more courageous and creative strategies that engage and inspire the public and the profession to promote the good of all.

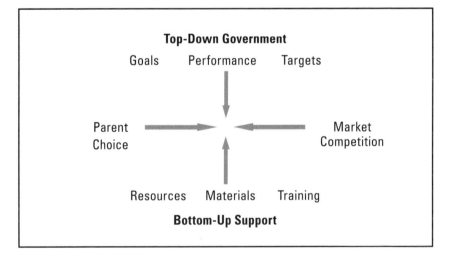

Figure 1: The Second Way

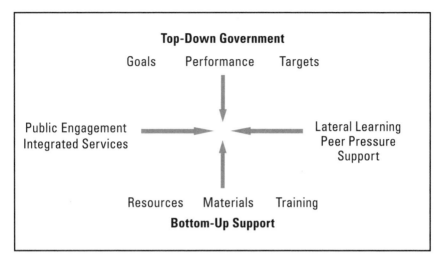

Figure 2: The Third Way

Building on past legacies and comparative success in various countries around the world, I propose an alternative path of change-in-action that can and should move us into an age of inspiration and sustainability. This Fourth Way brings together government policy with professional involvement and public engagement around an inspiring social and educational mission (Figure 3).

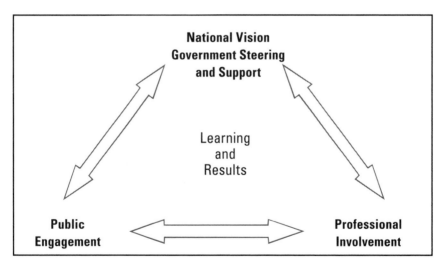

Figure 3: The Fourth Way

In a study of long-term change spanning more than 3 decades in eight innovative and traditional high schools in the United States and Canada (Hargreaves, 2003; Hargreaves & Fink, 2006; Hargreaves & Goodson, 2006), my colleagues and I found that the schools we studied had passed through three stages of change—optimism and innovation, complexity and contradiction, and standardization and marketization—that correspond with the three ways. I will begin with an overview of these stages, along with an examination of the transitional periods that arose between them. Then I propose The Fourth Way—an alternative path of change-in-action that can move education into an age of inspiration and sustainability. This theory-in-action consists of five pillars of purpose and partnership, three principles of professionalism, and four catalysts of coherence.

The First Way

From the 1960s to the late 1970s, a generation of young and enthusiastic teachers worked in an era of optimism and innovation for which many are now nostalgic. This period of economic expansion and state investment in initiatives such as America's War on Poverty legislation produced, in one teacher's words, "a golden age of education [where] there was money and respect and all kinds of things happening."

There are two nostalgias for this First Way. Teachers in more innovative schools are nostalgic for the freedom and flexibility to develop curriculum with attention to varying student needs as part of a mission to change the world. This mission was captured by the social justice–driven spirit of a time when social reform, the quest for women's equality, antiwar protests, and the struggle for civil rights were prominent. This group feels that the current standardized environment of high-stakes testing and a prescribed narrow curriculum stole this broader mission from them. Teachers in more traditional schools are also nostalgic for their lost professional autonomy, but they long to teach academic subjects as they choose, in schools that are smaller, where unmotivated students typically leave early for employment, and the rest want to learn.

The First Way highlighted freedom and flexibility, but it also created huge variations in focus and quality due to the lottery of leadership among individual school principals. The theories of change-in-action during this First Way could inspire innovation and even spread it among enthusiasts; however, the skills taught in teacher education rested more on intuition and ideology than on evidence, and there was no leadership development to create any consistency of impact or effort.

The Interregnum

After The First Way, a transitional period set in—an interregnum of complexity and contradiction. From the late 1970s to the mid 1990s, a declining economy quelled the thirst for innovation while encouraging a focus on market-driven competition among schools. Common educational standards and assessments (around which competition would be based) emerged as a way to create more coherence across the system. At the same time, people continued to preserve some of the ideals of The First Way. The results were complex and often contradictory.

Outcomes-based education and standards-based reform tried to build common understandings of and commitments to more challenging learning, but teachers struggled to translate these guidelines into practice. Portfolio assessments were paralleled by standardized tests, interdisciplinary initiatives ran alongside subject-based standards, and selective magnet schools also had to include students with special needs.

The theory of change-in-action was designed to increase standards and develop higher order knowledge by getting teachers and schools to address them together, while leaving enough room for intelligent professional judgment and interpretation in practice. The more innovative schools that had leaders who could help teachers interpret the complexity succeeded in maintaining their missions while still addressing the standards. The traditional schools, however, drifted into decline as their leaders overprotected their staffs and shielded them from the reform requirements until it was too late. This theory-in-action lacked investment in the systemwide professional development and leadership development that were required to build the strong and intelligent learning communities that could interpret the standards and define their purposes together (Hargreaves, Earl, Moore, & Manning, 2001).

The Second Way

Frustration with years of inconsistency, coupled with political and public nostalgia for tradition, competition, and certainty, helped propel many nations into a strident Second Way of standardization and market competition in the mid-1990s through the mid-2000s. In this period, many Anglo-Saxon governments with lesser or greater degrees of resources and support, witnessed the imposition of prescriptive and sometimes punitive reforms such as the following:

- Increased competition between schools fuelled by public rankings of high-stakes test and exam results

- Prescribed, paced, and sometimes scripted curriculum content in more narrowly defined areas and goals of learning

- Armies of literacy coaches along with periodic inspections and management walkthroughs to boost skill development and enforce classroom compliance

- Political targets and timetables for delivering improved results

- Sanctions such as involuntary teacher transfers, principal removal, or even school closure because of persistent failure

- Teacher training that increasingly moved away from the academy towards on-the-job training in schools
- Replacement of broad professional development by inservice training on government priorities

The paradox of this Second Way was that while parent consumers experienced freedom, professionals were subjected to greater control. Some feel The Second Way promoted a sense of urgency, attended to all students, increased teachers' skill levels, secured public support for educational investment, and moved the profession in a common and accountable direction. Others claim the goals could have been achieved by less negative means. Whatever the case, there is growing agreement that the strategy of standardization has been exhausted.

The Second Way of fear, force, prescription, competition, and intervention set a clear direction and could produce temporary lifts in measured achievement results, but it could not sustain them for more than a year or two. Moreover, the costs to the quality, depth, and breadth of learning—as well as to the sheer enjoyment in learning—were considerable. Student dropout increased, and teacher innovation declined. Also impacted was the caliber of teachers and leaders the profession could recruit and retain. The Second Way of standardization increased coherence, certainty, and accountability, but at the price of innovation, motivation, and creativity.

The Third Way

The limits of The Second Way have begun to herald in a new age or Third Way of post-standardization. The demands of knowledge economies call for more innovation and creativity (Hargreaves, 2003). The crisis of professional recruitment and retention makes it hard to maintain the emphasis on prescription and compliance. But in recent decades, many governments have become used to feeling in control. Therefore, while the paths emerging from the dark thicket of standardization point towards many new destinations of innovation, creativity, and professional engagement, their routes are nonetheless defined by the old imposed coordinates of targets and testing in literacy and mathematics. Three paths are intertwining to define this new orthodoxy or Third Way of post-standardization: autocracy, technocracy, and effervescence.

The Path of Autocracy

The path of autocracy acknowledges that new problems are emerging, including the need for a more innovative school system and economy. However, with one final surge, those who walk this path redouble their imposition of old, failed solutions by saying they were not pursued ruthlessly enough in the first place, and that more market competition between schools and teachers and tighter regulation in the areas of tested mathematics and literacy are still the only answer (Barber, 2007; New Commission on the Skills of the American Workforce, 2007).

The Path of Technocracy

The path of technocracy converts moral issues of inequality and social justice that are a shared social responsibility into technical calculations of achievement gaps for which teachers and schools are solely accountable. It invests faith in ever-increasing testing and voluminous amounts of numerical data collection so its Orwellian system can see everything, know everyone, and judge just when and where to intervene with any student, school, or classroom, at any time.

In the words of Michel Foucault—the ultimate authority on the surveillance society—"the constant pressure acts even before the offences, mistakes or crimes have been committed" (1977, p. 206). Schools do not just react to targets, testing, and adequate yearly progress, but they anticipate and prepare for them, scrutinizing and reorienting every program, curriculum choice, workshop, coaching session, and teaching strategy in order to accommodate them.

In any profession, practice and improvement should be guided by an intelligent conversation between hard evidence and intuitive judgment. Yet in systems of statistical surveillance, hastily assembled teams are driven by data in cultures of anxiety about instant results in tested subjects (namely literacy and mathematics). Data-driven instruction ends up driving educators to distraction.

The Path of Effervescence

The path of effervescence solves the motivation deficits created by top-down standardization by stimulating and spreading increased professional engagement and interaction. In these systems, schools learn from other schools, which can be an empowering and effective way to approach improvement. But in practice, what often transpires is a hyperactive professionalism where educators rush around, energetically and enthusiastically delivering the government's narrowly defined targets and purposes, rather than also developing and realizing inspiring purposes of their own.

In England, the Raising Achievement/Transforming Learning (RATL) project has devised an improvement model for more than 300 secondary schools that promotes improvement with peer-driven networks of lateral pressure and support. These networks:

- Combine the outside-in knowledge of experts at conferences with inside-out knowledge from successful and experienced practitioners working with less successful schools in transparent processes (not just outcomes) of assistance and support.

- Make mentor schools available to lower performing peers in lateral cultures of transparent improvement without mandating the details of the relationships.

- Supply modest resourcing to facilitate improvement and interaction.

- Provide practical menus of short-term, medium-term, and long-term strategies for improvement and transformation that have a practical record of proven success.

My joint evaluation of this network (Hargreaves & Shirley, in press-a; Hargreaves, Shirley, Evans, Johnson, & Riseman, 2006) reveals that two thirds of the schools improved at double the rate of the national secondary school average within 2 years. Yet it also shows that these laterally driven improvement processes are still constrained by the negative legacies of standardization in the surrounding policy environment—in the unrelenting emphasis on standardized test scores and targets in basic subjects, in short-term cycles of project funding, in hit-and-run inspections that over-rely on printed achievement data rather than direct observation to assess satisfactoriness, and in endless waves of short-term government initiatives. Despite the efforts of project leaders, most of the "collective effervescence" of energy is directed towards hurriedly and excitedly adopting short-term strategies to deliver existing forms of achievement rather than towards longer term attempts to transform teaching and learning (Hartley, 2007, p. 211).

A New Orthodoxy

This new orthodoxy of The Third Way that is coming to define the age of post-standardization integrates autocracy, technocracy, and effervescence. In this theory-in-action, a guiding governmental coalition defines the goals and targets in tested mathematics and literacy—even if the country or province is already one of the world's highest performers in these areas. But new means are employed to deliver the old political objectives. Data-driven improvement introduces a technocratic system of anticipatory surveillance where educators' energies are directed towards designing precise interventions that focus on meeting the next target, test, or outside inspection. School networks, SWAT teams of advice and support that abseil into schools with increasing urgency as the testing dates draw closer, and what Richard Sennett (1998) terms the "turnstile world of transient teamwork," introduce collective effervescence into swift exchanges and examinations of achievement data and improvement strategies to boost results and reverse the motivation deficits of standardization. The government's goals and targets are no longer imposed upon teachers but are instead delivered by educators themselves through self-surveillance and emotional effervescence.

The Legacy

The theory of change-in-action underpinning each way of educational change has its fatal flaws. But in eradicating the flaws, some real strengths can too easily be discarded as well. The spirit of innovation and flexibility of The First Way can restore the capacity of teachers to create much of their own curriculum and rekindle the inspiration of world-changing social and educational missions that bind teachers together and connect them to ideals beyond themselves. From the Interregnum, we can take the guiding power of broadly defined common standards and the technical advances of portfolio and performance assessments that began to make assessment part of learning. Even The Second Way of standardization has bequeathed a sense of urgency about standards and equity; drawn attention to the needs of all students in every school; improved the quality of some skill-specific training, coaching, and teaching; and highlighted the benefits of using achievement data to inform teachers' judgments and interventions. Finally, while the educational realization of The Third Way has departed from and distorted some of its highest ideals, it has also purged the shame that characterized The Second Way, increased resources for and confidence in public education, developed a more sophisticated evidence base for improvement, gained more support and recognition for the teaching profession, and stimulated professional learning, improvement, and support across schools. These legacies provide the foundation for the way ahead: The Fourth Way.

The Fourth Way

The theory-in-action of The Fourth Way has much in common with the new orthodoxy of educational change, but some of the elements are understood and implemented differently, and additional ones take a very different direction. This theory-in-action consists of five pillars of purpose and partnership, three principles of professionalism, and four catalysts of coherence.

Five Pillars of Purpose and Partnership

A viable theory-in-action of educational change must rest on the basic principles of sustainability. To sustain means not merely to maintain or endure, but also to hold up or bear the weight of something (Hargreaves & Fink, 2006). What ultimately bears the weight of sustainable educational change is not an overarching set of government policies and interventions, but people working together as partners around shared and compelling purposes. Sustainable educational change, therefore, rests on five pillars of purpose and partnership.

Pillar 1: An inspiring and inclusive vision. The most important and indispensable element of any theory-in-action of change is a compelling moral purpose. Finland ranks number 1 and 2 in the world in literacy, mathematics, and science among 15-year-old students, according to the influential Organisation for Economic Co-operation and Development Programme for International Student Assessment (OECD PISA) tables. It also ranks top in economic competitiveness and corporate transparency. In 2007, I took a team to Finland for OECD to report on the relationship between leadership and school improvement (Hargreaves, Halász, & Pont, 2007). One way Finland achieves its remarkable results is through a bold and inclusive vision that unites and energizes its people.

After high unemployment due to the loss of its Russian market in the early 1990s, Finland decentralized its educational system to help it become a more creative knowledge economy. The country's prime minister, university presidents, and corporate CEOs meet regularly to steer it toward its high-tech future. But most of the coherence comes from a common and inspiring vision that connects Finland's innovative technological future to its creative, craft-like past.

Elsewhere, during the age of optimism and innovation, many were drawn into teaching by a spirit of freedom and social justice that defined the world in which they came of age. Most Anglo-Saxon countries have now lost this sense of missionary purpose. They have defaulted to individualistic and self-protective goals of being strong and prosperous (Ontario), becoming an ownership society (United States), offering opportunity and security (Britain), or aspiring to world-class standards (all of them). None of these purposes are inclusively inspirational.

An inspiring and inclusive moral purpose steers a system, binds it together, and draws the best people to work in it. Literacy is sometimes such a purpose and should always be an educational priority. But it is not always the right reform priority—especially when schools and nations are already high performers in it, or when it sidelines other areas that need more attention. Nor can everything be achieved through literacy. For instance, while Canada ranks very high on tested literacy achievement as a measure of educational well-being, it performs very poorly in self, family, and peer-related or health-based well-being (UNICEF, 2007).

Raising the bar in tested literacy is too narrow a goal. If the posts that define the goal are too close together, the bar will eventually topple. Widen the goal posts too much, though, and the bar will sag. The challenge is to address more than one thing without doing everything at once.

What the inspiring mission might be should and will vary. It may be women's education in underdeveloped countries, learning to live together in post-conflict societies, or perhaps science, the arts, innovation, citizenship, or the United Nation's Education for

Sustainable Development initiative elsewhere. But there should not be one roaming and easily actionable solution—like literacy—just because it is the most politically convenient, whatever the context might be.

Pillar 2: Public engagement. The purposes that define a society's future vision are not for governments or their educational advisors to decide. They are a matter for public engagement and for leaders who can tap into and elevate the public's spirit. A good place to start is with a "Great Public Debate" about the future of education, say in 2020. This public engagement involves more than consulting a few focus groups, or including elite representatives in decision-making. It includes but also extends far beyond parent involvement. Instead, town by town, city by city, this debate should re-energize interest in public education.

Anxiety without information makes people nostalgic for the past, turns them against progress and change, and leads them to clutch at the straws of test scores as substitutes for richer relationships. Public engagement in education combats nostalgia by increasing involvement and understanding. Public engagement occurs one parent and community member at a time through a host of initiatives. These can include highlighting successes from local public schools in the media; contacting parents when their children are doing well and before problems occur; holding three-way parent meetings that involve teacher, parent, and child and reviewing portfolios of work together; and sharing data openly with the community so problems can be solved together. Open professionalism that includes the public builds awesome schools.

School quality can also benefit from political activism. For example, parents and students at one of the innovative schools in the Change Over Time study paraded in straitjackets outside the district office to protest the increased testing that threatened the richness of the learning in their school. Government is not always effective or always right. A vigorous public sphere guards against its excesses.

Pillar 3: No achievement without investment. The turn of the 21st century was marked by a shift from a shared social responsibility to support and create better opportunities for the poor, to an expectation that schools and teachers should raise all students' achievement and narrow the gaps between them entirely by themselves. The discourse of equality has degenerated into a demand to close numerical achievement gaps. Responsibility has been lifted from the wider community and placed exclusively on the schools. Too often we hear the mantras, "There are no excuses! Failure is not an option!"

However, years of research in school effectiveness still show that most of the explanation for differences in student outcomes exists outside the school, in families, communities, and society (Nichols & Berliner, 2007). Schools can and do make a significant difference, but not all or even most of it. They cannot excel alone; they need communities and society to work with them.

There is no achievement without investment. High-performing Finland and other Nordic countries benefit from a welfare state that makes strong public investment not just in education, but in housing, medical care, social services, and community development. While schools contribute a great deal, they are not expected to achieve miracles by themselves.

The British Building Schools for the Future initiative invests in rebuilding all the secondary schools in some of the country's most troubled towns and cities to use them as a point of community regeneration as well as to combat racism. In the United States, full-service schools integrate many welfare, health, early-childhood, lifelong-learning, public-library, and law-enforcement services all at one site.

Finally, greater professional accountability must be matched by increased parental responsibility. As Barack Obama urges, we must turn off the TV and the DVD and talk to children and play with them. Teachers cannot do everything. Parents must step up to the plate as well.

Pillar 4: Corporate educational responsibility. In the past, corporate partners in education have often been negligent, shallow, or self-seeking. Corporations have urged children's participation in skill-specific training for their benefit, not because it is best for the children. They have exploited children as captive consumers and peddled harmful products such as junk food as a trade for their investment. They have crowded critical thinking out of the curriculum by promoting programs that emphasize functional business communication rather than more rounded and critical language skills, for example.

The environmental movement has shifted many corporations' sense of responsibility. More and more businesses now practice corporate social responsibility. They take pride in where they rank on the Dow Jones Sustainability Indexes and in the practices that qualify them to be listed on it—reducing their emissions that affect the environment, improving the quality of work life for their employees, and contributing time and service to their communities (Hargreaves & Shaw, 2006). The businesses that get invited to participate in educational policymaking should be those that practice corporate social responsibility. Codes of practice already exist as a basis for business partnerships in many schools and districts. They now need to extend to the level of large-scale politics. Accountability between education and business should be mutual and transparent, not secret and one-sided.

Pillar 5: Students as partners in change. Students are usually the targets of change efforts and services; they are rarely change partners. But students are highly knowledgeable about the things that help them learn, such as teachers who know their material, care for them, have a sense of humor, and never give up on them. Finnish schools work very well in part because children are expected and prepared to be responsible from an early age. Most schools are remarkably calm and show respectful relationships between students and teachers. The innovative schools in our Change Over Time project also gave a prominent role to their students. Students must be a central part of any theory-in-action of educational change. Without students, there would be no teachers. They make up the biggest group in education, and their voices matter a lot.

Student involvement in change begins with the assessment *for* learning that develops student responsibility. This strategy allows them to plan their own learning, be more reflective about how they learn best, show their teachers how to help them, and enables them to negotiate next steps and set achievement targets with their teachers. Then they can help foster change in their peers by being involved in programs where they read to younger children, mentor struggling students, or stand up for children who are bullied.

Being partners in change also means being involved in school and district decision-making. This includes obvious areas such as contributing to the design of new behavior codes, but it also means being part of school-improvement planning, professional development days that focus on school change, the appointment of leaders in their schools, and—as in the case of Boston Public Schools—even negotiating teacher contracts.

Last but not least, if schools and school systems have a broader vision, and express it in their teaching and curriculum, their students will become more interested in and committed to changing the world. What better theory-in-action could there be than one that creates millions of change agents for the future?

Three Principles of Professionalism

Teachers are the ultimate arbiters of change. They are also often the initiators of change within their own schools and classrooms. The classroom door is the gateway to implementation or the drawbridge that holds it at bay. No theory-in-action of sustainable educational change can ignore or bypass the teacher. It must involve teachers not just in delivering pedagogical details, but also in determining the basic purposes of their work.

Principle 1: High-quality teachers. High-quality learning depends on high-quality and highly qualified teachers and teaching. Finnish teachers are attracted to the profession by their country's inspiring and inclusive vision that also accords high status to them as builders of their nation's future. Though teachers' pay in Finland is only at the OECD average, the profession is highly competitive, with just a 1-in-10 chance of acceptance. Retention is very high because conditions are good and teachers feel trusted. The Finns control quality at the most important point—the point of entry. Good working conditions, small class sizes, and cultures of trust and responsibility where schools are not subjected to constant interference ensure that this quality is not lost later on.

Supportive working conditions, sufficient pay, professional autonomy, and an inclusive educational and social mission are the foundations that support the development of high-quality teachers. Also, teacher training must be effective and properly accredited at a university standard that is becoming of a demanding profession. It should start late, after graduation, when highly motivated applicants are surer of their choices and when the probabilities of subsequent dropout are severely reduced. This increases quality, reduces training costs, and contributes to stability and sustainability within the system.

There are no quick fixes for creating quality teaching, such as sign-on bonuses or relabeling of qualifications. It is the mission, status, conditions, and rewards of the job as well as the quality and timing of training that matter most. This is how we get and keep the best teachers.

Principle 2: Powerful professionalism. Continuous professional learning helps retain teachers and further raises the standards of their work. A welcome part of the new orthodoxy of educational change is its increased attention to professional development. Two key areas in which this work can be extended are professional learning and professional standards.

Since the 1990s, most Anglo-Saxon countries have created self-regulating professional bodies in teaching, like those in medicine, law, or nursing, to register new members, deal with misconduct, play some role in teacher advocacy, and develop professional teaching standards. I was one of the group of 12 that created the Ontario College of Teachers and was responsible for designing its broad professional learning framework that extended beyond workshops and courses to include curriculum writing, engaging in inquiry, mentoring new teachers, or coaching colleagues, for example.

In The First Way, professional learning was individualized, scattered, and confused. From The Second Way of standardization to the emerging new orthodoxy, the emphasis on literacy and other basics has turned a focus into a fixation. Excessive proportions of professional learning time have been dedicated to inservice workshops for government priorities, supplemented by one-to-one coaching and visiting teams of specialists who offer support or enforce compliance. The Fourth Way, by contrast, supports a more diversified portfolio of professional learning that is guided by an inspiring and compelling mission, informed by the professional learning frameworks designed by self-regulating bodies and interpreted through local, distributed leadership in a culture of cooperation and responsibility, as schools and district communities determine their priorities together.

When self-regulating bodies were established, the promise of improved professional standards and increased professional recognition was considerable, but the results were disappointing. The most robust standards, recognized through peer review, were only evident in bodies with voluntary membership. Where membership was required, the standards were general and advisory, and only applied with any force to the profession's newest members (Hargreaves & Evans, 1997). Unions did not want the standards to be too specific and enforceable and to tread on their traditional turf. Governments like England's retained control over teaching standards, leaving professional bodies like the General Teaching Council with a role that was residual and symbolic. This was professionalism without power. By contrast, the Alberta Teachers' Association is pressing its provincial government to abandon the government's current accountability scheme for a Fourth Way solution that focuses on teacher-developed student assessment within professional standards of practice for which teachers are responsible—using lateral professional energy not to bolster government control, but to engage powerful professional responsibility to raise standards together.

Principle 3: Lively learning communities. Although teachers are often enthusiastic innovators individually or in small groups, collectively, their record on sustainable improvement is no better than that of their government. Dan Lortie (1975) classically noted that the classroom isolation of teachers led them to develop a noninnovative culture of presentism, conservatism, and individualism. In response to this problem, widespread efforts, including my own, have been made to promote more teacher collaboration (Fullan & Hargreaves, 1992; Hargreaves, 1994).

Collaborative cultures are strongly associated with increased student success (Rosenholtz, 1989) and also with improved retention among new teachers (Johnson, 2004). They promote mutual learning and provide moral support through the difficulties of change.

Finnish teachers work in professional cultures of trust, cooperation, and responsibility on behalf of all children, not just those in their own classes.

However, collaborative cultures are not always connected to learning and achievement, and their existence and success depend heavily on the quality of school and district leadership in supporting and steering the collaborative effort. During The Second Way of standardization, collaborative cultures were driven underground as resource reductions and reform requirements took away time for teachers to meet, and increased prescription over curriculum and even pedagogy meant there was little left for teachers to collaborate about (Hargreaves, 2003). Teacher collaboration is resurfacing as part of the new orthodoxy in the professional learning community (PLC) concept (DuFour, Eaker, & DuFour, 2008). PLCs have sharpened collaborative cultures by adding a clear school focus and providing performance data to guide teachers' joint reflections, discussions, and decisions, and to connect them to student achievement.

While these innovations have inspired great gains, much has also been lost. Relationship-driven cultures of collaboration have been converted into formula technologies of specifying clear goals and conducting regular meetings to analyze performance data and develop intervention plans so as to meet the targets connected to those goals. Far too often, cultures of collaboration have turned into the worst kind of contrived collegiality (Hargreaves, 1994). However, as innovative schools in the Change Over Time project demonstrated, the best PLCs are not merely an assemblage of teams. They are living communities and lively cultures dedicated to improving the lifelong learning of students and adults where data inform but do not drive judgments about practice. All teachers engage in multiple learning teams to improve their practice, not just in mandated meetings that are directly connected to test results. Teachers and administrators define their focus and set targets together rather than the principal or district doing it for them. The PLC includes students, parents, and support staff as well as teachers. And members of the community care not just about the outcomes of their short-term teams, but about each other as people, because they are in a long-term relationship (Giles & Hargreaves, 2006; Hargreaves, 2003).

In Finland, teachers work together not just to deliver curriculum, but also to develop it. With the broad steering of the state, highly qualified teachers create curriculum together in each municipality. Indeed, Germany and the Nordic countries make no distinction between curriculum and pedagogy/instruction. In their tradition of didactics, how a curriculum is developed is inseparable from thinking about how it should be taught. It is time to recapture some of the spirit that characterized The First Way and the early years of the standards and outcomes movements and recreate cultures where teachers in PLCs design significant parts of their curriculum and make decisions about pedagogy together, within clear and broad guidelines that steer them in a common direction.

Four Catalysts of Coherence

The hardest part of any theory of action in educational change is not how to start it, but how to make it spread. Detailed prescription and alignment increase consistency but at the cost of depth, breadth, and complexity. Pilot projects almost always show promise, but most attempts to increase their scale produce pale imitations of the original. Many projects are successful primarily with volunteers and enthusiasts and rarely reach the rest. And heroic leaders might be able to make dramatic turnarounds, but others find it hard to replicate their qualities and cannot find the same success.

The challenge of coherence is not to clone or align everything so it looks the same in all schools. Indeed, if we are all on the same page, then nobody is reading the whole book. The challenge, rather, is how to bring diverse people together to work skillfully and effectively for a common cause that lifts them up and has them moving in the same direction. The Fourth Way has four catalysts that create this coherence.

Catalyst 1: Sustainable leadership. Leadership is the afterthought of educational change. It is the cigarette that is smoked once the reform has been consummated. Institutions in crisis look for exceptional leaders to rescue them. Systemwide change efforts gather leaders together for a few meetings and hope they will follow through. Or governments bypass leadership altogether and go straight to the classroom through teacher-proof and leader-proof programs of prescribed delivery. It is extremely rare to have a more sustained strategy of leadership development connected to reform implementation. Yet change without leadership has no chance of sustainability.

The teachers in the Change Over Time study remembered their leaders during the age of optimism and innovation (The First Way) as larger-than-life characters, both in a good or a bad way, who knew everyone personally, made a mark on their school, were strongly attached to it, and stayed around for a long time. In the age of complexity and contradiction (The Interregnum), the good leaders acted as guides and the poor ones behaved like shields. In both cases, there was a random distribution of the strong and the weak.

By The Second Way of standardization, teachers were seeing their leaders as anonymous, interchangeable managers who were often at meetings away from their school or consumed by mountains of paperwork in their offices. They came and went with alarming frequency, and they were viewed as more attached to delivering the district's mandates or developing their own careers than they were to supporting their schools.

In The Third Way of educational change, leadership started to receive greater attention, but not in ways connected to other aspects of the reform strategy. Increased attention to leadership has been precipitated by a "perfect storm" of mass retirement of the boomer generation with few successors to fill open spaces; a different mission in the younger generation of potential leaders, which includes more women, is more assertive about its own needs, and is more concerned about work-life balance; and a reform environment that makes existing school leaders so overloaded and vulnerable that those who might be promoted are reluctant to take on the job.

Responses to this crisis of succession have involved creating aspiring and emerging leader programs to identify talent early, providing mentoring and coaching, and constructing clear routes of leadership opportunity. But this emphasis on developing leadership capacity concentrates only on increasing the supply side of the leadership pipeline. As Tom Hatch (2006) points out, leadership capacity, like water capacity, can also be developed by reducing unnecessary demand. When leadership turns into management of innumerable imposed initiatives, exposure to endless and unwanted interventions, and being evaluated according to unfair and inappropriate forms of accountability, the demand is unreasonable, and few people experience a calling to lead anymore.

So what can be done strategically when the demand is unappealing and the supply is scarce? One of the answers is distributed leadership. Distributed leadership creates large pools from which future high-level leaders come. It entails developing a lot of leadership early, and not just among the chosen few who show early potential. Leaders in high-performing Finland practice distributed leadership. All school leaders must have had experience teaching, and all leaders still do teach part of the time. They see themselves as part of a "society of experts" in their school. If they should falter or fall ill, then the teachers take over because the school, they say, belongs to them. Collective responsibility supersedes administrative accountability.

Distributed leadership draws change out of staff, rather than driving reforms through them. It is integral to curriculum and pedagogical development more than reform implementation and incompatible with meeting imposed targets related to external initiatives.

Catalyst 2: A net with no nanny. In most theories-in-action, improvement has been unequal and change has failed to spread. This is because people in schools learn best not by reading research reports, listening to speeches, or attending workshops, but by watching, listening to, and learning from each other. Experience counts; theory does not (Hargreaves, 1984). The art of spreading change is about building new relationships as much as disseminating new knowledge.

One way to disseminate knowledge through relationships is via networks. In natural and social systems, the most effective networks combine properties of emergence (the innovations that arise in open systems through spontaneous and unpredictable interactions) with the properties of design (shaping the interactions so that movement is in a desired direction) (Hargreaves & Fink, 2006). If there is too much emergence, networks become diffuse and they dissipate. Purposes are unclear. Talk does not turn into action. There is no proof of impact in products, practices, or results. Or networks attract only volunteers and enthusiasts, dividing those who are "in the net" from those outside it.

If there is too much design, networks turn into administratively constructed clusters of schools whose purpose is to implement or serve as a reference group for government policy. In the end, emerging ideas and innovations get suppressed when they conflict with mandated policies. Attempts to control networks ultimately kill them. Government networks are an oxymoron. As Internet network theorist Manuel Castells (2001) points out, governments cannot control networks, they can only disturb them by throwing in things for them to deal with.

The RATL network of 300 underperforming schools (plus their high-performing mentors) is one of the best examples of how to balance emergence with design. So is the Alberta Initiative for School Improvement (AISI), where large numbers of interconnected schools design their own improvements linked to shared targets and measurable gains in student achievement. Both have a clear, common, and urgent purpose linked to learning, achievement, and improvement. Neither has a hyperfocus on implementing policies and meeting external targets in imposed initiatives. Participation is by invitation rather than merely permissive. Governments initiate and fund the networks so that schools do not have to find their own resources and additional time, but they do not interfere in them. Experiential knowledge is circulated among respected practitioners, but these interactions are also invigorated and disturbed by the infusion of external ideas and expertise. The result is significant measurable improvement.

Even these best-case scenarios, though, pose two challenges. First, the unrelenting political emphasis on short-term system achievement targets in basic subjects can plunge networks into cultures of presentism where they circulate only short-term solutions and avoid undertaking more laborious, long-term efforts to transform teaching and learning (Hargreaves & Shirley, in press-b). The "nanny state" of constant surveillance and endless intervention is incompatible with the innovation of the network. Children need a nanny; professionals do not!

One of the greatest benefits of school networks is when stronger schools help similarly placed, weaker peers. But the greatest challenges are often between schools in contiguous neighborhoods in the same town or city. Divided by district boundaries that reflect class-based or race-related residential patterns, opposed by the ruthless competition of the market, and isolated by the fear of betraying secrets to the enemy, schools in the same town or city are the hardest to network of all.

Finnish school leaders share resources and support each other across schools through a sense of common responsibility for all young people. They have time to do this, they say, because unlike Anglo-Saxon countries, they are not always responding to waves of imposed initiatives. Elsewhere, more imagination is needed to reverse the market. Equity-based budgeting can allocate resources across a district or a state differentially according to need. Networking and partnerships may start best at a distance, and then move closer to home once the benefits of collaboration have been established. Local politicians can exercise inspirational leadership in bringing schools together to pursue a common mission, despite their differences. Since the inequities between districts are often much greater than within them, national and state governments can target increased funding to schools prepared to advance the interests of social justice by collaborating with less-favored schools across their immediate boundaries. Finally, as in some English schools, students might work in their home schools in the morning or on some days, but access specialist services and mix with other students across their local network of schools in the afternoons or on other days. The point of networks is to spread innovation, stimulate learning, increase professional motivation, and reduce inequities. They are a fundamental part of The Fourth Way.

Catalyst 3: Responsibility before accountability. Responsibility precedes accountability. Accountability is the remainder that is left when responsibility has been subtracted. The Finns are a good example. They have success because they are highly qualified professionals working together within and across schools on curriculum development and around the children they have in common, through a culture of trust, cooperation, and responsibility. Finnish schools do not perform well by creating geniuses, their teachers say. Rather, they lift every child up from the bottom, one at a time. Small classes increase teachers' personal knowledge of each child. An exceptionally inclusive definition of special education provides in-class support for any child requiring it. School welfare committees take concerted action on behalf of any child falling behind. A low-key reform climate also means that all teachers can concentrate on individual children, rather than dealing with paperwork, test preparation, and bureaucratic intervention.

The teachers and leaders in the RATL network operate in highly transparent systems of lateral engagement that automatically place pressure on them to act responsibly in finding and trying solutions that will help their students succeed. A rigorously self-regulating profession in partnership with representation of and openness to others increases collective responsibility.

Test scores and other student assessments are the most commonly used instruments of educational accountability. There is a place for them. At the moment, Finland has no standardized, high-stakes testing. But even here, my colleagues and I have advised that as the country accepts more immigration and ethnic diversity in order to provide a stronger tax base for its growing number of retirees, teachers may no longer find it easy to understand and intervene with students who do not intuitively look and act like them. Other, more objective data may be needed to gain insight and to motivate teachers who otherwise feel they are doing their best. Despite being top in the world, even Finland may need to consider a stronger role for educational testing.

In Western countries, test and examination data are often collected from all schools and children by census and used for comparison. Schools also collect this comprehensive data about their students so staff can determine where and how to improve. However, when high-stakes events like graduation depend on single or simple measures of performance that are linked to political targets, are cause for possible sanction, and are also made public, the chance that they will distort the learning process and lead to widespread corruption is high.

Fortunately, it is not necessary to ensure accountability through a census. It can be achieved more easily and also more effectively through a statistically valid sample. The National Assessment of Educational Progress (NAEP) test in the United States is just such a device. Interestingly, it has shown no significant achievement gains in recent years, while statewide tests applied through a census, for which students can be specifically prepared, have risen year after year. For accountability purposes, test samples are not merely substitutes for a census; they are superior. Even environmentalists check air quality and pollution levels by samples. This is quite enough to hold others accountable.

Yet governments hang on grimly to accountability by census, even though it is subject to widespread abuse. They do it even though it is exorbitantly expensive—diverting scarce resources from teaching and learning needs elsewhere. And they retain it despite the widely surveyed and well-reported objections of parents in England, for example, to their young children being the most tested in the world. Despite all the educational and democratic arguments against accountability by census, it bolsters political control. On the merging paths of autocracy and technocracy, it is used to patrol and police the profession, to push and prod it in the government's desired direction, and to monitor and intervene in schools and systems at any time.

A theory-in-action of educational change that is democratic and sustainable is one that supports assessment *for* learning in classrooms using a range of diagnostic tests and other assessments that give teachers feedback on individual student problems and progress, and that ensures systemwide accountability through prudent sampling rather than a profligate and politically controlling census.

But more than anything, The Fourth Way puts responsibility before accountability. It treats accountability as the conscience of the system that checks it, not the ego or the id that drives it.

Catalyst 4: Build from the bottom; steer from the top. The Fourth Way is not about letting a thousand flowers bloom or micromanaging everything in detail. It does not exalt the market or extol the virtues of an all-controlling state. Neither is it a way to retain top-down autocratic control over narrowly defined goals and targets with the assistance of technocratic surveillance and effervescent interactions. The Fourth Way, rather, is a democratic and sustainable path to improvement that builds from the bottom and steers from the top. Through high-quality teachers committed to and capable of creating deep and broad teaching and learning, it builds powerful, responsible, and lively professional communities in a largely self-regulating profession where teachers set high standards and shared targets and improve by learning through networks from evidence and with each other.

In The Fourth Way, a robust social democracy builds an inspiring and inclusive vision that draws teachers to the profession and grants them public status within it. It involves parents and the public as highly engaged partners and also draws on and contributes to the development of corporate educational responsibility. In The Fourth Way, a lot is expected of educators, but the burden of narrowing achievement gaps and achieving social justice does not rest on their shoulders alone. It is shared with a strongly supported health service, housing system, and social-service sector. In all this, students in The Fourth Way are not merely targets of change, but rather vigorous and active partners in its development.

The Fourth Way achieves coherence by assigning huge priority to the development of sustainable and distributed leadership that is knowledgeable about learning; by placing responsibility before accountability (with accountability serving as a conscience through sampling); by initiating and supporting but not over-regulating professional networks of improvement; and—most of all—by developing an inspiring and inclusive educational and societal vision that connects the future to the past and leaves teachers collectively responsible for pedagogical decisions and a lot of curriculum development.

The three converging yet slippery paths of autocracy, technocracy, and effervescence that make up the new orthodoxy of educational change (The Third Way) are largely about improving delivery. The Fourth Way takes a more vertiginous route that scales the heights of public, participatory democracy. The time is surely nigh for this. New generations of educators are moving into leadership positions, people are looking outside themselves, and the profession has never been more ready. The new orthodoxy has already done a great deal to demonstrate the power of increased professional energy. It is time for a Fourth Way to harness this to sustainability and democracy.

References and Resources

Barber, M. (2007). *Instruction to deliver: Tony Blair, the public services and the challenge of delivery.* London: Politico.

Castells, M. (2001). *The Internet galaxy: Reflections on the Internet, business, and society.* Oxford: Oxford University Press.

DuFour, R., Eaker, R., & DuFour, R. (2008). *Revisiting professional learning communities at work: New insights for improving schools.* Bloomington, IN: Solution Tree.

Foucault, M. (1977). *Discipline and punish: The birth of the prison.* New York: Pantheon.

Fullan, M., & Hargreaves, A. (1992). *What's worth fighting for in your school? Working together for improvement.* Buckingham, UK: Open University Press.

Giddens, A. (1999). *The third way: The renewal of social democracy.* Cambridge, MA: Polity Press.

Giles, C., & Hargreaves, A. (2006). The sustainability of innovative schools as learning organizations and professional learning communities during standardized reform. *Educational Administration Quarterly, 42*(1), 124–156.

Hargreaves, A. (1984). Experience counts, theory doesn't: How teachers talk about their work. *Sociology of Education, 57*(4), 244–254.

Hargreaves, A. (1994). *Changing teachers, changing times: Teachers' work and culture in the postmodern age.* New York: Teachers College Press.

Hargreaves, A. (2003). *Teaching in the knowledge society: Education in the age of insecurity.* New York: Teachers College Press.

Hargreaves, A., Earl, L., Moore, S., & Manning, S. (2001). *Learning to change: Teaching beyond subjects and standards.* San Francisco: Jossey-Bass.

Hargreaves, A., & Evans, R. (Eds.). (1997). *Beyond educational reform: Bringing teachers back in.* Buckingham, UK: Open University Press.

Hargreaves, A., & Fink, D. (2006). *Sustainable leadership.* San Francisco: Jossey-Bass.

Hargreaves, A., & Goodson, I. (2006). Educational change over time? The sustainability and non-sustainability of three decades of secondary school change and continuity. *Educational Administration Quarterly, 42*(1), 3–41.

Hargreaves, A., Halász, G., & Pont, B. (2007). *School leadership for systemic improvement in Finland.* Paris: Organisation for Economic Co-operation and Development.

Hargreaves, A., & Shaw, P. (2006). *Knowledge and skills development in developing and transitional economies: An analysis of World Bank/DfID Knowledge and Skills for the Modern Economy Project.* Washington, DC: World Bank.

Hargreaves, A., & Shirley, D. (in press, a). The coming of post-standardization. *Phi Delta Kappan.*

Hargreaves, A., & Shirley, D. (in press, b). The persistence of presentism. *Teachers College Record.*

Hargreaves, A., Shirley, D., Evans, M., Johnson, C., & Riseman, D. (2006). *The long and the short of raising achievement: Final report of the evaluation of the "Raising Achievement, Transforming Learning" project of the UK Specialist Schools and Academies Trust.* Chestnut Hill, MA: Boston College.

Hartley, D. (2007). The emergence of distributed leadership in education: Why now? *British Journal of Educational Studies, 55*(2), 202–214.

Hatch, T. (2006). Building capacity for school improvement. In T. Bacchetti & T. Ehrlich (Eds.), *Reconnecting education and foundations: Turning good intentions into educational capital* (pp. 163–171). San Francisco: Jossey-Bass.

Johnson, S. M. (2004). *Finders and keepers: Helping new teachers survive and thrive in our schools.* San Francisco: Jossey-Bass.

Lortie, D. C. (1975). *Schoolteacher: A sociological study.* Chicago: University of Chicago Press.

New Commission on the Skills of the American Workforce. (2007). *Tough choices or tough times: The report of the New Commission on the Skills of the American Workforce.* San Francisco: Wiley.

Nichols, S. L., & Berliner, D. C. (2007). *Collateral damage: How high-stakes testing corrupts America's schools.* Cambridge, MA: Harvard Education Press.

Rosenholtz, S. (1989). *Teachers' workplace.* New York: Longman.

Sennett, R. (1998). *The corrosion of character: The personal consequences of work in the new capitalism.* London: W. W. Norton.

UNICEF. (2007). *Child poverty in perspective: An overview of child well-being in rich countries, Innocenti Report Card 7.* Florence: UNICEF Innocenti Research Centre.

Linda Darling-Hammond

Dr. Linda Darling-Hammond is Charles E. Ducommun Professor of Education at Stanford University, where she has launched the Stanford Educational Leadership Institute and the School Redesign Network and served as faculty sponsor for the Stanford Teacher Education Program. She is a former president of the American Educational Research Association and member of the National Academy of Education. Her work focuses on issues of school restructuring, teacher quality, and educational equity. From 1994 to 2001, she served as executive director of the National Commission on Teaching and America's Future, whose 1996 report, *What Matters Most: Teaching for America's Future,* led to sweeping policy changes affecting teaching and teacher education. In 2006, this report was named one of the most influential affecting United States education, and Dr. Darling-Hammond was named one of the nation's 10 most influential people affecting educational policy over the past decade.

Among Dr. Darling-Hammond's more than 250 publications are *Preparing Teachers for a Changing World: What Teachers Should Learn and Be Able to Do* (2005), coedited with John Bransford for the National Academy of Education; *Powerful Teacher Education: Lessons From Exemplary Programs* (2006); *Teaching as the Learning Profession: Handbook of Policy and Practice* (1999), coedited with Gary Sykes; and *The Right to Learn: A Blueprint for Creating Schools That Work* (1997).

In this chapter, the author describes four approaches to school management and change. She argues that the purposeful pursuit of a democratic and professional approach to change is essential for the kinds of goals that now confront education systems. She provides recommendations for how a democratic, professional vision for educational systems can be pursued in the service of schools that empower learners with deep knowledge and the ability to problem-solve, invent, and guide their own learning. Dr. Linda Darling-Hammond can be reached at ldh@stanford.edu.

Chapter 2

Teaching and the Change Wars: The Professionalism Hypothesis

Linda Darling-Hammond

As the 21st century has dawned, nations around the world are undertaking major transformations of their governmental and education systems in response to changing economic, demographic, political, and social imperatives. Nearly all countries are engaged in serious school reform initiatives to address demands for much higher levels of education for a much greater number of citizens—demands created by a new information age, major economic shifts, and a resurgence and redefinition of democracy around the globe. The need to prepare future citizens and workers who can cope with complexity, use new technologies, and work cooperatively to frame and solve novel problems—and the need to do this for a much more diverse and inclusive group of learners—has stimulated efforts to rethink school goals and redesign school organizations.

Competing Theories of Change

There are competing views of how these massive changes should be pursued. Among the contending theories of action are the following:

- A *bureaucratic approach* to school management and change, which seeks solutions that can be centralized and hierarchically administered

- A *professional approach,* which seeks to invest in knowledgeable practitioners who can make sound decisions about how to shape education for the specific clients they serve

- A *market approach,* which looks to school choice and competition as drivers for educational reform

- A *democratic approach,* which seeks to involve students, parents, community members, and teachers in developing schools that are responsive to student needs and interests, as well as to distinctive visions of education

None of these concepts exists in an entirely pure form; rather, they describe approaches that operate from different paradigms of what makes schools effective and how productive change can occur. In this chapter, I argue that while there may be some role for bureaucratic and market elements, the more purposeful pursuit of a *democratic and professional* approach to change is essential for the kinds of goals that now confront education systems. In what follows, I describe the assumptions of these different approaches and offer evidence about the outcomes of various strategies. I close with recommendations for how a democratic, professional vision for educational systems may be pursued in the service of schools that empower learners with deep knowledge and the ability to problem-solve, invent, and guide their own learning—and do so in ways that support greater equity and social justice for democratic societies.

The Bureaucratic Approach

The traditional 20th-century approach to education in many countries, including the United States, relied heavily on bureaucratic management of schools: hierarchically administered decisions translated into rules and procedures for teachers to follow (prescribed curricula, textbooks, tests, class schedules, rules for promotion and assignment of students, and so on). There are several basic assumptions underlying this view:

- Students are sufficiently standardized that they will respond in identical and predictable ways to the "treatments" devised by policymakers and their agents.

- Sufficient knowledge of which treatments should be prescribed is both available and generalizable to all educational circumstances.

- This knowledge can be translated into standardized rules for practice.

- These rules can be operationalized through regulations and reporting and inspection systems.

- Administrators and teachers can and will faithfully implement the prescriptions for practice.

The fundamental assumption is that this process, if efficiently administered, will produce the desired outcomes. If the outcomes are not satisfactory, the circular assumption is that the prescriptions are not yet sufficiently detailed or the process of implementation is not sufficiently exact. Thus, the solutions to educational problems always lie in more precise regulation of educational or management processes: a more tightly specified curriculum, more frequent and intensive testing, more standardized approaches to teaching behaviors, more regulations over the uses of funds and the design of school organizations, and so on.

In the bureaucratic concept of teaching, teachers do not need to be highly knowledgeable about learning, teaching, or curriculum, because they do not, presumably, make the major decisions about these matters. Curriculum planning is done by administrators and specialists; teachers are to implement a curriculum planned for them. Inspection of teachers' work is conducted by superiors whose job it is to make sure that the teacher is implementing the curriculum and procedures of the district. Teachers do not plan or evaluate their own work; they merely perform it.

The central problem with the bureaucratic solution is that students are *not* standardized; thus, effective practice cannot be reduced to routines. By its very nature, bureaucratic management is incapable of providing appropriate education for students who do not fit the mold upon which all of the prescriptions for practice are based. As inputs, processes, and measures of outcomes are increasingly prescribed and standardized, the cracks into which students can fall grow larger rather than smaller. This is because the likelihood that each of the accumulated prescriptions is suitable for a given child grows smaller with each successive limitation of the teachers' ability to adapt instruction to the students' needs (Darling-Hammond, 1990). Ironically, prescriptive policies created in the name of public accountability ultimately reduce schools' responsiveness to the needs of students and the desires of parents. Faceless regulations become the scapegoats for school failure, since no person in the system takes responsibility for their effects on students.

Furthermore, as Ted Sizer (1984) aptly noted, the system of pyramidal governance created by bureaucratic approaches "forces us in large measure to overlook special local conditions, particularly school-by-school differences. . . . While central authorities almost always try to provide local options and 'consultation,' the framework of school remains permanently fixed. This framework includes the organization of schools by students' ages, by similar subject departments, by time blocks, by specialized job descriptions, by calendar, and in many states, by precise forms of staff contracts and licenses" (p. 207). Within this framework, much that fundamentally defines the process of education is predetermined. Changes within the framework can only be marginal.

While there are undoubtedly some routine aspects of schooling that are made more efficient by standardization, and some common expectations for what is taught are appropriate, core decisions about teaching cannot be effectively prescribed. Not only is bureaucratic management at odds with innovation, it is substantially at odds with student learning. Although many policymakers continue to rely on prescriptive approaches to reform, I argue that we have pushed the bureaucratic model of educational improvement as far as it can go, and it does not go far enough.

A Professional Approach

An alternative to the bureaucratic approach is a professional conception of teaching. Professionalism suggests an approach that is *knowledge-based* and *client-oriented*—one in which practitioners are accountable to their colleagues as well as to parents and students for using professionwide knowledge to meet the needs of students, and for continually improving their practice. A primary assumption is that since the work is too complex to be prescribed from afar, it must be structured so that practitioners can make responsible decisions, both individually and collectively. Professionalism aims to improve practice and enhance accountability by creating means for ensuring that practitioners will be competent and committed. Thus, they undergo rigorous preparation and socialization—through strong initial training, internships for novices, meaningful evaluation, professional development, and peer review of practice—so that the public can have high levels of confidence that they will behave in knowledgeable and ethical ways.

Professionals are obligated to do whatever is best for the client, not what is most expedient, and to base decisions about what is best on available knowledge—not just on knowledge acquired from personal experience, but also on clinical and research knowledge acquired by the occupation as a whole and represented in professional preparation, journals, and licensure systems. In policy terms, these requirements suggest greater regulation of *teachers*—ensuring their competence through more rigorous preparation, selection, and evaluation—in exchange for the deregulation of *teaching*—fewer external rules prescribing what is to be taught, when, and how. This is the bargain that all professions make with society: For occupations that require discretion and judgment in meeting the unique needs of clients, the profession guarantees the competence of members in exchange for the privilege of professional control over work structure and standards of practice.

The theory behind this equation is that professional control will improve the quality of services, because decision-making by well-trained professionals allows individual clients' needs to be met more precisely. Research illustrates how students differ in their approaches to learning, and how effective teaching techniques vary for students with different learning styles, at different stages of cognitive and psychological development, for different subject areas, and for different instructional goals (for review see Darling-Hammond & Bransford, 2005). Consequently, if students are to be well-taught, it will not be by virtue of bureaucratic mandate, but by virtue of knowledgeable professionals who can use good judgment to make sound decisions appropriate to the unique needs of children. Professionalism also promotes continual improvement in overall practice as "effectiveness" rather than "compliance" becomes the standard for judging competence.

Professional authority does not mean legitimizing the idiosyncratic or whimsical preferences of individual classroom teachers, however. Indeed, unfettered autonomy is the problem that professionalism is meant to address. It is precisely *because* practitioners operate autonomously that safeguards to protect the public interest—such as screens to membership and peer review of practice—are necessary. Collective authority to make decisions is achieved by creating collective *responsibility* through accountability mechanisms that enable the profession to define and transmit its knowledge base, evaluate and refine its practices, and enforce norms of ethical practice. As I discuss later, democratic engagement with partners in the educational enterprise is critical to ensure responsiveness to the needs and aspirations of students and their families.

The results of investments in teacher knowledge and skill have been demonstrated not only at the individual teacher level, but at the levels of the school, district, state, and nation. However, arming teachers with greater expertise is only part of what is needed for the kind of widespread educational change that is currently demanded. There must also be mechanisms for the change of school organizations and systems so that productive innovation is leveraged and public schools are kept responsive to the publics they serve.

A Market Approach

Arguments for greater choice and competition among schools— through public-school choices within or across districts, charter schools, or private-school vouchers—are intended to goad improvement as students and their parents select the schools that are best or most suited to their needs. Market mechanisms are supposed to improve schools and make them more accountable in at least two ways: First, by letting "customers" choose, schools are expected to work harder to provide services that parents or students want, and second, by allowing choice, the market should reveal for policymakers where there are problems they need to address in schools that are undersubscribed.

The existence of greater feedback to schools and policymakers and greater options for informed consumers are among the major potential benefits of choice plans. And there is evidence that some schools of choice in the public sector have been able to introduce important, educationally successful innovations, both through alternative, pilot, or magnet schools and through charters (French, 2008; Friedlaender & Darling-Hammond, 2007; Sizer & Wood, 2008).

However, not all schools of choice are successful. Evidence on charter schools, for example, is mixed, with both positive and negative findings depending both on the features of schools and the policy contexts in which they operate (Darling-Hammond & Montgomery, 2008; Imberman, 2007). Studies of voucher programs in the United States have found no evidence that private schools outperform public schools, even when public schools serve more educationally needy students (see, for example, Wolf, 2008).

Furthermore, choosing alone is not enough to ensure full client accountability. For one thing, not all modes of choice offer full, nondiscriminatory access or accountability for what gets taught, how students are treated, or how they succeed. In addition, when the most desirable schools have already been filled, there are still a great many students left to be served, and a number of schools, desired or not, that must serve them. If there are not other public-policy mechanisms in place to support improvements in all schools, then choice will only make marginal adjustments in the mix of students in some schools, rather than producing a general increase in the quality of education across the board. Conceptualizing education as a private good weakens educational guarantees for those with little clout in the marketplace.

Market-based conceptions have also been used to argue against professional standards with the notion that preparation and certification requirements are merely "regulatory barriers" to teaching that drive up costs and create unnecessary barriers to school choice (see, for example, Ballou & Podgursky, 1997). The client protection and societal investment offered by investments in professional knowledge and skill are viewed as unnecessary in an unfettered marketplace, even if some students are less well-educated as a result. In short, market mechanisms alone cannot ensure that all citizens will have access to high-quality education—especially those who have been traditionally underserved. While school choice that guarantees strong outreach and equitable access may be one part of an innovation agenda, additional strategies are needed to develop a supply of strong, responsive schools in all communities.

A Democratic Approach

The fundamental theory of action for systems of local public schools is that local ownership allows public schools "to be governed in a way that put them closest to the people they serve" (Sizer & Wood, 2008), thus making them more accountable and responsive to the needs and interests of their communities. While this has certainly occurred in many cases, we have also learned that local control by lay boards of education does not always translate into schools that are equitable, responsive, or reflective of the best knowledge available about how to educate children. Often, it has meant that the rights of minorities are unprotected and educational decisions are ill-informed. Boards of education have not always represented parents and students, nor have they always worked collaboratively with educators to understand and develop change.

New models of democratic governance of schools have begun to evolve—models that put more authority in the hands of local parents and students along with professional educators who are organized to work together to design and implement new models of schools. These approaches often incorporate choice among public schools for the purpose of innovation and distinctiveness of school mission, rather than for the purpose of competition (Darling-Hammond & Montgomery, 2008). They incorporate school-site governance that involves parents and students, as well as teachers and administrators, in decision-making that is grounded in principles of consensus and parity and built on norms of trust, openness, and equity.

The assumption underlying democratic site-based forms of school governance is that decisions about the uses of school resources made by faculty, principals, and parents will better address community needs and local problems. In large school bureaucracies, authority for decisions and responsibility for practice are widely separated, usually by many layers of hierarchy. Boards and top-level administrators make decisions while teachers, principals, and students are responsible for carrying them out. In such a system, accountability for results is hard to achieve. When the desired outcomes of hierarchically imposed policies are not realized, policymakers blame the people responsible for implementation, and practitioners blame their inability to devise or pursue better solutions on the constraints of policy. No one can be fully accountable for the results of practice when authority and responsibility are dispersed.

Furthermore, when authority for decision-making is far removed from practitioners and parents, and is regulatory in nature, change comes slowly. Dysfunctional consequences for students cannot be quickly remedied while edicts hang on, immune from the realities of school life and protected by the forces of inertia and constituencies both inside and outside the bureaucracy. The amount of effort and influence required to change a school-system policy is so great that most teachers, principals, and parents find it impossible to deflect their energies from their primary jobs to the arduous and often unrewarding task of moving the behemoth. They sigh and strive to cope, looking for loopholes that might allow unobtrusive alternatives to grow for a time.

Thus, adjustments in programs, course requirements, schedules, staffing, and materials to meet the needs of students are difficult to make; the knowledge of school staff and parents about more productive alternatives is not used; and time is deflected from teaching to paperwork, monitoring, and reporting systems. Even where flexibility might exist, the pressures for conformity are so strong that principals and teachers are often afraid to test the limits of the regulatory structure. The end result is that when problems are identified, practitioners often claim they have no authority to change the status quo. Eventually a general acceptance of the failings of the system comes to prevail, and cynicism overwhelms problem-solving initiatives by principals, teachers, or parents.

Finally, the assumption is that when authority is removed from the school, so is accountability for learning. Until authority for making decisions is granted to those who have responsibility for performing the work—those who are living with these decisions on a daily basis—reform of practice cannot occur. But ensuring that good decisions are made depends, once again, on the availability of solid professional knowledge and strong moral commitments within the school, suggesting the critical importance of combining a professional agenda with one to secure more democratic decision-making. Indeed, studies that document the successes of schools that enable more personalized education and more democratic governance at the site level also illustrate that improved practice and student achievement are accompanied by a strong professional learning component (Darling-Hammond, Ancess, & Ort; 2002; Friedlaender & Darling-Hammond, 2007; Lieberman, 1995; Smiley, Lazarus, & Brownlee-Conyers, 1996).

Evidence and Strategies for Professionally-Supported Democratic Schools

There is considerable evidence that investment in teachers' knowledge and expertise makes a difference for student learning—and that skilled teachers' efforts can be even more effective in the context of democratically organized schools. Significant links between measures of teachers' knowledge (including education coursework, professional development opportunities, certification status, and scores on professional knowledge tests) and student achievement have been found at the level of the individual teacher, the school, the school district, and the state (for reviews, see Darling-Hammond, 2000; Wilson, Floden, & Ferrini-Mundy, 2002).

How Investments in Teachers and Teaching Matter

The influence of teacher expertise can be quite large. For example, in a study of 900 Texas districts, Ronald Ferguson (1991) found that combined measures of teachers' expertise—scores on a licensing examination and teachers' education level and experience—accounted for more of the interdistrict variation in students' reading and mathematics achievement in grades 1 through 11 than student socioeconomic status. He concluded that investments in the quality of teachers secure greater improvements in achievement than any other use of a marginal education dollar.

Similarly, a recent large-scale study in North Carolina found that teachers are more effective if they are fully prepared when they enter the profession, are certified in the specific field they teach, have higher scores on a teacher licensing test, have taught for more than 2 years, have graduated from a more competitive college, and are National Board–certified after having passed a portfolio assessment of their teaching performance (Clotfelter, Ladd, & Vigdor, 2007). Together, the combined effects on student achievement of these teacher qualifications exceed the substantial effects of race and parent education. In other words, having highly skilled teachers can help overcome the societal inequalities that are generally reinforced by schools.

On-the-job professional learning increases teachers' influence even further. A review of well-designed studies found that teachers who receive substantial professional development—an average of 49 hours annually across the nine studies reviewed—boosted their students' achievement by about 21 percentile points (Yoon, Duncan, Lee, Scarloss, & Shapley, 2007). A study of 25 of the world's school systems, including 10 of the top performers, found that investments in teachers and teaching are central to improving student outcomes. Top school systems emphasize 1) getting the right people to become teachers, 2) developing them into effective instructors, and 3) ensuring that the system is able to deliver the best possible instruction for every child (Barber & Mourshed, 2007).

Strategies That Enable Systemwide Professional Practice

The need to invest in teachers is a lesson that has been well-learned by societies that top the international rankings in education. The highest-achieving countries around the world—Finland, Sweden, Ireland, the Netherlands, Hong Kong, Singapore, South Korea, Japan, Australia, and New Zealand—have poured resources into teacher training and support over the last decade. These countries routinely prepare their teachers more extensively, pay them well in relation to competing occupations, and provide them with lots of time for professional learning. They also distribute well-trained teachers to all students—rather than allowing some to be taught by untrained novices—by offering equitable salaries and sometimes adding incentives for harder-to-staff locations.

In Scandinavian countries like Finland, Sweden, Norway, and the Netherlands, all teachers now receive 2 to 3 years of graduate-level preparation for teaching, completely at the government's expense, plus a living stipend. Typically, this includes a full year of training in a school connected to the university, like the professional development school partnerships created by some programs in the United States, along with extensive coursework in pedagogy and a thesis researching an educational problem in the schools. Unlike the United States, where teachers either go into debt to prepare for a profession that will pay them poorly or enter with little or no training, these countries made the decision to invest in a uniformly well-prepared teaching force by recruiting top candidates and paying them to go to school. Slots in teacher training programs are highly coveted, and shortages of teachers are unheard of.

Finland has been a poster child for school improvement since it rapidly climbed to the top of the international rankings after it emerged from the Soviet Union's shadow. Leaders in Finland attribute these gains to their intensive investments in teacher education. Over 10 years, the country overhauled preparation to focus more on teaching for higher order skills like problem-solving and critical thinking. Teachers learn how to create challenging curriculum and how to develop and evaluate local performance assessments that engage students in research and inquiry on a regular basis. Teacher training emphasizes learning how to teach students who learn in different ways, including those with special needs. The egalitarian Finns reasoned that if teachers learn to help students who struggle, they will be able to teach all students more effectively and will indeed leave no child behind (Buchberger & Buchberger, 2004; Kaiser, 2005).

Policymakers also decided that if they invested in very skillful teachers, they could allow local schools more autonomy to make decisions about what and how to teach—a reaction against the bureaucratically heavy, centralized system they sought to overhaul. This bet seems to have paid off. Teachers are sophisticated diagnosticians, and they work together collegially to design instruction that meets the demands of the subject matter as well as the needs of their students. Finnish schools are not governed by standardized tests, which are absent until the very end of high school, but instead by teachers' strong knowledge about how students learn, engaged in the context of locally managed democratically run schools.

Top-ranked Singapore, by contrast, is more centralized, but it treats teaching similarly. The National Institute of Education—the country's only teacher training institution—is strongly focused on preparing teachers to teach a curriculum focused on critical thinking and inquiry—the 21st-century skills needed in a high-tech economy. To get the best teachers, students from the top third of each graduating high school class are recruited into a fully paid 4-year teacher education program (or, if they enter later, a 1- to 2-year graduate program) and immediately put on the Ministry's payroll.

When they enter the profession, teachers' salaries are higher than those of beginning doctors.

As in other highly ranked countries, novices are not left to sink or swim. Expert teachers are given released time to serve as mentors to help beginners learn their craft. The government pays for 100 hours of professional development each year for all teachers in addition to the 20 hours a week they have to work with other teachers and visit each others' classrooms to study teaching. Currently, teachers are being trained to undertake action research projects in the classroom so that they can examine teaching and learning problems, and find solutions that can be disseminated to others. And teachers continue to advance throughout their careers. With help from the government, teachers in Singapore can pursue three separate career ladders that help them become curriculum specialists, mentors for other teachers, or school principals. These opportunities bring recognition, extra compensation, and new challenges that keep teaching exciting.

While national curriculum standards guide instruction in Singapore, schools are governed through a variety of local school-site management and operating committees that engage community members, parents, teachers, and administrators in student recruitment (all public schools are schools of choice), budgeting and fundraising, curriculum refinement, program development, and instructional improvement. Local businesses and community organizations frequently work closely with schools to secure resources and organize a variety of supports and programs. Parents are involved both through committees and frequent parent-teacher-student conferences and events at the school.

In these and other high-achieving countries, schools are organized to support teacher success. Typically, teachers have 15 to 20 hours a week to work with colleagues on developing lessons, participating in research and study groups, and engaging in seminars and visits to other classrooms and schools. Often this collegial work includes lesson study and development around the state or national standards or curriculum framework, usually a lean document that outlines what major concepts or skills should be taught and leaves to teachers the development of the finer-grained pedagogical strategies that will be responsive to individual classrooms and students. In the course of developing and refining lessons and analyzing student work, teachers become more thoughtful and reflective in their practice, and hence more able to connect evidence of student learning to their planning and teaching.

In their study of mathematics teaching and learning in Japan, Taiwan, and the United States, Jim Stigler and Harold Stevenson (1991) described the intensively collegial approach to lesson study and development they observed in Japan and China, noting that "Asian class lessons are so well crafted [because] there is a very systematic effort to pass on the accumulated wisdom of teaching practice to each new generation of teachers and to keep perfecting that practice by providing teachers the opportunities to continually learn from each other" (p. 43).

A recent analysis of the strong learning gains in Cuba, which has the highest literacy rate and school achievement in Central or South America, also attributed the country's extraordinary educational success to strong professional preparation of teachers and investments in ongoing professional learning, coupled with small, personalized schools that are closely connected to local parents and communities. By contrast, much wealthier Chile, which has relied on a market-based system of public and private choice and little investment in teacher knowledge, has both much greater inequality and lower average achievement, despite its affluence (Carnoy, 2007).

These kinds of strategies have also been successful where they have been attempted in the United States. Beginning in the 1980s, for example, Connecticut and North Carolina enacted ambitious efforts to improve teaching. On the heels of these efforts, these states, which serve sizable numbers of low-income and minority students, registered striking gains in overall student learning and narrowed achievement gaps between advantaged and disadvantaged pupils. During the 1990s, for example, North Carolina posted the largest student achievement gains of any state in math and sizable advances in reading, while narrowing the black-white achievement gap (Baron, 1999). In Connecticut, also following steep gains throughout the decade, fourth-grade students ranked first in the nation by 1998 in reading and math on the National Assessment of Educational Progress, despite increased poverty and language diversity among its public school students, and the state earned top rankings in science and writing as well. Its achievement gap, too, narrowed notably (National Education Goals Panel, 1998, 1999).

Among the reforms that contributed to such gains were the significant improvements in both states' teaching forces, including in inner cities and rural areas. These were accomplished with ambitious teacher initiatives that introduced standards and incentives and professional learning for teachers, along with curriculum and assessment reforms for schools (Darling-Hammond, 2000).

Both states strengthened teacher education and licensure. For a teaching license, for example, Connecticut insisted on additional preparation at entry: a major in the content area and more pedagogical training as well as learning to teach reading and pupils with special needs. Teachers must complete a master's degree and a rigorous performance assessment modeled on that of the National Board for Professional Teaching Standards to gain a professional license. North Carolina likewise increased licensing requirements for teachers and principals. It increased coursework in content and pedagogy as well as licensing tests, required schools of education to undertake professional accreditation, invested in improvements in teacher-education curricula, and supported the creation of professional development schools (PDSs) connected to schools of education in which candidates could complete a year-long clinical experience interwoven with their coursework.

By creating settings that merge theoretical and practical learning, PDSs help transmit a common set of expectations that link preparation and practice. They also address the age-old problem of educational change: If teacher educators prepare teachers for schools as they are, they will be unable to teach more effectively or help schools become more effective than the status quo permits. Professional development schools create a means to prepare teachers for schools that do not currently exist in large numbers by combining the work of preservice education, staff development, school restructuring, and research (Fullan, 1993).

While raising standards, both states also increased and equalized salaries and initiated programs to subsidize teacher education costs in return for multiyear teaching commitments in high-need fields and locations. The highly selective North Carolina Teaching Fellows program, for example, pays all college costs, including an enhanced teacher education program, for thousands of high-ability students in return for several years of teaching. After 7 years, retention rates for these teachers exceed 75%, with many of the remaining alumni holding leadership positions (NCTAF, 1996). Both states launched mentoring programs for new teachers and greatly strengthened professional development for veterans, supporting teacher academies, teacher networks such as the National Writing Project, and coaching models, as well as incentives for National Board Certification.

Such teacher reforms paid off rapidly. Within 3 years of Connecticut's initiative, for instance, the state not only had eliminated teacher shortages, but had created surpluses. A National Education Goals Panel report (Baron, 1999) found that in districts with sharply improved achievement, educators cited the high quality of teachers and administrators as a critical reason for their gains, and noted that "when there is a teaching opening in a Connecticut elementary school, there are often several hundred applicants" (p. 28). Most notably, both states held to the course of teacher improvement over a sustained period—more than 15 years—thus demonstrating what policy in support of good teaching can accomplish.

There is more to these state and national success stories, including systems of curriculum and assessment focused on higher order thinking and problem-solving. These systems engage teachers in the development and scoring of performance-based assessments— student research papers, essays, inquiries, and problem-solving tasks—that provide productive goals and formative information about learning, as well as ongoing opportunities for student and teacher reflection and revision of work, which is another critical engine for professional practice. In schools where students publicly exhibit the work resulting from these assessments, with jurors drawn from the community, parent body, and higher education institutions, a democratic conversation about what schools are seeking to do and what constitutes high-quality work is also stimulated, producing both public support and ongoing improvement (Darling-Hammond, Ancess, & Falk, 1995; Murnane & Levy, 1996).

Recommendations

The critical need for investments in teacher learning has been made clear again and again in efforts at educational change. Those who have worked to improve schools have found that every aspect of school reform—the creation of more challenging curriculum, the use of more thoughtful assessments, the implementation of decentralized management, the invention of new model schools and programs—depends on highly skilled teachers, working in tandem with families (Fullan, 2007). In the final analysis, there are no policies that can improve schools if the people in them are not armed with the knowledge and skills they need.

Policymakers interested in reforming whole systems for greater performance must invest in strong initial preparation and ongoing professional development for all teachers that is grounded in ethical commitments to children and the knowledge needed to teach diverse learners well. Preparation must be tightly connected to instructional reform in schools that enables students to develop critical-thinking skills and the ability to manage their own learning, and teachers must be prepared to work productively with families in schools that are collaboratively and democratically run.

Ensuring that all practitioners have the supports to become expert also requires investments in the conditions of the teaching career, in particular the salaries, teaching conditions, and learning opportunities needed to maintain a strong pool of teachers and give them access to the knowledge they need to be successful. These include financial supports for candidates to become well-prepared, competitive and equitable salaries to attract and retain teachers where they are needed, and the material conditions needed to teach well (appropriate teaching assignments, reasonable class sizes and pupil loads, long-term relationships with students, curriculum materials, texts, computers, and so on).

In addition, if teacher learning is to be productive, coaching must be guided by meaningful, expert analysis of practice. This depends substantially on school leaders who are also knowledgeable about instruction and how to support adult and organizational learning. Teacher isolation must be overcome so that opportunities to study teaching and discuss problems of practice can be frequent and regular. Teachers need opportunities to develop and evaluate curriculum and assessments with colleagues—and engage students in authentic demonstrations of learning, so that learning standards come alive, are publicly shared, and shape ongoing diagnosis and improvement of practice. Finally, teachers must be involved in evaluation of student learning and in decision-making about policies and practices, so that they can change curriculum, teaching, and schooling practices as they learn more about what is effective and what is not.

Rather than piecemeal innovations that try to reform only one element of schools, such *systems* of support for high-quality teaching and learning will not only prepare teachers for the challenging work they are asked to do, but also ensure that schools are organized to support student and teacher learning, and that the standards, curriculum, and assessments that guide their work, in turn, support the kind of teaching and learning needed in the 21st century. While such initiatives have been difficult to sustain over the last century, the prospects for change guided by democratic professionalism are enhanced in this age of globalization by the evidence that nations and states experiencing dramatic improvement are investing in a strong teaching profession and are developing means for participation of local communities in supporting and designing schools that are increasingly responsive to the demands of an unpredictable new world. Their successes reinforce a theory of action that knowledgeable and committed educators working in close collaboration with local communities can help to secure the right to learn that is increasingly essential to the survival and success of individuals and societies.

References

Ballou, D., & Podgursky, M. (1997). Reforming teacher training and recruitment. *Government Union Review, 17*(4), 1–47.

Barber, M., & Mourshed, M. (2007). *How the world's best-performing school systems come out on top.* London: McKinsey & Company.

Baron, J. (1999). *Exploring high and improving reading achievement in Connecticut.* Washington, DC: National Education Goals Panel.

Buchberger, F., & Buchberger, I. (2004). Problem solving capacity of a teacher education system as condition of success? An analysis of the "Finnish case." In F. Buchberger & S. Berghammer (Eds.), *Education policy analysis in a comparative perspective* (pp. 222–237). Linz, Austria: Trauner.

Carnoy, M. (2007). *Cuba's academic advantage: Why students in Cuba do better in school.* Palo Alto, CA: Stanford University Press.

Clotfelter, C. T., Ladd, H. F., & Vigdor, J. L. (2007). *Teacher credentials and student achievement in high school: A cross-subject analysis with student fixed effects.* National Bureau of Economic Research Working Paper 13617. Cambridge, MA: National Bureau of Economic Research.

Darling-Hammond, L. (1990). Teacher professionalism: Why and how? In Ann Lieberman (Ed.), *Schools as collaborative cultures* (pp. 25–50). New York: Falmer Press.

Darling-Hammond, L. (2000). Teacher quality and student achievement: A review of state policy evidence. *Educational Policy Analysis Archives, 8*(1). Accessed at http://epaa.asu.edu/epaa/v8n1 on May 22, 2008.

Darling-Hammond, L., Ancess, J., & Falk, B. (Eds.). (1995). *Authentic assessment in action: Studies of schools and students at work.* New York: Teachers College Press.

Darling-Hammond, L., Ancess, J., & Ort, S. (2002). Reinventing high school: Outcomes of the Coalition Campus Schools Project. *American Educational Research Journal, 39*(3), 639–673.

Darling-Hammond, L., & Bransford, J. (2005). *Preparing teachers for a changing world: What teachers should learn and be able to do.* San Francisco: Jossey-Bass.

Darling-Hammond, L., & Montgomery, K. (2008). Keeping the promise: The role of policy in reform. In L. Dingerson, B. Miner, B. Peterson, & S. Waters (Eds.), *Keeping the promise? The debate over charter schools* (pp. 91–110). Milwaukee, WI: Rethinking Schools.

Ferguson, R. F. (1991). Paying for public education: New evidence on how and why money matters. *Harvard Journal on Legislation, 28*(2), 465–498.

French, D. (2008). Boston's pilot schools: An alternative to charter schools. In L. Dingerson (Ed.), *Charter schools: Keeping the promise*

or dismantling communities? (pp. 67–80). Milwaukee, WI: Rethinking Schools.

Friedlaender, D., & Darling-Hammond, L. (2007). *High schools for equity: Policy supports for student learning in communities of color.* Palo Alto, CA: School Redesign Network at Stanford University.

Fullan, M. (1993). *Change forces: Probing the depths of educational reform.* London: Falmer Press.

Fullan, M. (2007). *The new meaning of educational change* (4th ed.). New York: Teachers College Press.

Imberman, S. (2007). *Achievement and behavior in charter schools: Drawing a more complete picture.* Occasional Paper 142. New York: National Center for the Study of Privatization in Education.

Kaiser, R. B. (2005, August 7). In Finland's footsteps: If we're so rich and smart why aren't we more like them? *Washington Post,* B01.

Lieberman, A. (1995). *The work of restructuring schools: Building from the ground up,* pp. 87–110. New York: Teachers College Press.

Murnane, R., & Levy, F. (1996). *Teaching the new basic skills: Principles for educating children to thrive in a changing economy.* New York: The Free Press.

National Commission on Teaching and America's Future (NCTAF). (1996). *What matters most: Teaching for America's future.* New York: Author.

National Education Goals Panel. (1998). *Data volume for the National Education Goals Report, 1998.* Washington, DC: U.S. Government Printing Office.

National Education Goals Panel. (1999). *Reading achievement state by state, 1999.* Washington, DC: U.S. Government Printing Office.

Sizer, T. R. (1984). *Horace's compromise: The dilemma of the American high school.* Boston: Houghton Mifflin.

Sizer, T. R., & Wood, G. (2008). Charter schools and the American dream. In L. Dingerson, B. Miner, B. Peterson, & S. Waters (Eds.), *Keeping the promise? The debate over charter schools* (pp. 3–16). Milwaukee, WI: Rethinking Schools.

Smiley, M., Lazarus, V., & Brownlee-Conyers, J. (1996). Instructional outcomes of school-based participative decision making. *Educational Evaluation and Policy Analysis, 18*(3), 181–198.

Stigler, J. W., & Stevenson, H. W. (1991, Spring). How Asian teachers polish each lesson to perfection. *American Educator, 15*(1), 12–21, 43–47.

Wilson, S., Floden, R., & Ferrini-Mundy, J. (2002, February). *Teacher preparation research: Current knowledge, gaps, and recommendations.* Working Paper. Seattle: Center for the Study of Teaching and Policy, University of Washington.

Wolf, P. J. (2008). *The comprehensive longitudinal evaluation of the Milwaukee parental choice program: Summary of baseline reports.* Fayetteville, AR: University of Arkansas, School Choice Demonstration Project.

Yoon, K. S., Duncan, T., Lee, S. W.-Y., Scarloss, B., & Shapley, K. (2007). *Reviewing the evidence on how teacher professional development affects student achievement.* Washington, DC: U.S. Department of Education, Institute of Education Sciences. Accessed at http://ies. ed.gov/ncee/edlabs on May 22, 2008.

Sir Michael Barber

Sir Michael Barber is an expert partner at an international consultancy leading its global education practice. He has been working on major challenges of performance, organization, and reform in government and the public services, especially education, in the United States, Great Britain, and other countries.

From 2001–2005, he was the founder and first head of the Prime Minister's Delivery Unit, where he was responsible for the oversight of implementation of Prime Minister Tony Blair's priority programs, including education, among others. From 1997–2001, Sir Michael was chief adviser to the U.K. Secretary of State for Education and was responsible for the implementation of the government's school reform program.

Prior to joining government, Sir Michael was a professor at the Institute of Education, University of London. He is the author of *Instruction to Deliver: Fighting to Transform Britain's Public Services* (2008) and numerous other books and articles.

In this chapter, the author describes three paradigms of public service reform—what he calls "21st-century solutions"—and gives examples of system improvement from around the world. He extends his argument with an analysis of the relationship between government and professions, a central issue in all education reform and one that the three paradigms on their own do not sufficiently explain. He then draws conclusions both for government and for leaders of the teaching profession.

Sir Michael Barber can be reached at Michael_Barber@mckinsey.com.

Chapter 3

From System Effectiveness to System Improvement: Reform Paradigms and Relationships

Sir Michael Barber

In the 1980s, a series of major reports from leading academics such as Michael Rutter and Peter Mortimore gave us for the first time a clear definition of school effectiveness. The picture they painted then has been refined somewhat in the decades since, but it has not been substantially altered. In the mid-1990s, the focus shifted from school effectiveness (what an effective school looks like) to school improvement (how to achieve effectiveness). Currently, research about whole education systems, not just individual schools, is reaching a similar point. We are becoming much clearer about what effective systems look like. The current picture will surely be clarified and refined in decades to come, but the central question now is this: What kind of reforms and what approaches to implementation will be most successful in enabling systems to *achieve* effectiveness? This debate is only just beginning, and there is much more to learn. The thirst for this knowledge in governments around the world is very great because a significant and perhaps decisive factor in the future economic and social success of countries is the quality of their education systems.

In this chapter, I will set out some admittedly early thinking on the question of system improvement based in part on the research, in part on my participation in debates of education reform in more than 20 countries around the world, and in part on my direct experience in England with both managing reform of the education system (from 1997 to 2001) and leading the Prime Minister's Delivery Unit (from 2001 to 2005) for Tony Blair, which provided the opportunity to learn about reform of other large public systems. The value here is that while some of the knowledge about improving education systems will, of course, come from within education research, much, I believe, also comes from examination of the reform of large systems in general. What they have in common may well be more important than their differences. In this chapter, I will do the following:

- Describe the three paradigms of public service reform—"21st-century solutions"—which I have put forward in previous and recent publications, relating them throughout to education reform and giving examples from around the world.

- Extend the argument by analyzing the relationship between government and professions, a central issue in all education reform and one that the three paradigms on their own do not sufficiently explain.

- Draw some conclusions both for government and for leaders of the teaching profession.

The first two sections draw heavily on my pamphlet *Three Paradigms of Public-Sector Reform* (2007), while the third and fourth parts draw similarly on the postscript in my book *Instruction to Deliver* (2008). This, however, is the only place where full argument about education system improvement is laid out.

21st-Century Solutions

How do we go about ensuring that the public services, especially education, are good enough that increasing numbers of wealthy people still choose them, thus binding them to the system and thereby securing the necessary support to generate enough revenue to ensure both steadily improving performance and increasing equity? Successful efforts to create effective education, health, policing, and social security systems suggest that there are three paradigms for reform in large-scale systems, that each is suitable in different circumstances, and that, regardless of which approach is selected, the government at the center of the system has a crucial role to play. I should say at the outset, therefore, that full-scale privatization has not been included as an option. While it is theoretically feasible, no government of a developed country has applied it to education for the good reason that while it might theoretically deliver efficiencies, it would be entirely inconsistent with equity.

Three Paradigms for Large-Scale Public Service

There are three paradigms for the reform of any large-scale public service: command and control, quasi-markets, and devolution and transparency.

Command and Control

Command and control is often the first choice of governments that want urgently to enact change—and to be seen enacting it. As the phrase implies, it involves top-down management approaches and conveys at least an impression of government taking charge. If executed well, it can be highly effective. Good examples of this paradigm include the U.K. government's National Literacy Strategy from 1997 to 2001 and its approach to reducing health service waiting times from 2000 to 2005. It should be noted, however, that there is nothing worse than command and control incompetently implemented.

A refinement of this paradigm is also top-down, but it is built and designed much more explicitly in consultation and potentially in collaboration with other key stakeholders, such as teachers and local authorities. Perhaps, rather than top-down, it should be described as "government-led." A good example of this is the education reform in Ontario since 2003, where educators have been successfully led by the government to pursue the moral purpose of higher standards of literacy and numeracy.

The danger of this variation is that it becomes a soft, pragmatic compromise and can therefore be ineffective. In Ontario, the existence of clear targets, strong emphasis on capacity-building, and the fact that the strategy was a reaction to a period of bitterness and conflict have all contributed to avoiding such an outcome. The question faced there is whether in the next phase the government can build effectively on the strong foundations already laid, because as performance improves, further improvements may depend on greater specification of teaching approaches—always a sensitive issue in relations between the teaching profession and the government.

Quasi-Markets

The second paradigm is quasi-markets. Given the stunning gains in productivity and customer services brought about in recent decades by the global market economy, and the difficulty governments have had in delivering improved public services, the idea of applying market forces to public systems without full-scale privatization has obvious attractions. Quasi-markets make the introduction of elements of the private sector feasible by introducing options such as retaining public control of the commissioning of services but having private providers deliver them. Examples include Medicare in the U.S., encouraging the use of independent-sector providers of routine operations in the U.K. healthcare system, and private providers of public schools in Philadelphia, which, recent evidence suggests, have been modestly successful. The academies that have been part of the education reform in England—and which are similar in concept to charter schools in the U.S.—also to some extent fit here.

However, applying market-like pressures within a public service is not always straightforward. One must be able to define a clear customer, offer customer choice, bring in new providers, and ensure that the use of money reflects the choices made by the customer. Charter school programs in New York State and California and voucher programs in Milwaukee, Wisconsin, and Florida are examples of quasi-markets in action. Evidence of impact is so far mixed, however, and success seems to depend on the precise design of the program. For example, Swedish education reform, which has brought in new providers and offered much greater choice, appears to have had modest positive effects, while the radical restructuring of England's National Health Service along quasi-market lines has brought some early benefits but is still far from complete. Meanwhile, evidence from the OECD-PISA international benchmarking is neutral on the benefits or otherwise of quasi-market reforms.

What of situations in which a government wishes to reform a service without resorting to command and control, but where the conditions for the success of quasi-markets are not present? For example, in the provision of prisons, courts, or policing, it is either not possible or not desirable to define a customer and offer choice from a range of providers. In relation to education, a government may seek a means of improvement, but for political, ideological, or indeed pragmatic reasons, it may reject market thinking.

Devolution and Transparency

In the third paradigm, devolution and transparency, the government can devolve responsibility to the frontline units delivering the relevant service and then use transparency—making public the results in a way that allows comparisons to be made—to drive performance. Units that succeed can be rewarded and potentially expanded; failing units can be made subject to interventions and ultimately shut down. To work, this model depends on genuine devolution of operational control along with accountability. The benefits have been limited at best in some U.S. school districts where accountability has been devolved to principals without offering them commensurate operational flexibility. The New Zealand school reforms of the early 1990s, those in Victoria, Australia, under the Kennett government of the late 1990s, and England's reforms from 1988 onwards are examples of this philosophy being applied to public education systems.

The model can operate in a fully public system—the most famous example being the New York City Police Department, where the CompStat process generated competition between precinct commanders—or within a service in which a mix of public and private providers compete on equal terms. This can be done by separating payer and provider and encouraging competition for contracts offered by the government or its agencies. This approach has been widely adopted with significant success in a variety of public services. Examples include the use of private prisons and the contracting out of local education services in the U.K. It seems clear that it can only work if, in those cases where performance is very poor in specific schools or local systems in education, the government has both the will and means to intervene effectively. This is by no means straightforward, and many American states are struggling with this challenge as the impact of the No Child Left Behind legislation is increasingly felt.

Where fully applied, the devolution and transparency model has proved sufficiently beneficial that some informed commentators have suggested applying it fully to all government services (see Osborne & Hutchinson, 2004). Moreover, it has the advantage that it can be applied in combination with the quasi-market approach. For example, while the quasi-market approach has been put in place in some public school systems, it is important to acknowledge that it has limitations in this sector. In a true market, the customer may change providers regularly. But parents are naturally reluctant, for good reason, to change their child's school often. For this reason, market pressures on schools tend to be weak. If, however, as is the case in England, New Zealand, and Holland, devolution and transparency are also introduced, pressure for school improvement tends to be significantly strengthened. The evidence from OECD-PISA, particularly its most recent report (OECD, 2007), suggests that moves in favor of both devolution and transparency are generally associated with better performance—though of course much depends on the precise detail.

To some degree, these paradigms will be familiar to any government, and there is intense ideological and political debate about the merits of each. The truth is that each model is appropriate in different circumstances, and all may be deployed within a system, with the balance between them changing over time.

A Four-Point Scale for Public Service

In *Good to Great* (2001), Jim Collins explains the characteristics that distinguish great companies from good ones. More recently in *Good to Great and the Social Sectors* (2005), he has explained that similar characteristics apply to all good organizations, regardless of whether they are in the business or social sector. Unfortunately, some organizations, including many of those that have historically been insulated from the pressures of the market, cannot yet call themselves "good." In the U.K. Prime Minister's Delivery Unit, we developed an extended, four-point scale designed to encompass the full range of performance for the various public services whose improvement was sought (Figure 1, page 78). The scale also suggests what the consumer reaction is likely to be at each point on the scale.

This categorization is crude but useful. Generally speaking, when services are "awful" and users are exiting the system, command and control solutions are appropriate. This is certainly true in a crisis, but it also applies in circumstances of endemic underperformance.

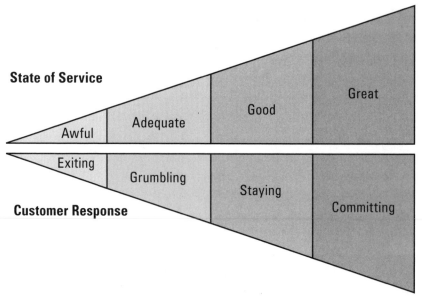

Figure 1: A Four-Point Scale for Public Services

In such cases, the public, and even the workforce within the service, will usually accept (albeit perhaps reluctantly) strong government intervention as long as it is effective. This is, after all, how the market handles bankrupt companies and how CEOs deal with underperforming companies. England's National Literacy and Numeracy Strategies, for example, were justified by the fact that elementary school literacy had barely improved in the 50 years leading up to the mid-1990s and the country's math standards lagged behind those in comparable countries.

Once adequate performance is established—which in itself is a huge task—the benefits of command and control are less clear. Governments find it hard to sustain the focus and drive on which command and control depends. Frontline leaders find themselves constrained by government regulation. Moreover, while shifting performance from "awful" to "adequate" is a substantial achievement, it does not satisfy the consumer, who continues to grumble until performance improves substantially. In the end, achieving "great" performance in the public sector requires unlocking the initiative, creativity, and motivation of leaders throughout the system, rather than just those at the top. This cannot be done without substantial devolution and/or providing the freedoms of a quasi-market. In short, as Joel Klein, Chancellor of the New York City school system, says, "You can mandate 'awful' to 'adequate,' but you cannot mandate 'greatness'; it must be unleashed" (quoted in Barber, 2008, p. 337)

The Role of Government

Reforming a large public service is a sophisticated challenge. Whichever paradigm is chosen, it will work only if three underlying roles are performed by government (Figure 2): capability, capacity, and culture; performance management; and strategic direction.

The first requirement relates to the capability, capacity, and culture of the service in question. This means that the people who provide the service must have or must acquire the right skills. It means sufficient resources must be allocated to get the job done. And it means an appropriate performance mindset must be established

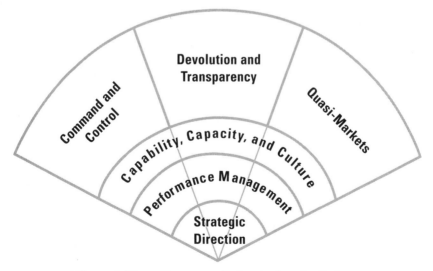

Figure 2: Three Necessary Underpinnings for Reform

among those providing the service. The precise nature of the required mindset will differ depending on the stage of reform. The final section of this chapter debates this issue in depth.

The second requirement is that the government secures rigorous performance management. None of the three paradigms can work without it. Performance management starts with information: Data on performance are essential so that service providers can see how they are doing and can benchmark their performance against others. The public, the ultimate funder of the service, also needs to see the return it is getting on its investment. Neither parents nor patients can exercise choice without good information. And as governments move away from command and control, the capacity to intervene when part of a service is underperforming remains crucial. Again, this cannot be done without reliable, up-to-date information on performance.

Third, because public-service reform is complex and only possible over several years, strategic direction is necessary. Developing a good strategy is a sophisticated challenge for a large business. In a political environment, with all its attendant pressures, this challenge is even more daunting. A small, well-qualified, courageous group—a kind of "guiding coalition" (Kotter, 1996) must oversee the sequencing and implementation of reform. The group that oversees the education reform in Ontario is a fine example. Given the controversy such reform often generates, only a sustained, well-thought-out strategy will work. Moreover, those responsible need to learn as they go because not all outcomes can be anticipated. This means designing processes to ensure rapid learning about what is working, what is not working, and how the environment is changing. In short, what the literature calls adaptive leadership (see Ronald Heifetz's work, for example) needs to be exercised by this group. The support for the strategy should build over time, both within the public service itself and among the public.

Government and the Teaching Profession

Whichever of the paradigms are chosen, the nature of a government's relationship with the teaching profession is central and needs analysis. There was some frustration among many teachers in England in the 1990s and early 2000s as the education reform unfolded, though it has now diminished. Even now, much more could be achieved if the relationship between the teaching profession and government was one that—in the word of the 2008 Ontario white Paper—"energized" all those involved (Ontario Ministry of Education, 2008).

The status quo ante in the late 1980s and early 1990s was unacceptable; performance fell short of both public expectations and the demands of the economy, so reform was necessary. There is no doubt government made mistakes along the way—governments always will. But despite mistakes, the education service significantly improved in England, not just for pupils, but also for teachers and other staff because of, not in spite of, the government's efforts. No one faced with the facts can dispute this, but it does not solve the problem of the strained relationship between the teaching profession and government over that 20-year period; the question is whether we can learn from that experience—and parallel reform efforts elsewhere—to develop a conceptual framework for thinking about this relationship, which is at the heart of education reform.

Unless the relationship between teachers and government is soundly based, it is a problem for everyone. It is a problem for government because the credibility of a teacher will always be much higher than that of a Minister or a civil servant and, even more importantly, because well-motivated teachers will do a better job. It is a problem for the professionals themselves because if they are dissatisfied, their careers will be less rewarding than they might have been, and by suggesting to people that reform is not working, they undermine the long-term prospects of fully tax-funded services. Above all, it is a problem for citizens because even if it does not affect the quality of their services—which in some cases it might—they will often feel a sense of confusion about what is happening and where the services for which they pay their taxes are headed.

Getting to the Root of the Problem

Part of the answer to this problem lies with globalization and technology, which are transforming services of all kinds everywhere. Those who work in media and communications or financial services, for example, have seen their working lives and organizations transformed since the 1980s. This is true for many professions in the private sector—architects, accountants, and lawyers, for example— whose working methods have been changed utterly. Globalization and technology influence services such as health, policing, and education, which are in the public sector, just as much as they shape those in the private sector. The difference is that in the public services, the changes that result are inevitably—precisely because the services are public—mediated through government. When governments urge educators to be "world class," they are giving voice to what the global market demands in other services. When doctors struggle with the impact of technology on medicine, they are facing what the market drives in other sectors. When police try to keep pace with organized crime, they are competing directly with an endlessly innovating— albeit in this case illegal and immoral—global business.

Charles Clarke, former Secretary of State for Education in England, makes this case in his chapter in *Public Matters: The Renewal of the Public Realm* (2007). He argues that technological and scientific innovation, empowered and assertive consumers, and growing concern about professional standards have dramatically changed the rules of the game and contributed to a mutual lack of confidence between government and the professions.

So when public service professionals complain that government has driven too much change, often the drivers (hidden though they might be) are these wider forces. This does not excuse a government from coming up with too many initiatives or making mistakes, but it does help to explain why governments around the world generally want more change while simultaneously public service professionals complain about overload. Moreover, while it is true that there has been immense change in many education systems since the 1980s, it is not true that it is more than in other sectors; indeed it may overall have been less.

For example, one of the most glaring gaps between the public and business sectors is in the attitude to customers. Public service professionals still too often take customers for granted and expect them to be grateful; very few professionals in the business sector can afford to take this attitude. In another example, in relation to the widespread availability of information, many people are now able to be their own lawyer or doctor or teacher up to a point, thanks to the Internet. It is easy for the professional, once revered specifically for his or her expertise, to feel threatened or defensive in these circumstances—but in fact the existence of many better-informed citizens or customers is potentially a major gain. The challenge for teachers is to build unshakeable partnerships for performance with those they serve—that is, pupils and parents.

Consider performance data: Most teachers and headteachers I know hate league tables (in the U.K., these are published charts or lists that compare institutions by ranking them in order of their progress or results), but this is the era of global media and freedom of information. University vice-chancellors do not like league tables, either, and government does not publish them for higher education, but *The Times* does, student websites do, and so do several outlets on a global basis. When I was in Berlin recently, the front-page headline on the city's main paper related to a website where schoolchildren were able to rank their teachers across the city. Comparative data will out. Moreover, citizens and customers demand it and will not give it up. The only question, therefore, for teachers is whether they would prefer government to organize and provide reliable, published comparative performance information—in which case there can be an ongoing dialogue with them about what is included and how it is presented—or a major media organization to do it instead, in which case there will be no such dialogue.

I emphasize this point because I believe that the two main drivers of teachers' frustration in England, as in the Unites States, since the 1980s have been the pressures of accountability and the pace of change, yet both of these are ultimately spurred on not just by government, but by globalization and technology. When government makes mistakes or suffers "initiative-itis," it compounds the problem, and government hugely influences how these forces play out, so of course it bears huge responsibility. But unless this bigger picture is understood, we will never unravel the complexities of the relationship between government and professions.

The central issue, therefore, beyond the competence of government, is how to construct a more effective relationship between government and teachers—one in which they develop a deeper understanding not just of each other's views of the world, but also of the profound forces that are reshaping everyone's world and the implications of these forces for education.

In the first broadly successful phase of Blair's education reform between 1997 and 2000, one of the government's mistakes in relation to the teaching profession was, in the words of John Kotter, "under-communicating the vision by a factor of 10 (or 100 or even 1000)" (1996, p. 4). To be sure, the government wrote what was widely recognized to be an ambitious white paper and promoted it. It consulted widely in its formation, too. It sent out pages of regulations and guidance on everything from the far-flung corners of school governance (unimportant) to the sequence of teaching phonics (vital). In what was widely seen as an innovation (remarkably), Ministers and officials visited schools all the time. Alongside these efforts to communicate directly with the school workforce, government also ran a largely successful media strategy aimed, of course, at parents and taxpayers rather than teachers. The message here was that performance in the education system was not good enough, failure would be tackled vigorously, and poor schools would be closed. Parents and taxpayers heard and generally warmed to the message. The problem was a simple and obvious one: Teachers read the newspapers like everyone else and heard the government's message to parents loud and clear; understandably they did not pay as much attention to the guidance and white papers so they did not necessarily understand the strategy or the moral purpose of the strategy.

The government understood this challenge soon enough and began to respond. It reduced the paper going into schools dramatically, but obviously this did not convey the vision in the way Kotter suggests. It realized that in order to do this, it needed intermediaries. Government could not communicate directly with more than 400,000 teachers, so it focused on headteachers. For example, in September 2000, it took a road show around the country: five cities in 5 days, 500 heads in each venue—like a band on tour. Ministers, leading officials, and successful headteachers explained the vision and the strategy and debated them vigorously with the very engaged participants. These events were a great step forward and were valued greatly by those who attended, but what about Kotter's point? This was the boldest direct communication exercise ever attempted by the Department for Education in England up to that time, yet that week just 10% of headteachers in the country participated in the events.

The government needed briefer, clearer, more memorable messages that resonated. It needed to spend even more time than it did on the road. It needed to integrate the media and direct communications approaches. It needed to sustain the same messages for longer. It needed fewer distractions. It needed constant, genuine interaction, and it needed more intermediaries. The purpose, after all, was a better society—not, as many teachers understandably thought, hitting government targets. Others in addition to head-teachers should have been effectively mobilized, such as local authority chief executives, chief education officers (now called Directors of Children's Services), and heads of university schools of education. Not all of these people would have agreed with the government by any means, but it would have greatly helped if they had understood.

I have spent some time discussing these communication efforts to make a more general point about the need to invest in much greater, deeper communication between professions and the government. Moreover, it needs to be two-way, interactive, and sustained. Much of policy in England from 1997 to 2000 was of the "shock therapy" variety. The government had set out to jolt a system from its comfort zone and deliver some results. It was largely successful, but could it have achieved what it did with a different approach, investing more deeply (and inevitably more slowly) in two-way communication early on? Or would it have lost momentum and found the cutting edges beveled off its policies? There is no easy answer to this uncomfortable question.

This takes us back to the idea of a guiding coalition. It is necessary to have a small group at the center of a change whose members know what they want to do and how they plan to go about it, but over time this group must widen. This is why Michael Fullan and I talk about "ever-widening circles of leadership"; the guiding coalition can stay at the center, but it needs consciously and constantly to build leadership capacity throughout the service for which it is responsible (Barber, 2008, p. 372). In Ontario's education reform, this has been done well.

In the second Blair term, Estelle Morris began and then Charles Clarke and David Miliband completed a process of building a social partnership with teacher leaders. In return for active involvement in the policy process, the unions (all but one of them) agreed to greater flexibility in working practices. This inspired the foundation of something that could be much more radical; imagine a joint declaration that, for example, the teaching profession and government would strive to achieve world-class performance—defined and specified—with both accepting their share of responsibility for achieving it. This points the way to the next phase of my argument: What is needed is not just better communication, but a shared understanding of what is required to achieve world-class public services and a shared commitment, given the huge investment over the past decade in England (and still flowing, albeit more slowly, in the next decade), that this is what this country needs to see delivered. Making this happen will require courageous leadership—not just in government, but also in the professions. Whether it will emerge remains to be seen, but given that the alternative, over a generation, could be frustration, conflict, disappointing performance, the flight from the public realm of those who can afford the private alternative and thus a residual set of poor public services for poor people, it must be worth a try.

Moving Toward World-Class Education

In this final section, I want to set out a conceptual framework that might provide an underpinning for this long-term shared understanding between government and the professions. The basis of the framework is that the nature of reform and therefore the nature of the relationship between professions and government needs to change and adapt as services improve.

The starting point is the scale presented in Figure 1. As discussed previously, this crude scale establishes four states: awful, adequate, good, and great. In terms of reform, it establishes three phases or transitions: 1) awful to adequate, 2) adequate to good, and 3) good to great.

My argument is that as systems pass through these three transitions, the nature of the relationship between government and the professions needs to adapt and the dialogue between them needs to develop accordingly.

To take a large education system through these three transitions is a major task by any standards. To take them all the way from "awful" to "great" is surely at least a decade's work. Any government, along with its allies in the professions, needs to be committed for the long haul. Indeed, given the vagaries of democracy, it is always possible that governments of differing parties will be involved, as in the 1990s in education reforms in England, Texas, and North Carolina. Given the long timelines, the key is for those leading the reforms to have two timetables in mind: one leading to short-term results, the other leading ultimately to world-class performance. Both are essential; the former because without short-term results, neither those within the system nor those using it will have any confidence that progress is being made, and the latter because world-class is the ultimate goal. Thus, in the awful-to-adequate phase, it is right to emphasize reducing outright failure and achieving a jump in the next year's test results, just as the management of a failing company must first stop leaking cash and then build some confidence among investors. The key, though, is to take these sometimes drastic actions in a way that does not undermine progress towards the long-term goal. For example, Michael Fullan and I emphasize in our conversations the importance of building the underlying capability and capacity of a workforce and a system through *every* policy.

Since 2003, the Government of Ontario has consciously modeled its strategy for improving literacy and numeracy in schools on our experience in England between 1997 and 2001, but it has also consciously varied the strategy, with greater emphasis on partnership, less prescription, fewer "distracters" (as they call them), and a language about capacity-building and sustainability. They still have targets, but the government does not publish league tables (it leaves that to the newspapers), which means it can deflect this criticism. Interestingly, the results so far in Ontario are very similar to England's—really substantial progress beginning to plateau, but so far not enough to hit an ambitious target. The test will be whether in the next phase they can avoid the long plateau seen in England. I believe they have a strong chance, partly because performance in Ontario was already better than in England when they began, so shock therapy was not judged necessary, and partly because leaders there have been careful to bear the long term in mind throughout the first phase. It will depend whether it can sustain partnership as the strategy becomes more precise and specific. Certainly, the dialogue throughout with the teacher unions, principals, and school boards has been focused on building partnership and appears to have developed and sustained a shared sense of moral purpose.

This is just one interesting contrast. On the basis of education reforms such as these in other countries and my own experience in England in health and policing as well as education, it is possible to set out a framework for the changing nature of the dialogue between government professions that moves the conversation on as the system goes through the transitions toward world class. The basic premise is that awful-to-adequate may involve shock therapy and therefore a top-down approach, but the further you move towards world class, the less a government's role is prescriptive and the more it becomes enabling. Meanwhile, the professions need to move in the other direction from being on the receiving end of the shock therapy to, at the world-class end, leading or driving the reform.

At the outset, though, we need some understanding of what it takes to be world class. In education, we have this knowledge from a series of international benchmarking studies. What marks out the best systems in the world is that they recruit great people into teaching, and invest in their skills effectively both at the start of their careers and throughout them so that they teach lessons of consistently high quality. Consistency is the key word from our point of view in England, for these same international benchmarking exercises reveal that England's education system has many of the qualities of great systems, but far too much variation from classroom to classroom and school to school. In fact, as Andreas Schleicher, who organizes the OECD's benchmarking of school systems says, "Few if any systems are doing more of the right things in policy terms than England's, but this has yet to translate into consistent quality at classroom level" (cited in Barber, 2008, p. 376).

If in England we want world-class education, building this reliability will be crucial, and it begins and ends in teachers' classrooms. In other words, it can only be brought about by frontline professionals who share the mission, benefit from excellent management, and are given the tools and incentives to deliver consistent high quality by an enabling government. With this background, then, the framework described in Table 1 can be developed as the starting point for dialogue.

At the very least, a framework such as this could provide a common language for the dialogue between government and the professions. That alone would be a major improvement on talking past each other, which has seemed so common in many countries. Two factors should enable it: One is that even when a system is awful, there are plenty of headteachers and teachers who are doing an outstanding job. Right from the outset, government needs to foster a strong relationship with those in any service who are out in front. If these school leaders can express impatience with the slow pace of change, it helps to counterbalance the drag effect of those who want to slow things down. Indeed, this alliance with successful leaders is a key part of that process of building ever-widening circles of leadership, as previously mentioned. The second enabling factor is the vastly improved information available about the performance of

	Phase of Development		
	Awful → Adequate	Adequate → Good	Good → Great
Chief Focus of the System	• Tackling under-performance	• Transparency • Spreading best-practice	• World-class performance • Continuous learning and innovation
Role of Government	• Prescribing • Justifying	• Regulating • Capacity-building	• Enabling • Incentivizing
Role of Professions	• Implementing • Accepting evidence • Adopting minimum standards	• Accommodating • Evidence-based • Adopting best-practice	• Leading • Evidence-driven • Achieving high reliability and innovation
Nature of Relationship Between Government and Professions	• Top-down • Antagonistic	• Negotiated • Pragmatic	• Principled • Strategic partnership
Time Horizon	• Immediate	• Short and medium term	• Continuous
Chief Outcomes	• Improvement in outcomes • Reduction of public anxiety	• Steady improvement • Growing public satisfaction	• Consistent quality • Public engagement and co-production
What the Public Thinks	• "You should have done that years ago."	• "Maybe. . . . We'll believe it when we see it."	• "That's what we wanted all along."

Table 1: How the Relationship Between Government and Professions Could Transform Public Service

public services. These data—everything from the published performance data to the growing range of international benchmarks—provide (and in the future will provide even better) the evidence base on which to have this conversation. Charles Clarke, former Secretary of State for Education in England, argues that part of the new relationship would need to be long-term pay settlements, which are both more flexible and more explicit about professionals' responsibilities to develop their skills continuously, with government accepting responsibility for making this possible. The 3-year pay settlement for teachers in England announced in January 2008 may point the way. In Ontario, similarly, a long-term (4 year) pay deal was agreed upon in 2005 as a conscious step toward removing a "distracter."

Certainly it is in everyone's interest to make the attempt to create a principled relationship between government and the public service professions. The demand for public services of real quality that are available to all is overwhelming; those who work in the public services would surely prefer to be more motivated and more successful (rather than less), while governments in the next decade will find they need to sign up to this vision too if they are to succeed in meeting bold aspirations. Without something along these lines, we are likely to see public education systems collectively—government and the school workforce—fail to implement reform successfully or to communicate to the users and to those who pay for the services where they are heading and how they are doing. As a consequence, a spiral of decline would set in. If government and the teaching profession aim their messages only at each other and appear to be at loggerheads, then the public will inevitably be both skeptical and confused.

If instead they combine in implementation and communication, they could be unstoppable. Easy to say, but very hard to do in practice, since this will require major culture change all around. It will require professions that embrace transparency, recognize the value of consistently high-quality and reliable processes, as well as personalization, and instead of saying "slow down," they would promote greater urgency. It will require governments to engage in constant, informed dialogue, stick to priorities, avoid gimmicks, and admit mistakes. Delivering sustained system improvement and consistent world-class performance will be an exacting challenge for whole systems. System leaders around the world are just beginning to understand what it will take.

So what is the change model being advocated here? It can be summarized as follows:

- There is more than one possible means of reforming a system—the three paradigms—and choosing between them is a matter in part of political judgment and in part an assessment of current performance in the system. Not having any model at all—just initiatives—will not work.

- Whichever paradigm or combination of paradigms is chosen, as long as the service remains public, there is a role for government, which consists of three elements: strategic oversight, performance management, and developing the culture, capability, and capacity of the overall systems.

- As a reform proceeds, continuous, powerful two-way communication between government stakeholders—especially frontline professionals—and between all those in the system and the wider public is essential. Very few governments get this right.

In addition to being clear about the approach to reform, government needs an account of its relationship to the teaching profession that is more sophisticated than the traditional "hard" or "soft" stance. The nature of this relationship should change as the strategy unfolds and the performance of the system improves. The task of building and sustaining this relationship is a responsibility of the leaders of the profession as well as the government. In this chapter, I have described a conceptual framework for the way this relationship might develop. I do not for a minute think this is conclusive; rather, I hope it will start a more sophisticated conversation than we have had hitherto.

References

Barber, M. (2007). *Three paradigms of public-sector reform.* London: McKinsey & Company.

Barber, M. (2008). *Instruction to deliver: Fighting to transform Britain's public services.* London: Methuen.

Clarke, C. (2007). Competition for social justice: Markets and contestability in public services. In P. Diamond (Ed.), *Public matters: The renewal of the public realm.* London: Politico.

Collins, J. (2001). *Good to great.* New York: Harper Business.

Collins, J. (2005). *Good to great and the social sectors: Why business thinking is not the answer: A monograph to accompany* Good to Great. New York: Collins.

Heifetz, R. A. (1994). *Leadership without easy answers.* Cambridge, MA: Belknap.

Kotter, J. (1996). *Leading change.* Boston: Harvard Business School.

Mortimore, P., Sammons, P., Stoll, L., Lewis, D., & Ecoh, R. (1988). *School matters: The junior years.* London: Open Books.

Ontario Ministry of Education. (2008). *Energizing Ontario education: Reach every student.* Toronto: Author.

Osborne, D., & Hutchinson, P. (2004). *The price of government: Getting the results we need in an age of permanent crisis.* New York: Basic Books.

Peterson, P. E., & Gringas, M. M. (2007). *Impact of for-profit and nonprofit management in student achievement: The Philadelphia experiment.* Boston: Harvard University.

Rutter, M. (1979). *Fifteen thousand hours: Secondary schools and their effect on children.* London: Open Books.

Andreas Schleicher

Andreas Schleicher is head of the Indicators and Analysis Division of the Organisation for Economic Co-operation and Development (OECD) Directorate for Education. In this role, he is responsible for the development and analysis of benchmarks on the performance of education systems, which includes the management of the OECD Programme for International Student Assessment (PISA), the OECD Programme for the International Assessment of Adult Competencies (PIAAC), the OECD Teaching and Learning International Survey (TALIS), and the OECD International Indicators of National Education Systems program (INES). Before joining the OECD in 1994, he was director for analysis at the International Association for the Evaluation of Educational Achievement (IEA). He studied physics in Germany and received a degree in mathematics and statistics in Australia. He is an honorary professor at the University of Heidelberg.

In this chapter, the author examines the merits of international comparative benchmarks as drivers for educational change. He begins by setting out a rationale and theory of action and then illustrates the role and functioning of international benchmarks with the example of PISA, which the OECD launched in 2000 to monitor learning outcomes on a regular basis in the principal industrialized countries. The example of PISA suggests that international benchmarks feeding peer pressure and public accountability may at times be more powerful than legislation, rules, and regulations. Within less than a decade, international benchmarks such as PISA have established themselves as indispensable for reform in the field of education, which thus far has been conceived of as essentially domestic.

Andreas Schleicher can be reached at Andreas.Schleicher@oecd.org. For more information about the Organisation for Economic Co-operation and Development and the Programme for International Student Assessment, visit www.oecd.org.

Chapter 4

International Benchmarking as a Lever for Policy Reform*

Andreas Schleicher

The world is rapidly becoming a different place; the demands of globalization and modernization on individuals and societies include the challenges stemming from diverse and interconnected populations, rapid technological change in the workplace and in everyday life, and the instantaneous availability of vast amounts of information. In this globalized world, individuals and countries that invest heavily in education benefit both socially and economically. For example, among the countries studied by the Organisation for Economic Co-operation and Development (OECD), those that have experienced the largest increase in the percentage of their populations receiving a college education in the last decade have often continued to see rising earning differentials for college graduates. On average across 25 OECD countries with available data, the earnings premium of a college degree is now more than 50%, and all but six countries saw increases in the relative earnings of college

---

*The views expressed in this chapter are solely those of the author and do not necessarily reflect the views of the Organisation for Economic Co-operation and Development.

graduates over the last decade. In Hungary, Germany, and Italy this increase exceeded 30 percentage points (OECD, 2008). Similarly, while unemployment is substantially higher than the average among those with low qualifications, it has not increased in those countries that have expanded college education, suggesting that the better qualified are not simply crowding out those with lower qualifications in labor markets.

Technological development also depends on education, not just because tomorrow's knowledge workers and innovators require high levels of education, but also because a highly educated workforce is a prerequisite for adopting and absorbing new technologies and increasing productivity. Together, skills and technology have flattened the world such that all work that can be digitized, automated, and outsourced can now be done by the most effective and competitive individuals, enterprises, or countries—regardless of where they are located.

In contrast to this global reality, education still remains a very local business that often looks inward. This is not just because the educational process centers on local human interaction, but also because different types of walls tend to separate students, educators, institutions, and education systems. Some of these walls are natural, established by language or culture. Others result from poor knowledge management in education systems or beliefs, traditions, and ideologies that remain dominant in education. As a result, education systems can face difficulties in their attempts to enable schools and teachers to share, jointly develop, and implement knowledge about their work and performance. While those who run education systems may have access to some evidence on school performance, those who deliver educational services at the front line in schools often do not, or they face obstacles in translating such knowledge into effective classroom practices.

Similar walls exist between education systems and the world beyond their national borders. Few instruments exist for countries to look outward to educational policies and practices developed and implemented beyond their immediate experience and control. This is a particular challenge since, in the field of education, ethical and practical considerations limit the use of experimental methods to explore alternative policies and practices. Thus, school systems can operate like food silos: Every few years a new reform idea is put on top, creating below it 10 to 15 years of layers of often unfinished and incoherent reforms. This is because with an approach where educators at the frontline implement ideas conceived at higher levels of an organization through cascades of regulation and training, this is the amount of time it takes to implement change. At the end of the process, students, teachers, and schools can then be confronted with a blend of past directions they often do not understand and own.

How much further could education systems develop if they could integrate and build on the human potential that lies in their global workforce, as is the case in other economic and social sectors? Education has always been a knowledge industry in the sense that it is concerned with the transmission of knowledge, but it is still far from becoming a knowledge industry where its own practices are transformed by knowledge gained at the frontlines about their efficacy. This is in contrast to many other fields where people begin their professional lives expecting their practice to be transformed by research. Half a century ago, a surgeon, like the teachers of today, would manage his or her job with a limited set of tools and the knowledge acquired during his or her studies. Today, the surgeon is embedded in a profession that continually transforms itself through global research and development, with knowledge developed in one part of the world spreading rapidly and absorbed globally. He or she now works in a sophisticated technological environment, exchanges ideas and experiences with others in the professional community, and manages his or her work in a team. Very little of that change in the work environment (and in incentive systems, as well) has happened in the field of education. In contrast to other sectors, productivity in education has tended to decline over recent decades because increases in educational expenditure—which among OECD countries amounted to 35% in real terms per student over the last decade alone—have often not been matched with improved outcomes, with only a few countries showing a significant rise in student performance.

International Comparative Benchmarking: Breaking Down the Walls

International comparative benchmarking provides one way to break through some of these walls, and it has become a powerful instrument for policy reform and transformational change. It allows education systems to look at themselves through the lenses of policies planned, implemented, and achieved elsewhere in the world. International benchmarks can show what is possible in education in terms of the quality, equity, and efficiency of educational services, and they can foster better understanding of how different education systems address similar problems. While international benchmarks alone cannot identify cause-and-effect relationships between inputs, processes, and educational outcomes, they can shed light on key features in which education systems show similarities and differences, and make those key features visible among educators, policymakers, and the general public.

In the Dark, All Schools and Education Systems Look the Same

Some contend that international benchmarking encourages an undesirable process of degrading cultural and educational diversity among institutions and education systems, but the opposite can be argued as well: In the dark, all institutions and education systems look the same. It is comparative benchmarking that sheds light on the differences on which reform efforts can then capitalize.

For example, the OECD's Programme for International Student Assessment (PISA) revealed the success of very different education systems in Finland, Canada, and Japan in terms of the quality, equity, and coherence of learning outcomes. Before PISA, these successes went unnoticed often.

But international comparative benchmarks have their pitfalls, too. Policymakers tend to use them selectively, often in support of existing policies rather than as instruments to challenge them and explore alternatives. Moreover, highlighting specific features of educational performance may detract attention from other features that are equally as important, thus potentially influencing individual, institutional, or systemic behavior in ineffective or even undesirable ways. This can be likened to a drunken driver who looks for his lost car keys under a street lantern; when questioned whether he lost them there, he responds no, but it was the only place he could see. This risk of undesirable consequences of inadequately defined performance benchmarks is very real, as teachers and policymakers are led to focus their work on those issues that performance benchmarks value and put into the spotlight of the public debate. This does not detract from the value of benchmarks, but it urges policymakers and researchers to benchmark on the basis of relevant indicators while keeping a close eye on their limits.

This chapter examines the merits of international comparative benchmarks as drivers for educational change. It begins by setting out a rationale and theory of action and illustrates the role and function of international benchmarks using the example of PISA, which the OECD launched in 2000 to monitor learning outcomes in the principal industrialized countries on a regular basis.

The example of PISA is interesting in this context because in contrast to other organizations, the OECD has no legislative or financial powers with which to exert influence on national policies. The OECD only provides the evidence, analysis, and advice generated by PISA. Nevertheless, it seems that in some countries, PISA has spurred educational reform and sometimes transformational change in unprecedented ways. By shifting the focus from the inputs and the ways in which education systems are run toward the outputs and outcomes of education systems, and by making these outcomes publicly visible in an internationally comparative framework, PISA has made the work of education systems—and the work of politicians—globally transparent. The example of PISA suggests that international benchmarks feeding peer pressure and public accountability may at times be more powerful for reform than legislation, rules, and regulations. Within less than a decade, it seems that international benchmarks such as those highlighted by PISA have, for better or worse, established themselves as crucial for reform in the field of education, which thus far has been thought of as an essentially domestic system.

Know Why You Are Looking: A Theory of Action

The rationale for developing and employing international educational benchmarks as levers for educational change has several dimensions:

- **Showing what is possible in education**—International benchmarks can help to optimize and transform existing policies by allowing reflection on the paradigms and beliefs underlying current policies, which become apparent when contrasted with policy alternatives.

- **Putting national targets into a broader perspective**—International benchmarks can help set policy targets by identifying measurable goals achieved by other systems, identifying policy levers, and establishing trajectories for reform.

- **Assessing the pace of change**—International benchmarks can assist with gauging the pace of educational progress and reviewing the reality of educational delivery on the front lines.

- **Supporting the political economy of reform**—These benchmarks can be a powerful tool to make educational change happen—even where there are major obstacles—which is a major challenge in education since the benefits of educational reform almost inevitably accrue to successive governments, if not generations.

These dimensions are examined more closely in the following sections.

Showing What Is Possible in Education

The impact of international benchmarks is usually most profound when they reveal that a country performs comparatively poorly. Although it is sometimes argued that weighing the pig does not make it fatter, diagnosing its status as underweight can be an important first step towards treating malnutrition. Moreover, the level of public awareness raised by comparisons like PISA has in some countries created an important political momentum and engaged educational stakeholders, including teacher or employer organizations, in support of policy reform. By raising the stakes, it has also increased the cost of failure for educational reform.

Equally as important, international benchmarks have had a significant impact in some countries that did not do poorly in absolute terms, but were confronted with results that differed from how educational performance was generally perceived. In Germany, for example, equity in learning opportunities across schools had often been taken for granted, as significant efforts were devoted to ensuring that schools were adequately and equally resourced. The PISA 2000 results, however, revealed large socioeconomic disparities in educational outcomes between schools. Further analyses that separated equity-related issues from those related to the socioeconomic heterogeneity within schools and those related to socioeconomic segregation through the school system suggested that German students from more privileged social backgrounds were directed into the more prestigious academic schools that yielded superior educational outcomes. It was found that students from less privileged social backgrounds—even when their performance on the PISA assessment was similar—were directed into less prestigious vocational schools that yielded poorer educational outcomes. This raised the specter that the education system was reinforcing rather than moderating socioeconomic background factors. These results, and the ensuing public debate, inspired a wide range of equity-related reform efforts in Germany, some of which have been transformational in nature. These changes included providing early childhood programs with an educational orientation (they had previously been considered largely an aspect of social welfare), establishing national educational standards in a country where regional and local autonomy had long been the overriding paradigm, and enhancing targeted support for disadvantaged students, such as those who had immigrated to the country (whose poor performance had previously gone unnoticed).

For many educators and experts in Germany, the socioeconomic disparities that PISA revealed were not necessarily surprising; however, it was often taken for granted and seen as outside the scope of public policy that disadvantaged children would fare less well in school. The fact that PISA revealed that the impact of socioeconomic background on students and school performance varied so considerably across countries, and that other countries appeared to moderate socioeconomic disparities so much more effectively, showed that improvement was possible, provided the momentum for policy change, and took away excuses for not pursuing change.

Showing that strong educational performance, and indeed improvement, is possible seems to be one of the most important merits of international benchmarks. Whether in Asia (like Japan or Korea), in Europe (like Finland), or in North America (like Canada), many countries displayed strong overall performance in PISA and, equally important, showed that poor performance in school does not automatically follow from a disadvantaged socioeconomic background.

International benchmarking has also shown that in some countries, success can become a consistent and predictable educational outcome. For example, in Finland, the country with the strongest overall results in PISA, the performance variation between schools in 2006 amounted to only 5% of students' overall performance variation. Thus, Finnish parents can expect high and consistent performance standards in whatever school they choose to enroll their children. Considerable research has been invested in the features of successful education systems. In some countries, governments have used knowledge provided by PISA about their relative standing internationally as a starting point for peer review to study policies and practices in countries operating under similar circumstances that achieve better results (Döbert et al., 2004). Such peer reviews, resulting in a set of specific policy recommendations for educational improvement, are also being carried out by the OECD, and have been published so far for Denmark and Scotland (Organisation for Economic Co-operation and Development, 2004, 2007b).

As a result of all of this the yardsticks for public policy in education are no longer national goals or standards alone, but instead increasingly based on the performance of the most successful education systems internationally. Public visibility of international benchmarks has sometimes transformed a specialized educational debate into a public debate, with citizens recognizing that their country's educational performance will need not to simply match average performance, but to exceed it, if they want their children to earn above-average wages.

Putting National Targets Into a Broader Perspective

International benchmarks can also play an important role in putting national performance targets into perspective. Educators are often faced with a dilemma: If the percentage of students obtaining degrees in school increases, some will claim that the school system has improved. Others, however, will claim that standards must have been lowered, and behind the suspicion that better results reflect lowered standards is often a belief that overall performance in education cannot be raised. International performance benchmarks give us a wider frame of reference by allowing schools and education systems to look at themselves through the lens of the performance of schools and education systems in other countries. Some countries have actively embraced this perspective and systematically related national performance to international performance benchmarks, for example, by embedding components of the PISA assessments into their national assessments.

Assessing the Pace of Change

A third important aspect of international benchmarking is that comparisons provide a frame of reference to assess the pace of change in educational improvement. While a national framework allows assessment of progress in absolute terms, an internationally comparative perspective allows assessment of whether or not that progress matches the pace of change observed elsewhere. Indeed, while all education systems in the OECD network have seen quantitative growth over past decades, international comparisons reveal that the pace of change in educational output has varied markedly. For example, among those 55 to 64 years old, the United States is well ahead of all other OECD countries in terms of the proportion of individuals with both secondary and post-secondary schooling. However, international comparisons show that this advantage is largely a result of the "first-mover advantage" that the United States gained after Word War II by massively increasing enrollment in schooling. Their lead has lessened over recent decades as more and more countries have reached and surpassed qualification levels in the United States in more recent cohorts. While many countries are now close to ensuring that virtually all young adults leave their schooling with at least

a high-school degree—the baseline qualification for reasonable earnings and employment prospects according to the OECD—the United
States has not improved significantly on this measure. Among
OECD countries, only New Zealand, Spain, Turkey, and Mexico
now have lower high-school completion rates than the United States
(Organisation of Economic Co-operation and Development, 2008a).
Even when including qualifications that people can acquire later in
life to make up for unsuccessful school completion, the United States
has slipped from first among OECD countries for adults born in the
1940s to 12th among those born in the 1970s. That is not because
completion rates in the United States declined, but rather because
they have risen so much faster in many other countries. For example,
two generations ago, South Korea ranked 24th in schooling output
among OECD countries, and had the level of economic output of
Afghanistan today; however, South Korea is now the top performer
in proportion of successful schooling, with 96% of an age cohort
obtaining a high-school degree. In college education, the pace of
change has been even more dramatic, and so has been its impact
on the relative standing of countries: Within less than a decade, the
United States has slipped from first to 15th place for college graduation among the relevant age group. The point is that, while progress
in a national perspective matters, in a global framework, an internationally comparative perspective is having a growing impact not just
on public policy but on institutional behavior as well.

Supporting the Political Economy of Reform

Last but not least, international benchmarks can support the
political economy of reform by helping to make change happen,
even in the face of important obstacles or when the returns may
not be immediately apparent. In the 2007 Mexican national survey
of parents, 77% of parents interviewed reported that the quality of
educational services provided by their children's school was good
or very good, even though, as measured by OECD's PISA 2006

assessment, roughly half of the Mexican 15-year-olds enrolled in school performed at or below the lowest level of proficiency established by PISA (IFIE-ALDUCIN, 2007; Organisation for Economic Co-operation and Development, 2007a). There may be many reasons for such a discrepancy between perceived educational quality and performance on international benchmarks. For example, this may be due to the fact that the quality of educational services and schooling that Mexican children now receive is significantly better than what their parents experienced. However, it is difficult to justify the investment of public resources into areas for which there seems to be limited public demand. This poses challenges for the political economy of reform.

One recent response by the Mexican presidential office has been to include a "PISA performance target" into the new Mexican reform plan. This internationally benchmarked performance target (to be achieved by 2012) will highlight the gap between national performance and international standards and monitor how educational improvement contributes to closing this gap. It is associated with a reform trajectory and delivery chain of support systems and incentive structures, as well as with improved access to professional development to assist school leaders and teachers in meeting the target, with much of this drawing on the experiences of other countries. Brazil has taken a similar route, providing each secondary school with information on the level of progress that is needed to perform at the OECD average performance level on PISA in 2021.

Japan is one of the best performing education systems on international comparisons. However, PISA revealed that while Japanese students tended to do very well on tasks that require reproducing subject matter content, they did much less well on open-ended constructed tasks that require demonstrating the capacity to extrapolate from what they know and apply their knowledge in novel settings. Conveying that to parents and a general public that are used to certain types of tests poses another type of challenge for the political economy of reform. The policy response in Japan has been to incorporate PISA-type open-constructed tasks into the national assessment, with the aim that skills that are considered important become valued in the education system. Similarly, Korea has recently incorporated advanced PISA-type literacy tasks in its university entrance examinations to enhance excellence in the capacity of its students to access, manage, integrate, and evaluate written material. In both countries, these are transformational changes that would have been much harder to imagine without the challenges revealed by international benchmarking.

Know What You Are Looking For, and Know How to Recognize It: Putting Theory Into Practice and Validating It

It is one thing to recognize the relevance of international benchmarks. It is another thing to develop the right benchmarks that facilitate educational improvement. International benchmarks need to fulfill different and sometimes competing demands. First of all, they should relate to the central and enduring parts of education systems to ensure that they are relevant and remain relevant. This ensures that short-lived policy concerns do not distort the priorities and operation of educational institutions. Second, benchmarks should also relate to performance or behavior that can be improved by policy and practice, and the international comparative perspective should offer added value to what can be accomplished through national analysis. Third, while international benchmarks need to be as comparable as possible, they also need to be as country-specific as is necessary to capture historical, systemic, and cultural variation among countries. Fourth, such benchmarks need to be as simple as possible to be widely understood, while remaining as complex as necessary to reflect multifaceted educational realities. Fifth, while there is a general desire to keep any set benchmarks as small as possible, the set needs to be large enough to be useful to policymakers across countries that face different educational challenges.

To provide effective tools for public policy that balance these various demands, the OECD has established a framework for international benchmarks (see Table 1, page 112). This framework builds on the recognition that central features of the development, functioning, and impact of education require information on learning outcomes. OECD's measurement and benchmarking tools in education, such as PISA, derive from this framework.

OECD's framework distinguishes between four levels of the education system that speak to different types of stakeholders (the left column in Table 1):

I.   The individual participants in education and learning—the learning environment within the institutions and the learners themselves

II. The instructional settings

III. The providers of educational services

IV. The education system as a whole

The framework groups each of these levels into three classes of benchmarks (the top row in Table 1):

1.   **Education and learning outputs and outcomes**—This is often perceived to comprise the most important class of benchmarks as it relates to direct measures of learning outcomes as well as to measures of the impact of knowledge and skills for individuals, societies, and economies.

2.   **Policy levers and contexts shaping educational outcomes at each level of the education system**—This includes measures of attitudes and behavior at the student level, measures of student learning and teacher working conditions at the instructional and institutional level, and measures of structures and resource allocation policies and practices at the education system level.

3. **Antecedents or constraints that contextualize policy and practice**—This third class provides information that is particularly important in a comparative context, as it ensures "like with like" comparisons. For example, it might provide information on the socioeconomic context of students, schools, or systems to promote comparisons of schools that have students of similar socioeconomic background or countries that operate under similar socioeconomic constraints.

These dimensions are then cross-classified and the resulting information used to address a variety of issues from different policy perspectives (see items 1.I to 3.IV in Table 1). These issues relate to:

- The quality of educational outcomes and educational provision

- The quality of educational outcomes and equity in educational opportunities

- Adequacy, effectiveness, and efficiency of resource management

Recognizing the effective functioning of internationally comparative benchmarks and ensuring their cross-national validity is a significant challenge, and there is considerable evidence of distortions that result from poorly conceived benchmarks (Hazelkorn, in press). For example, the most significant challenge of OECD's PISA was to define and operationalize a set of key skills that could serve as criteria to compare educational performance in ways that are cross-culturally appropriate and valid and reliable across countries and languages. Since there is no overarching agreement on what fundamental competencies 15-year-olds should possess, since an assessment such as PISA can only capture a selection of competencies, and since various methodological constraints limit the nature of competencies that are currently amenable to large-scale assessment, it was clear from the outset that the resulting benchmarks would never

	(1) Education and Learning Outputs and Outcomes	(2) Policy Levers and Contexts Shaping Educational Outcomes	(3) Antecedents or Constraints That Contextualize Policy
(I) Individual Participants in Education and Learning	(1.I) The quality and distribution of individual educational outcomes	(2.I) Individual attitudes, engagement, and behavior	(3.I) Background characteristics of the individual learners
(II) Instructional Settings	(1.II) The quality of instructional delivery	(2.II) Pedagogy and learning practices and classroom climate	(3.II) Student learning conditions and teacher working conditions
(III) Providers of Educational Services	(1.III) The output of educational institutions and institutional performance	(2.III) School environment and organization	(3.III) Characteristics of service providers and their communities
(IV) The Education System as a Whole	(1.IV) The overall performance of the education system	(2.IV) Systemwide institutional settings, resource allocations, and policies	(3.IV) National educational, social, economic, and demographic contexts

Table 1: The Organisation for Economic Co-operation and Development's Framework for International Benchmarks

capture the *entirety* of competencies that will make young people successful. The question then remained whether those competencies that were being assessed could be considered predictive for the future success of students.

The Canadian Youth in Transition Survey (YITS), a longitudinal survey that investigates patterns of and influences on major educational, training, and work transitions in young people's lives, provided a way to examine this empirically. In 2000, 29,330 15-year-old students in Canada participated both in YITS and PISA. Four years later, the educational outcomes of the same students, then aged 19, were assessed, and the association of these outcomes with PISA reading performance at age 15 was investigated (Knighton & Bussière, 2006). The results show that students who mastered PISA performance level 2 on the PISA reading test at age 15 were twice as likely to participate in postsecondary education at age 19 than those who performed at level 1 or below, even after accounting for school engagement, gender, native language, place of residence, parental education, and family income. The odds increased to eight-fold for those students who had mastered PISA level 4 and to sixteen-fold for those who had mastered PISA level 5. It is noteworthy that the analysis also showed that performance on the PISA test was a better predictor for subsequent educational success than teachers' judgment as reflected in the school marks of 15-year-olds. A similar study undertaken in Denmark led to similar results. The percentage of youth who had completed postcompulsory, general, or vocational upper-secondary education by age 19 increased significantly with their reading ability assessed at age 15 (see http://www. sfi.dk/sw19649.asp). Also, the International Adult Literacy Study related reading and numeracy skills that were defined in similar ways as those measured by PISA to earnings and employment outcomes in the adult population. The analyses showed that such competencies were generally a better predictor for individual earnings and employment status than the level of formal qualification individuals had attained (OECD and Statistics Canada, 2000).

A Powerful Instrument for Policy Reform

In a globalized world, the yardsticks for public policy in education are no longer national goals or standards alone, but increasingly the performance of the most successful education systems internationally. International comparative benchmarking can be a powerful instrument for policy reform and transformational change by allowing education systems to look at themselves in the light of policies (intended, implemented, and achieved) elsewhere in the world. It can show what is possible in education in terms of quality, equity, and efficiency in educational services, and it can foster a better understanding of how different education systems address similar problems. Most importantly, by providing an opportunity for policymakers and practitioners to look beyond their own experiences and reflect on underlying paradigms and beliefs, international benchmarks hold out the promise of transformational change.

Last but not least, the level of public awareness raised by international benchmarks has often created an important political momentum and engaged educational stakeholders, including teacher or employer organizations, in support of policy reform in ways that would otherwise have been difficult to achieve—and by raising the stakes, it has also increased the cost of failure.

While the development of international benchmarks is fraught with difficulties and their comparability remains open to challenges, cultural differences among individuals, institutions, and systems should not suffice as a justification to reject their use, given that the success of individuals and nations increasingly depends on their global competitiveness. The world is indifferent to tradition and past reputations, unforgiving of frailty, and ignorant of custom or practice. Success will go to those individuals, institutions, and countries that are swift to adapt, slow to complain, and open to change. The task for governments will be to ensure that their citizens, institutions, and education systems rise to this challenge, and international benchmarks can provide useful instruments to this end.

References

Döbert, H., et al. (2004). *Vertiefender Vergleich der Schulsysteme ausgewählter PISA-Teilnehmerstaaten*. Frankfurt am Main: Deutsches Institut für pädagogische Forschung.

Hazelkorn, E. (in press). Learning to live with league tables and ranking: The experience of institutional leaders. *Higher Education Policy*.

IFIE-ALDUCIN. (2007). *Mexican national survey to parents regarding the quality of basic education*. Mexico City: Author.

Knighton, T., & Bussière, P. (2006). *Educational outcomes at age 19 associated with reading ability at age 15* (research paper). Ottawa: Statistics Canada.

Organisation for Economic Co-operation and Development. (2004). *Reviews of national policies for education—Denmark: Lessons from PISA 2000*. Paris: Author.

Organisation for Economic Co-operation and Development. (2008). *Education at a Glance—OECD indicators 2008*. Paris: Author.

Organisation for Economic Co-operation and Development. (2007a). *PISA 2006: Science competencies for tomorrow's world*. Paris: Author.

Organisation for Economic Co-operation and Development. (2007b). *Reviews of national policies for education: Quality and equity of schooling in Scotland*. Paris: Author.

Organisation for Economic Co-operation and Development and Statistics Canada. (2000). *Literacy skills for the information age*. Ottawa and Paris: Author.

Marc S. Tucker

Marc S. Tucker is the president and chief executive officer of the National Center on Education and the Economy (NCEE). In addition to his work with the NCEE, Tucker has been instrumental in creating the Commission on the Skills of the American Workforce, the New Commission on the Skills of the American Workforce, the New Standards Consortium, the National Skill Standards Board, America's Choice, and the National Institute for School Leadership. He has also served as author, coauthor, or editor of many articles and several books and reports, including *America's Choice: High Skills or Low Wages* (1990); *Thinking for a Living: Education and the Wealth of Nations* (1992); *Standards for Our Schools: How to Set Them, Measure Them, and Reach Them* (1998); *The Principal Challenge: Leading and Managing Schools in an Era of Accountability* (2002); and *Tough Choices or Tough Times: The Report of the New Commission on the Skills of the American Workforce* (2006). Tucker has testified frequently to the United States Congress and state legislatures.

In this chapter, the author describes his experiences with industrial benchmarking—a research technique borrowed from industry to examine what makes education systems successful in countries across the world. The author points out that there is great variation among nations in the ability of their students to do well on international assessments of student achievement, but surprisingly little of the variance in results can be explained by per capita education spending, gross domestic product per capita, or differences in instructional methods. Rather, a substantial amount of the variance can be explained by the design of education systems. He explores some examples of the differences in system design that account for the variations in national education performance and how researchers from the National Center on Education and the Economy find these variations through a seven-step process.

Marc Tucker can be reached at mtucker@ncee.org.

Chapter 5

Industrial Benchmarking: A Research Method for Education

Marc S. Tucker

Educators take it as an article of faith that research can guide us to improved student achievement. We think that if researchers can show that practice A is consistently superior to practice B, then educators and policymakers will replace practice B with practice A and student performance will improve. But the relationship between research and practice is not often so straightforward.

The general approach to research in education is derived from research in the field of medicine. We identify a "treatment" of interest and compare its effectiveness to the effectiveness of other treatments (or no treatment at all) on a sample of "subjects." In medical research, it is relatively easy—that is, in comparison to education—to establish conditions in which only the variables being studied change, making it possible to isolate and gauge the effects of the potential treatments being researched with a high degree of confidence. In education, we do our best to hold everything else in the environment constant, and, if that is not possible, to correct as much as possible for those other factors in the environment, typically with statistical strategies. The strongest method we have found for doing such research is to randomly assign subjects to treatments.

In education, it is easiest to employ such methods when looking directly at interventions in the instructional process itself, such as, for example, when trying to assess the relative effectiveness of a particular method of teaching young children to read. But the farther we get from such settings, the more difficult it is to get conclusive results from our research. There are too many intervening variables interacting with one another in too many ways to produce strong conclusions.

This is particularly true when research seeks to understand the relative effectiveness of entire national education systems. It is now apparent that there is great variation among nations in the ability of their students to do well on international assessments of student achievement. Surprisingly, little of the variance in results can be explained by the per capita education spending of these countries, their gross domestic product per capita, or differences in instructional methods. Many researchers suspect that a substantial amount of the variance can be explained by the design—intentional or otherwise—of their education systems. Thus, it is the system itself that is of interest. So we ask, "What are the differences in system design that account for the variations in national education performance, and how would we find the answer to that question?"

It is patently impossible to randomly assign national populations to the "treatments" provided by different countries' education systems. Nor is it possible to use the quasi-experimental methods typically used in education research, except in rare instances, a point to which I will return at the end of this chapter. So what is to be done? The method I want to advance in this chapter is the method known as *industrial benchmarking* research.

Industrial Benchmarking

At the end of the 1970s, David Kearns was hired from IBM by Xerox to be its new CEO and chairman. Xerox had risen to the top ranks of American corporations faster than any company in history. It was the darling of the business magazines, much as Apple and Google are today. Almost as soon as Kearns arrived on the scene, a small group of Xerox engineers returned from a trip to Japan and told their new boss that a little-known company called Ricoh had figured out how to build a copier and market and sell it at a profit for less than it cost Xerox just to manufacture such a machine. And it took Ricoh less than half the time that it took Xerox to design and build a comparable machine. They said to Kearns that in their opinion, there was simply no way that Xerox could compete with such a company, so Xerox might just as well prepare for its inevitable failure in the market.

Kearns was not having any of it. He instructed the engineers to go back to Japan prepared to find out in detail exactly how the Japanese did it. He did not want them to copy what the Japanese did, but rather to learn from them. Their job was not just to match Japanese performance, but to figure out how to surpass it. This was the birth of industrial benchmarking in the United States.

In conventional education research, the aim, as in medicine, is to identify and then replicate the most effective strategies. Kearns was not interested in replication; he was interested in improving on best practice, on beating the competition. He was not trying to find the most effective Japanese company and duplicate its methods and systems. He was smart enough to know that no company would be superior on all points. He would need to study many of them and pick out the best features of each, combine them, and while combining them, mix in some distinctly American contributions, thereby building an approach that could beat any and all competitors.

Kearns also knew that Japan and the Japanese are very different from the United States and Americans. What worked for the Japanese might not work for us, because of differences in culture, tradition, institutional structure, regulatory systems, and much more. So his engineers could not just blindly copy what they saw. They would have to sort out those strategies that worked because of conditions that could be duplicated in the United States from those conditions that we could not hope to duplicate, and then identify those things that would be much easier for us to do than it was for them to do. They would have to imagine what might happen if we took an approach to a problem that worked very well for the Japanese and married it to a technique where we seemed to have an edge.

This is very far indeed from replication, which is the highest aim of American educational research. For Kearns, replication would be the most direct route to permanent second best. Why take a technique honed to match to a particular cultural and institutional setting we could not hope to replicate and try to replicate it in the United States? The results could never be as successful as those obtained by the Japanese. For us in the United States, the aim in our education research is to show beyond a shadow of a doubt that practice A produces results superior to those of practice B. Kearns did not need that proof. He knew that he could not succeed by blindly copying his competitor, but he could beat him by learning from him. The question was how to do that.

Translating a Business Approach for Education: How the National Center on Education and the Economy Does It

Rather than explain further what businesses do, I will describe how the National Center on Education and the Economy (NCEE) has translated business techniques to fit our own education research objectives. The goal of the NCEE is to learn enough from the most successful countries in the world to fashion designs for our own education systems that would make them competitive with and possibly superior to the best in the world. To do this, the organization follows a seven-step process.

1. Choose Countries to Study

The first step is to identify the countries for study. At one level, this is easy. It involves looking at the league tables offered by the most highly regarded international comparative studies of national primary and secondary education system performance. But not all countries of interest participate in these studies. So we look for other evidence. During our studies of the Hong Kong system, for example, we were told by multiple informants with an intimate knowledge of the mainland Chinese system that if the rest of the country were to participate in the international studies, it would surely rank very high in mathematics and science, possibly even outperforming Hong Kong itself. In the case of India, we came across data showing that fully one quarter of the chief scientists and chief executive officers of the Silicon Valley firms in the 1990s were of Indian origin. This was arguably the functional equivalent of Ricoh building copiers that could be sold for a profit below Xerox's cost. It led us to mount a serious—and very fruitful—study of the Indian education system.

When companies benchmark the competition, they look not just at their direct competitors in their own market, but also at other companies that perform functions that they also perform, even if those companies are not competitors. For a long time, companies all over the United States benchmarked L.L. Bean for its inventory management system—not because they were in the business of inventory management, but because they knew that they could improve their margins and be better overall competitors if they did a better job of managing their inventory.

So we are constantly looking for countries that have only part of the picture right, but are doing that part very well. They might be exceptionally efficient in terms of achievement per dollar, or they might have an exceptionally effective method of recruiting and retaining unusually talented teachers, or they might arguably have the best vocational education system in the world.

We have developed a worldwide network of informants who have direct knowledge of various aspects of national education systems and draw on this network to identify countries of interest, in addition to using the league tables and specialized research reports from all over the world.

2. Build a Library of Relevant Data, Information, and Analysis

In this step, we throw a very wide net; we collect and analyze data and information on education, but we also seek out a broader range of data and information. This typically includes the following (and often much more):

- Country studies from the Organisation for Economic Co-operation and Development (OECD), *The Economist*, and the Central Intelligence Agency (CIA)

- Relevant data from international comparative studies of student performance

- Workforce and economic data

- Histories of the country

- Detailed descriptions of the country's education system, government speeches, and white papers and other position papers on education and other issues, as well as critiques of the government's positions on these issues by the opposition party and independent analysts and scholars

- Research papers and reports from in-country researchers and research organizations

- Studies by international scholars

- Reports from teams of Americans and other foreign visitors

We want to understand as much as we possibly can about the country's history, social structure, economic situation, education system, current issues in education, education performance profile, and prospects before even boarding the airplane to visit the country.

3. Identify In-Country Experts

In this step, we work hard to figure out which individuals in the country are likely to be the best informants on the issues in which we are most interested. We learn both from the materials we read and from phone conversations with people in the country, which we organize in a "snowball" research technique: We want to talk with the top officials, but also with the people one or two layers closer to the action—those who actually make the system work day to day. We want key informants from inside the education system, and the government, but we also want to talk with their most incisive critics in the press, the opposition parties, and in the research and policy analysis establishment. When we establish our schedule for the visit, we want to leave enough time to find out what we need to know from our key informants, but it is also very important to leave enough unscheduled time to follow up on what we learn after we arrive. You must expect the unexpected and be able to take advantage of every opportunity to achieve a successful visit.

4. Build a Framework

As in any research of this sort, you must have a conceptual framework in your head in order to decide what data and analysis are relevant. The framework must be very loose at the beginning of the research and get progressively tighter as the team delves deeper into their examination of the subject country. This is a process of making guesses about what is relevant until the narrative line— the story about what is actually happening in the country that is relevant to our overarching question, what features of national education systems in what combinations are the most important determinants of national education system performance—becomes clear. Thus, the framework is constantly adjusted in light of new data, which will in turn lead to the collection of even more new data that will improve the predictive power of the framework.

5. Pick Your Team

The visiting team is designed to bring a wide range of perspectives to the research. At a minimum, we include a school practitioner, often a school principal who has been a highly competent teacher, and an education policy analyst. When appropriate, we bring others. The group might include an economist, a state or district superintendent of schools, or someone well-versed in workforce systems issues. When we do not understand the language of the country we are visiting, we bring a translator. Sometimes we bring someone who has done comparative research on the country we are visiting.

But, ordinarily, we try to keep the number to no more than three people. On one hand, we greatly value multiple perspectives. On the other, if there are more than two or three people on the team, it becomes very difficult for any one member of the team to follow up on a line of questioning of an informant, and it is usually through doggedly persisting in a line of questioning that the most valuable information and insights are obtained. It is possible to solve this problem by dividing a larger team up into smaller teams, each of which meets with its own thread of informants. But then it becomes very difficult for any one member of the team to put the whole picture together, and it is in putting together the whole picture that the payoff comes.

6. Prep the Team

When our team is identified and the visit is set up, we make a book of the most important material we have collected and share it with the team. Each member is required to read it carefully before arriving on site. At many points during the trip, we reassemble the team to debrief, share our growing understanding, identify what is puzzling, and decide what appears to be most important for us to learn next.

7. Allow Enough Time to Get Confused, and Then, If You Are Lucky, to Put the Whole Picture Together

The next step is the visit: schools, district offices, government officials, experts of many kinds, and so on. Benchmarking of this sort is inherently confusing. If it is not confusing, you are not learning anything worthwhile and have almost certainly missed what is most important. Most of the benchmarking trips I take to a country are at least a week long. The first day is typically exhilarating, as new and fascinating information floods in. By the end of the second day, I believe I have a decent general grasp of the shape of the system, the nature of its main strengths and weaknesses, and the big issues, although there are some important gaps and puzzles. By the end of the third day, I am hopelessly confused and doubtful that I will ever be able to form a satisfactory view of the system itself or the issues it faces. Then, if I am lucky, the fog begins to clear on the fourth day, and by the end of the trip I have most of what I came for.

The reasons for this trajectory are important: In the beginning, no matter how good the briefing materials, you understand what you have read and listened to by adding it to your stock of knowledge about your own system. So you construct a picture of the other country's teacher education system by simply imagining your own system and replacing the one aspect of it with a detail about the other country's system that you have just learned. It is almost impossible not to do this. In fact, however, very important features of the country's teacher education system may be very different from the corresponding features of your system, and so you have unwittingly created a very erroneous picture of the country's system—not because you have misunderstood something your informants have told you, but because you have substituted your reality for theirs without realizing it.

At the end of every day during a benchmarking tour, I force myself to construct a detailed description of how their education system works, as well as an explanatory map for the country's profile of student performance. In the early stages of the trip, I discover that there are big pieces of the picture I have constructed that do not mesh together at all. These lacunae become the basis of the questions that I bring to the following day's informants. By doing this every day, I am able to progressively identify the pieces of the puzzle that are missing and put them in place.

The puzzle I am constructing is a picture of how the system really works, and of the structures of causation that have led to the outstanding performances we have observed in the data that led us to visit the country in the first place. This is very hard to do. Few informants within a country have any idea why they are more successful at what they do than other countries. The formal properties of their education system may or may not explain their success. If these properties are an important part of the explanation, that may be true only when those features are combined with some aspect of their country that has nothing to do with the formal properties of their education system.

Perhaps the best example of this sort of problem comes from Finland. Like many others, we, too, made the pilgrimage to Finland after that country led OECD's Programme for International Student Assessment (PISA) league tables for the first time. By the time we left for Finland, a number of other researchers had preceded us, and many had shared their explanations for the country's unexpected success. We read their papers carefully and set up extensive interviews to test their hypotheses. None panned out. One of the most popular was that their success came from the large investments they had made in their teachers and their teacher education system. But when we looked closely, those investments had only brought Finland into the company of many other industrialized countries. Nothing we observed inside their formal education system could explain the outstanding performance of their students. We had a very pleasant dinner with the former Minister of Education who served during the years in which the foundation of the present system had been put in place. Nothing he or his principal aide, who was also our guest at dinner, told us could possibly explain the Finns' scores on the international tests.

But we later learned a key piece of information. Prior to the fall of the Berlin Wall between the communist East and the capitalist West, much of Finnish production was sold to the Soviet Union. When the wall fell, those trading agreements were terminated, and the Finnish economy went into free fall. Soon the Finns were suffering more economically than they had during the Great Depression. The Finnish people are best understood as a close-knit tribe. When they are threatened, the tribe's elders gather and decide on a strategy for their people. That is what happened when their economy tanked. The elders concluded that given the current dynamics of the global economy and the Finns' lack of any natural resources that could sustain them, their only hope lay in carving out a niche in high technology and in creating the very highly educated workforce that would be required in an economy that would live or die on its ability to compete in high technology. The nation was in crisis, and the best of the young people of this tribe behaved as the best of the young people in tribes throughout history have behaved when their countries have called on them in a crisis. In this case, they became teachers. It can best be described as an act of patriotism. Overnight, the status of teachers went through the roof. The world observed the result of this story in the astonishing success of Nokia and the no-less-astonishing success of their high school students in the PISA league tables.

This story confirms once again how important it is to have a highly capable teaching force if the goal is to have consistently high student performance, but we concluded that we could learn little from Finland that would translate to the American scene about how to produce a superb national teaching force. We are the very opposite of a tribe; we are the most polyglot nation in the world, and we are not about to entrust our future to the country's elders in the same way that Finland did. Our path, whatever it is, will be different from Finland's.

And then there is the problem of defining "success." In health matters, reducing mortality rates and increasing life spans are universal goals. In education, what constitutes success is a little more ambiguous.

Some years ago, a colleague and I went to Asia for a month to see if we could begin to understand why this collection of Asian countries rose again and again to the top of the league tables in comparative studies of math and science achievement. But the people we talked with in Hong Kong, Tokyo, Singapore, and Shanghai universally dismissed their success on the Third International Mathematics and Science Study reports as unimportant. They pushed us hard for information on how the United States teaches creativity. Of course, we do not. We venerate the individual and are suspicious of authority. They place a higher value on the group than on the individual and venerate their elders and those in authority. We left this exchange persuaded that the country with the best chance in the coming international economic competition would be the country that combines our ability to produce original thinkers and skilled entrepreneurs with the ability of the Asian countries to develop very solid foundations of knowledge and skill in their students. But that may not be possible.

The Asians we spoke with would like the advantages we derive from our free-thinking culture, but they are very much afraid of the social costs they see associated with it. We would like to enjoy their high levels of skill and knowledge in the core subjects in the curriculum, but not if it comes at the cost of a conformist, unimaginative society.

One might conclude from what I have said so far what many Americans, in fact, conclude: Cultural differences among nations are so great that there is no point in benchmarking; it is simply impossible to transfer techniques and systems from one country to another and get similar results. But that is not our experience at all. Consider the twin issues of testing and accountability.

American teachers decry teaching to the test. Teachers in most of the other countries we have visited simply do not understand that. For them, testing is how they find out whether the student has learned what the teacher has been trying to teach. When we unpack this difference in perspective, we find that in other countries, testing is part of a larger system in which the state defines the curriculum that the teachers are expected to teach, and the tests are designed to match that curriculum. In those other countries, it is assumed that the purpose of teacher training is to train the teacher to teach the state curriculum. And the textbooks sold in those countries are also designed to match the state curriculum. In the United States, there is no state curriculum, so the teachers' colleges have no obligation to teach their teachers to teach the state curriculum, and the teachers are not teaching it. The textbooks are not geared to it. The tests used in the United States are far cheaper than those used in most advanced industrial countries and are likely to miss all the nuance in good teaching. It is little wonder that American teachers resent being told to teach to a test that greatly narrows the curriculum they think they should be teaching.

But the issues run deeper than this. In most advanced industrial countries, students' progression through the system and their success later in life is determined by their performance on state examinations. In the United States, it is largely determined by their time in the seat. In most advanced industrial countries, therefore, students have a strong incentive to take tough courses and to study hard. In the United States, they do not. Thus, teachers in the United States face students with very weak incentives to work hard in school, whereas teachers in most other advanced industrial countries face students with much stronger motivations to study hard in school. These are, of course, broad generalizations. The specifics vary significantly from country to country, but the general point is very important. One can only conclude that a country whose system systematically deprives its teachers of motivated students is a country that is not likely to match the performance of its peers, no matter what else it does. The mechanisms that it uses to motivate students may or may not be the same as those used by its peers, but it ignores the issue at its peril.

This is hardly the only issue raised by these brief observations. We have seen no country that has high standing in the international league tables where student motivation to work hard in school is high that does not also have high-quality, relatively expensive examinations. To the extent that one gets what one measures, the quality of the examinations turns out to be a crucial variable. This is a very important lesson for the United States, where the per-pupil, per-subject cost of state accountability tests is, according to our calculations, on the order of one-fifth of the cost in countries with high-quality examination systems.

Or take the matter of teacher quality. Virtually every country that we have studied that has consistently high student performance recruits its teachers from the top third of its college graduates. The United States does not.

These are just a few examples in which there are clear conclusions concerning parameters for system design that can be drawn from the kind of benchmarking studies we do that are not subject to the charge that cultural differences invalidate international comparisons. There are many, many more examples. The fact of the matter is that the cultural differences between Massachusetts and Mississippi are arguably as great as the cultural differences between Massachusetts and Denmark, to say nothing of Great Britain. That does not prevent us from sending American researchers to Massachusetts to study the determinants of reading proficiency or the effectiveness of certain innovations in school organization and draw conclusions that are expected to apply to Mississippi.

But the obverse is also true. Notwithstanding the American commitment to local control, the general design parameters of the American education system are far more similar from state to state than are those of any state to those of any other education systems in the world. So it should not surprise us that almost all interventions designed to improve the outcomes for our students—very few of which change the design parameters of the system—produce only modest differences in student outcomes. To recall a point made earlier, why should we expect a big difference from altered curriculum in a state if it is still true that the incentives for students to take tough courses and work hard in school are very weak? To put it another way, if the principal sources of academic weakness lie in the basic design of our system, and that system is fairly consistent across this country, why would we expect to significantly improve student outcomes unless we change the system?

The American educational research paradigm has been largely blind to this question, with a few notable exceptions, such as the studies of Jim Stigler and Harold Stevenson, Liping Ma, and William Schmidt and his associates. But this is the heartland of industrial benchmarking: If we want to match or exceed the performance of our most able competitors, then we have no choice but to study how they do it. Learning from them is most emphatically not copying them, but rather carefully studying the causal relationships involved and using our understanding of those causal relationships to adapt their designs to our own circumstances.

A Method to Inform Design

The reader might at this point wonder why the title for this article speaks of *industrial* benchmarking rather than *international* benchmarking, since much of the article focuses on what is to be learned by looking to the experience of other nations with stronger education records than ours. It is surely true that I have worked hard here to help you see why international comparative studies are important. But the method of doing it has nothing to do with particular locales. The argument for the use of that method hinges on the primacy of design, the importance of the knowledge needed to inform design, and the crucial significance of the role of the system itself in determining educational outcomes. As I close this essay, I will try to draw these threads together.

Industrial benchmarking begins with the assertion that the most important question for education research now is why some national education systems outperform others with respect to access, completion rates, efficiency, and student performance. The primary goal of education research should be to provide the kind of information that would make it possible for state and national policymakers to design a system that will outperform any of those now existing. But current education research methods are poorly suited to the task of informing design. Indeed, the current gold standard of education research methodology is patently inapplicable to the problem of identifying those factors that best explain the relative success of national education systems. The method that holds the most promise for achieving this goal is industrial benchmarking, a tool developed by industrial organizations for outperforming their best and most successful competitors. This method involves a carefully disciplined study of the larger context in which the object of study is embedded, as well as detailed field examination by teams of experts of the actual workings of the system at all levels, with special attention to the connections among the elements of the systems that account for the superior outcomes of interest.

In this case, because we are after an understanding of a whole system, it is crucial to remember that it is the gestalt of the system that is the Holy Grail of this kind of study. The dictionary defines *gestalt* as a physical or biological pattern of elements so unified that its properties cannot be derived from the sum of its parts. That means, of course, that it is not the parts that determine the properties of the system, but rather the way they interact with one another. It is for precisely this reason that one abstracts best practices (the parts) at one's peril and why it is so important to understand the whole system in its context. And it is from the comparative analysis of these systems, properly understood, that we can derive the specifications for the design of superior systems, which is our goal.

None of this is to suggest that industrial benchmarking ought to replace traditional methods of educational research where those methods are appropriate to the questions being asked. The data produced by the Trends in International Mathematics and Science Study (TIMSS), and now PISA, will prove essential in the years ahead, as benchmarkers define and refine their hypotheses and broaden their frames of reference. A good industrial benchmarker will use all the available high-quality research that is applicable to the inquiry at hand. I would argue only that for the kind of purposes described here, the methods of industrial benchmarking be used to find the gestalt of these systems and to identify the elements of design which, when assembled, will prove superior to all that has gone before.

Dennis Shirley

Dr. Dennis Shirley's work in education spans from the microlevel of assisting beginning teachers to the macrolevel of designing and guiding large-scale research and intervention projects for school districts, states, and non-profit agencies. Dr. Shirley recently collaborated with Andy Hargreaves on a study of the Specialist Schools and Academies Trust Raising Achievement Transforming Learning project, which raised pupil learning results in over 200 schools in England at double the national rate in a 2-year period. The findings of that research will be presented in Hargreaves' and Shirley's first collaboratively authored book, *The Fourth Way* (ASCD, 2009).

For 3 years, Dr. Shirley has led a teacher inquiry project along with Boston Public Schools teacher-leader Elizabeth MacDonald; their research will be published in *The Mindful Teacher* (Teachers College Press, 2009). Dr. Shirley serves on the Scholars Forum of the Public Education Network, advises the One Square Kilometer of Education school improvement project of the Freudenberg Foundation in Berlin, and collaborates with the California Teachers Association on improving 480 struggling schools. He has led three school improvement efforts with more than 13 million dollars in funding, and his research has been translated into German, Spanish, and French. He holds a doctorate from Harvard University.

In this chapter, the author discusses why American educators have turned against recent reforms, and he contends that to correct course, multiple strands of educational change need to be interwoven. He highlights the strands of change most important for long-term, sustainable learning. These include developing a focus on learning, signature practices, and a network of strategies merging bottom-up community organizing with top-down antipoverty programs. He then describes how the strands need to be embedded by multiple social sectors if they are to attain a truly systemic level of impact. Dr. Dennis Shirley can be reached at shirleyd@bc.edu, or visit www.dennisshirley.net.

Chapter 6

The Music of Democracy: Emerging Strategies for a New Era of Post-Standardization

Dennis Shirley

The standards and accountability movements that have reigned supreme in the United States for decades have reached a moment of truth: A mere 15% of American educators believe that No Child Left Behind (NCLB) is improving American education (Public Agenda, 2006). Scores in reading and writing that have not improved and gains in math that have been modest at best indicate that these educators may be right (Lee, Grigg, & Dion, 2007). According to a recent RAND study (Hamilton et al., 2007), while standards in and of themselves are popular among educators, significant numbers of educators—more than 30% in some states—find that their state's standards are capricious, reflecting the hectic nature of a fast-

The author gratefully acknowledges the generosity of the Federal Chancellors Fellowship of the Alexander von Humboldt Foundation in Bonn, Germany, and the Rockefeller Study and Conference Center in Bellagio, Italy, for supporting the research presented in this chapter.

tracked reform initiative that grabbed headlines but neglected intellectual depth. Even Bill Riley and Rod Paige, both former United States Secretaries of Education, signed on to a major new report that decries America's excessive reliance on standardized tests that have undermined creativity and rewarded rote memorization (New Commission on the Skills of the American Workforce, 2007). Consider the following:

- In spite of a major federal initiative in the United States, test scores of fourth graders, eighth graders, and 15-year-olds on the National Assessment of Educational Progress (NAEP) and the Programme for International Student Assessment (PISA) have remained basically the same in recent years, thereby casting into doubt the validity of the strategic emphasis on standards, testing, and accountability favored by NCLB (Fuller, Wright, Gesicki, & Kang, 2007; National Center for Educational Statistics, 2007).

- Even the most tenacious advocates of standards and accountability are now expressing concerns about some aspects of the movement, such as its tendency to narrow the curriculum, to teach to the test, and to mandate prescriptive and unimaginative approaches to teaching and learning (New Commission on the Skills of the American Workforce, 2007; Rennie Center for Education Research & Policy, 2005; Rothstein, 2007).

- Even when trends are positive and strong on the standardized tests administered by states, enormous variability in definitions of proficiency, fluctuations in the number of English-language learners and special education students assessed by the test, and low or nonexistent correlations between student achievement results on state tests and the NAEP raise numerous unsettling questions about test score inflation and the role of districts and states as abettors in this to meet their adequate yearly progress (AYP) goals (Center on Education Policy, 2007a, 2007b; Koretz, 2008).

- The approach of using accountability data to create an exogenous shock to propel educators to embark upon ambitious reforms all too often sparks short-term gains that plateau after a few years and fail to build momentum and capacity for sustainable learning over time (Hopkins, 2007; MacBeath et al., 2007).

But despite these statistics that expose the problems with a focus on standardized testing as legislated by NCLB, some researchers, advocacy groups, and educators have found positive elements in the legislation. Consider the following:

- Advocacy groups for traditionally disenfranchised students in the United States—such as the National Council of La Raza, the Citizens' Commission on Civil Rights, and the National Center for Learning Disabilities—all support strong federal leadership in regard to testing and accountability as essential in promoting educational equity and transparency about student achievement and have forged links with business leaders from the Chamber of Commerce and the Business Roundtable to advance their agenda (see www.nclbworks.org).

- High levels of public concern about education, the administration of national and international tests, and their clockwork appearance in paper and digital media throughout the year indicate that policymakers cannot afford to ignore slumps in achievement, and those who do will be punished by voters (Levin, 2008).

- School districts have been working hard and making progress transforming data into information that can be used by educators to gain more precision in their instruction.

As districts transition from "status models" comparing one cohort of students to another to "growth models" tracing individual students' learning gains over time, educators' opposition to accountability measures is likely to decline (Hoff, 2007).

- Broader and apparently unstoppable social transformations in the direction of greater transparency and technological advances about all facets of social and institutional life have led the public to expect easy access to information as part of the emergence of a new transnational "audit society" (Power, 1997).

These realities indicate that the arguments of some commentators (Kohn, 1999; Ohanian, 1999) who have called for the standards and accountability reforms to be halted in their entirety are likely to be ignored. As Manuel Castells (1996, 1997, 1998) has argued in detail and Michael Barber has observed elsewhere in this volume, we are living in the midst of a bold new information age in which the free flow of all kinds of data has rapidly become a defining characteristic of everyday life. No one, it appears, can escape this macrolevel change in our new global society. Furthermore, as Archon Fung, Mary Graham, and David Weil (2007) have noted, there are many aspects of the new transparency that promote valuable social goals, such as the ability of citizens to judge the efficacy of their governments and to participate on an informed basis in the political process.

Given this contradictory evidence, will the standards and accountability movement go the way of the self-esteem movement, outcomes-based education, total quality management, and other educational analogues of the wooly mammoth? If so, how do we prepare for a new era of greater complexity, one that has been designated as a shift to a period of "post-standardization" (Hargreaves & Shirley, 2007)? The framework of this new era is already emerging.

It is becoming increasingly clear that educators' classroom-level resistance to certain aspects of the recent reforms has reached such a critical mass that a redesign of school-improvement strategies is a matter of the utmost urgency. When 70% of American teachers indicate that students in their schools are required to take too many standardized tests, and another 70% state that reforms such as NCLB are causing problems rather than improving education, advocates of reforms such as NCLB have a major problem: They have lost the support of the very people who are most needed to make their reforms work (Public Agenda, 2006). But countervailing tendencies indicate that the next phase of educational change most likely will *not* entail a nostalgic return to the kinds of conditions that existed, for example, in the United States before the report *A Nation at Risk* was issued in 1983. When predicting the future course of reform, it is helpful to first consider why educators have turned against recent reforms.

Declining Support for NCLB

At one point, NCLB had broad support by educators. The National Education Association and the American Federation of Teachers were part of a broad consensus coalition that supported NCLB, and one could even argue that American Federation of Teachers President Al Shanker, more than anyone else, pushed for the launching of the standards movement in the 1980s and 1990s (Ravitch, 2000). Despite this early support along with initial sizeable gains on state-mandated tests, educators have not remained convinced that the standardized tests legislated through NCLB are beneficial for students. Why not? Andy Hargreaves (2004) found in an intriguing study of Canadian teachers that teachers actually expect governments to lead and do not have fundamental objections to their roles as implementers of government policy—*provided that* government policies are "professionally inclusive and supportive and demonstrably beneficial for students" (p. 303). This seems to be true in the United States as well. One reason educators have given for their lack of support of the legislation is that while there were initial gains on state-mandated tests, there were no corresponding gains seen on the NAEP and PISA (Koretz, 2008; National Center for Education Statistics, 2005).

The ultimate measure of a high-quality test is whether its findings are generalizable: Does student knowledge as measured on tests reflect students' actual knowledge of a discipline and their ability to apply that knowledge in unfamiliar settings, or is the knowledge only evident on a narrow range of items on which students have been carefully coached, with encouragement and support from their teachers and district and state leaders? If the NAEP is used as an audit test to check the generalizability of student knowledge, then it is difficult to avoid a damning conclusion: Test score gains as reflected on state tests likely are spurious, reflecting careful pruning of the schools' curricula to tested items and teachers' development of targeted instruction to achieve desirable results.

Another reason for classroom teachers' disenchantment with NCLB is that apparently widespread practices of "educational triage" have led educators to focus on those students who can best reach proficiency. This undermines educators' sense of moral purpose to provide an equally high level of instruction for all of their students (Booher-Jennings, 2005; Neal & Schanzenbach, 2007). While one study (Springer, in press) has found no evidence of such practices in one western state in the United States, it does appear that large percentages of teachers feel that recent reforms have led them to teach in ways that they feel are not beneficial for their students (Pedulla et al., 2003). Since NCLB's measurement system for gauging AYP puts all of the emphasis on reaching proficiency and does not recognize gains among students who move from low performance to a moderate level of performance, for example, one should hardly be surprised if educators "game the system" by adapting triage strategies to meet AYP.

The Next Phase of Reform: Post-Standardization

Despite the problems associated with standardization in the current reform efforts, the next phase of reform will likely include a continued emphasis on standardized testing. We already know many of the components of what will be needed in a new era of post-standardization, and in regard to some of them, a remarkable policy convergence is already evident. With others, the battle lines are drawn. I contend that the next era of education reform must include multiple strands of change that are interwoven and embedded within multiple social sectors if they are to attain a truly systemic impact. In this chapter, I highlight three strands of change that I believe are most important for students' long-term, sustainable learning: the development of a focus on student learning, signature practices, and a network of community organizing and public engagement.

A Focus on Student Learning

The first step in any meaningful change effort is to ensure that each part of the system is supporting the ultimate goal of the enterprise; in the case of schools, this is *student learning*. To address this first step, we must acknowledge that the state testing systems created since the 1980s have dubious track records for improving student achievement. Michael Fullan's observation that "being in the limelight of change may bear no resemblance to substantial enduring reform" (1993, p. 54) certainly appears to be true in the case of the current legislation.

What if we asked teachers what they would prefer instead of standardized testing? Their responses could no doubt vary greatly, from an even greater emphasis on testing and accountability, to abolishing tests altogether, to tinkering with existing systems. In one study, teachers indicated that they would prefer smaller scale assessments administered throughout the year with results that they can receive immediately to provide greater precision in their instruction (Rennie Center for Education Research & Policy, 2005). Positive results from this strategy have been reported from Germany, where two major foundations sponsor a competition each year for the best schools in the country. The gathering and targeted instructional use of such formative assessment data by teachers is a cornerstone of the selection process for the competition (Fauser, Prenzel, & Schrantz, 2007). This model focuses not on student achievement data on a high-stakes test that is administered once a year, but rather on the slow and deliberate accretion of students' skills and knowledge over time. In this model, teachers have to incorporate serious study and analysis of student work into the normal and everyday fabric of their work lives. Best of all, such practices extend core components of teaching as a profession from within, rather than providing an exogenous shock to it from the outside.

To develop schools that truly are focused on student learning, one must acknowledge that the role of national governments in prompting high levels of learning in schools is limited. Although schools could become educational analogues of the army or the air force, in which the commander in chief says what goes, no one really argues that such a model is promising for preparing citizens for leadership roles in a pluralistic and free civil society. Rather, teachers as professionals need a much more vigorous and assertive role in developing craft knowledge and sharing it across schools through networks of lateral learning and leading. To evolve to this next level, teachers must abandon a passive stance that puts them in the role of uncritical implementers of the policymakers' latest nostrums. They must be much more intellectual about their work—reading research, engaging in public debates, and communicating with others about the impact of federal and state policies on the children with whom they interact on a daily basis.

This work will be difficult. After beginning their careers with high levels of idealism, many teachers become hardened and skeptical (Huberman, Grounauer, & Marti, 1993). One heartbreaking finding from a recent survey of beginning teachers is that close to half of them thought that "making it easier to terminate unmotivated or incompetent teachers" would be one of the most effective steps toward improving teacher quality (National Comprehensive Center for Teacher Quality and Public Agenda, 2007). Findings such as these indicate that beyond the relatively straightforward, mechanistic chatter of restructuring lies the far more difficult terrain of what Michael Fullan (2001) termed "reculturing." We have to move beyond reform du jour compliance, flavor-of-the-month change strategies, and educational tourism that seeks the "next big thing." If we really look at ourselves and our cultures, we cannot circumvent deep personal introspection in companionship with one's colleagues, and the most painful and poignant of all questions: When things go wrong in my school or in my system, could it have something to do not only with how I am acting, but also perhaps even with my deepest presuppositions and biases?

Daunting and delicate as such questions may be, we now have a new opportunity to pursue them in all earnestness. There is an amazing convergence right now: Advocates as well as critics of standards-based reforms have come to understand that there is no way forward if teachers are condemned to simply implement "command and control" policies (Barber, 2008; Hopkins, 2007). Hence, the major challenge in the new era of post-standardization will be to help teachers to develop professional expertise, autonomy, and leadership.

Of course, post-standardization will still require some formal assessments of student achievement, and here again a remarkable convergence is underway: Both critics and advocates of high-stakes testing are welcoming the abandonment of first-generation status models of student achievement and encouraging the development of second-generation growth models. These will allow educators to track individual student learning over time with less concern about their peer groups and more concern for the individual's own continuing development. If accompanying achievement benchmarks can be established for individual learners or cohorts of learners, and if we move beyond a simple definition of proficiency in assessing student learning, teachers will have less incentive to manipulate the system and more incentive to help individual learners achieve at their very best, wherever they might stand in relationship to proficiency. Yet even here, we should learn from our most recent experiences that over-reliance on data to tell us what to do is misplaced faith, because data always are embedded in a specific institutional and political context. Rarely, if ever, do the numbers speak for themselves, which leads us to the necessity of adapting what Jörg Schlömerkemper of the University of Frankfurt has called a veritable "hermeneutics of data analysis" (2007, p. 4).

Signature Practices

A second component of post-standardization is far greater emphasis on cultural change and capacity enhancement than in the recent past. This is the concept of finding and nurturing a given school's own signature practices and particularistic identity (Morocco, Brigham, & Aguilar, 2006). Educators need forums for swapping best practices, visiting one another's classrooms, and pooling knowledge. This year's winner of the prize for the best school in Germany stands out precisely because teachers there developed their own rubric for assessing instructional quality, developed their own schedules for visiting each others' classrooms, and created a 5-year plan for ongoing professional development based upon their evolving needs and interests (Robert-Bosch-Gesamtschule, 2008).

Educational leaders have to be careful with such practices, however, because teachers vary widely in quality. Hence, the preparation and support of educational leaders must hone their skills to differentiate between various kinds of teaching; sharpen their abilities to enter into difficult conversations with practitioners, both new and seasoned, about what is going well and what is not with their teaching, and devote special attention to helping them help teachers identify and develop precise and rapid responses to struggling students. Nothing could be more disastrous for the future education of any nation than to heed the impetuous, ill-advised exhortations of Arthur Levine, the former president of the Teachers College of Columbia University, who has argued that the preparation of educational leaders should essentially be based upon the model of a master's degree in business administration (Levine, 2005). It really is amazing, and deplorable, after the disasters of Enron, Arthur Andersen, and skyrocketing CEO salaries during times of recession that educators continue to feel the need to mimic the corporate sector at all costs, even on matters as removed from profit motives as educating our children.

We need an alternative strategy to ensure teachers are guided by strong instructional leaders who will work with them tactfully to correct poor pedagogy, to select more demanding and differentiated curricula, and to accelerate learning and achievement (Fullan, 2006). We know that educational leadership makes an enormous difference in raising or depressing student achievement (Waters, Marzano, & McNulty, 2003). Innovative leaders provide teachers with opportunities to observe other teachers so they can develop other frames of reference on their teaching. When they are given these opportunities, even excellent teachers report that they find valuable new ideas for diversifying their instructional repertoire (Hargreaves, Shirley, Evans, Stone-Johnson, & Riseman, 2007).

Community Organizing and Public Engagement

A third and separate dimension of post-standardization must entail community organizing, especially within and across poorer communities. A disappointing feature of several authors and reform advocates who focus on "system leadership" (Barber, 2008; Hopkins, 2007) is a complete omission of any reference to the role of social class, race, or ethnicity in education. Yet as David Berliner (2006) has demonstrated, and as test score data continually show, student achievement results continually reflect the powerful role of race, class, and ethnicity in shaping educational outcomes. American educators who teach children from poor and working-class backgrounds can only look with envy at the broad social safety net enjoyed by children and youth in other Western nations where educators are not expected to achieve everything by themselves (UNICEF, 2007; Wilkinson, 2005). Rather than learn from other nations about polices that increase economic performance and social cohesion, reduce income disparities, and expand educational access for all, American policymakers have endorsed the untested and ideologically driven strategy of markets, testing, and unilateral accountability as the path to academic achievement.

Yet policymakers are not the only shapers of public education. One of the more inspiring developments of recent years in the United States has been the emergence of community and youth organizing as drivers of change and creators of "civic capacity" in urban education (Stone, Henig, Jones, & Pierannunzi, 2001). For years, these local initiatives were bit players in school reform. Symbolic language about parent involvement rarely went beyond one-on-one deals between individual parents and the educators who served their children (Shirley, 1997, 2002). Larger efforts to organize parents indicated they were usually divided amongst themselves, incapable of galvanizing anything beyond episodic protests, and sidestepped in the push for standardization and control. Moreover, this pattern of fragmented and fractious engagement occurs more recently within a new context of "diminished democracy" (Skocpol, 2004), in which fewer Americans participate in the older forms of civic life and more prefer to contribute to large voluntary associations that represent their interests but do not bring them into deliberative processes in the public sphere.

Despite this, however, the tide is starting to turn. A new wave of community and youth organizing, supported by funders such as the Ford, Hazen, Mott, and Gates Foundations, is helping to get us beyond the "deep reforms with shallow roots" that Michael Usdan and Larry Cuban (2003) decried as endemic patterns in American change efforts. In New York City, the Community Collaborative to Improve District 9 Schools in the South Bronx developed a teacher support program with that city's public schools that reduced teacher attrition from 28% to 6.5% in targeted schools in the space of a single year (Academy for Educational Development, 2006). In Philadelphia, high-school activists with the group Youth United for Change exposed the way in which one of the only three secondary schools in the city that achieved AYP did so by coaching students on test items and posting answers to anticipated test questions on walls in rooms where tests were administered (Shah & Mediratta, in press). In Chicago, the Logan Square Neighborhood Association and other community groups have created Grow Your Own Teachers, a preparatory program linked with area universities to prepare poor and working-class parents to become certified teachers (Warren, 2005). In these and other cases, organizers affiliated with the nation's 7.5 million grassroots associations have moved beyond 1960s-style protest politics to conduct research with university allies, provide professional development for teachers, and educate parents in how to combine data analyses of student achievement with in-class observations of teaching and learning (Shirley & Evans, 2007).

We do not yet know whether these diverse efforts will prove to be sustainable; nor should we romanticize them. To become institutionalized, bottom-up social movements should evolve to drive and shape top-down, public-forming policies at the highest of federal levels. Many of the most progressive events in the history of the United States—such as Amendment XIII to the Constitution abolishing slavery, Brown versus Board of Education, and the Civil

Rights Act of 1964—could all be construed as top-down measures. Yet precisely because of strong federal leadership, revolu-
tionary consequences followed that dramatically advanced African
Americans' struggle for freedom and increased opportunities of all
for the better.

The Music of Democracy

One of the most challenging aspects of educational change is
the way in which reforms can be implemented in superficial ways
that leave the basic "grammar" of traditional education intact (Tyack
& Tobin, 1994). Indeed, perhaps the most troubling finding from
the last 30 years of research on educational change is that the most
promising reform initiatives are often undermined by a wide variety of actors who have, intentionally or not, prevented students
from acquiring higher order critical thinking skills (Fruchter, 2007;
Fullan, 2001, 2006; Sarason, 1995). From these findings, change theorists have recognized that episodic and isolated approaches to change
have little chance to succeed. Only if reforms advance simultaneously
and are interwoven in morally purposeful ways can the complexity
of overcoming traditional practices actually be achieved.

The necessary implication is that political strategies must be
developed to support the three change strands identified here—
developing a focus on student learning, signature practices within
schools, and the capacity for community organizing and public
engagement—if they are to produce results. This implication introduces a host of challenges:

1. Is it asking too much of policymakers and the public to
   understand the fine points of educational research and
   measurement? Will they be able to understand why coping
   strategies such as teaching to the test are undesirable?

2. The NCLB genie is already out of the bottle, so to speak, and
   the United States has now had decades of experience with

standards and accountability. Can it be expected that those reforms will really be dismissed in a putative new era of post-standardization?

3. How do we know that teachers will not exploit their autonomy? Signature practices can encompass bad practices as well. What safeguards do we have that this will not occur?

4. Activists inspired by the social movements of the 1960s have been waiting for the renaissance of the civil rights movement for decades, but poor and working-class people actually are more disengaged from the civil arena than others. Why should we expect that to change at any point in the near future?

In regard to the first concern, it appears that the public already does understand some of the issues associated with educational research and measurement. The public understands that coaching students to achieve on a given state test can produce a limited set of skills that does not transfer to other tests assessing similar bodies of knowledge. In 2007, for the first time, 40% of the public turned against NCLB as measured on a survey conducted by the Gallup Poll and Phi Delta Kappa, with 30% in favor and 30% not sure of their opinion. Perhaps more significantly, the public does not see raising standards or adding more tests as effective strategies for raising student achievement; 39% would place more emphasis upon giving schools more money and 39% on improving pupil attitudes towards teachers, with only 15% believing that standards are too low (Public Agenda, 2006).

It will be crucial for leaders to emphasize that the term *post-standardization* is a neologism that must be understood accurately. It does not mean the *end* of standards, but rather *moving beyond an emphasis upon standards* as a leading-edge change strategy. This addresses the second concern: There is no going back to pre-NCLB conditions with more relaxed accountability systems. The declining popularity of NCLB with voters and especially with teachers has complicated this issue. No Child Left Behind has become so associated with heavy-handed policies and a lack of student achievement that it is politically risky for anyone—politicians, school leaders, and so on—to identify themselves with a policy with at best uneven results. It is hardly surprising that the reauthorization of NCLB has become bogged down with little chance of any real movement until the next president enters the White House. It is concerning to face the challenge of distilling the good from such a problematic structure and moving ahead with support in the new era.

The third concern about teacher autonomy reflects a major challenge of the post-standardization era. We must remember that while we have many examples from the change literature of teachers distorting reforms aimed at enhancing their autonomy (Achinstein, 2002; Campbell, 2005; Lima, 2001; Fruchter, 2007), we also have 20 years of research and activism focusing on teacher inquiry and leadership that can provide a solid foundation for such changes in professional practices (Cochran-Smith & Lytle, 1993; Lieberman & Miller, 2004; Nieto, 2003). Hence, the major challenge for teachers will be truly to become professionals who are driven by the high levels of internal accountability described by Elmore (2004). Such teachers will need to be willing to challenge and overcome traditional teacher cultures of unquestioning solidarity in regard to one another's practice. In some situations, data will help teachers to identify problem areas, but in other jurisdictions (such as in high-achieving Finland), teachers seem to work effectively without high amounts of external accountability data because their internalized sense of accountability, reinforced by high levels of social trust from the public at large, has given them a foundational professional identity predicated upon student achievement (Aho, Pitkanen, & Sahlberg, 2006; Hargreaves, Halasz, & Pont, 2007; Sahlberg, 2006, 2007).

But teachers can only go so far. At a certain point, educational leaders will have to use the power of their offices to help develop cohesion and consistency in instruction, and to help develop those signature practices that lead a school beyond a loose collection of classrooms to acquire a common cultural identity. Such practices cannot be developed by those who limit their roles to management and administration, but rather must be undertaken by those who do not shy away from leadership in the sense of establishing a common vision, rallying diverse constituencies, and engaging students, parents, and community members in manifesting over time their core values—in this case, focusing on student learning.

Finally, in regard to efforts to increase community engagement in education, one should note that such undertakings regularly fall short because they underestimate just how serious the problem of public disengagement is among the poorest and most disenfranchised constituencies, and they assume that mere structural changes without accompanying technical assistance will catalyze student achievement. Local school councils that were created in Chicago during the administration of Mayor Harold Washington succeeded in improving elementary schools, but at the high school level, parents lacked the capacity to understand complex, low-trust institutions and failed to have any impact on the system (Bryk, Sebring, Kerbow, Rollow, & Easton, 1999). A myriad of factors—the greater complexity of the curriculum, the sheer size of high schools, and the difficulty of engaging the many teachers a student encounters in the course of a day—scuttled parents' efforts to improve high schools. In my own writing on the politics of school committee meetings, I have described how community-based organizations sometimes overstep professional boundaries and seek to dictate policies related to literacy or to manipulate teachers to take specific stances (Shirley, 2002; Shirley & Evans, 2007). Perhaps most troubling of all, some scholars (Oakes & Lipton, 2002; Welner, 2001) have found that when educators issue calls for greater public engagement in education, privileged parents find ways to use such rhetoric to block the very reforms that could lead to more equitable student learning.

The world of educational change is indeed a battleground where individuals often stake out their turf and defend it reactively and tenaciously; the public good can become lost in the fight for interest group politics. Max Weber (1918/1946) once famously described such political struggles as akin to the "strong and slow boring of hard boards" (p. 128)—an unappealing image, to be sure. Yet unlike some who find such political battles alienating and turn to marketplace models of reform as potential alternatives, I counter that circumventions of democracy carry their own costs, which generally outweigh the benefits of any given reform. Saul Alinsky (1965) once famously referred to dissonance as "the music of democracy" (p. 42), and Robert Putnam (1993, 2000) and theorists of civic capacity (Stone et al., 2001) repeatedly have shown that conflict, when managed properly, can enhance rather than diminish the social trust that is a crucial dimension of the positive school climate that is a foundation for student achievement (Bryk & Schneider, 2004). Especially when population groups traditionally have been marginalized from positions of power, participatory democratic social movements can provide venues that bring individuals out of their isolation, distribute and enhance group problem-solving, and advance public learning by bringing diverse constituencies into new forms of communication with one another (Polletta, 2002).

Moving Into the New Era

If post-standardization is to become a true augur of good things to come—good things that actually *are* beginning to come together in many instances—it will, I believe, have to build upon the three core organizing principles outlined here. *Focus on learning,* and if your assessment systems are getting in the way of student learning, then modify or discard them. *Develop signature practices in schools* that promote the special strengths and talents of students, teachers, parents, and community members, and lead teachers to expect that lifelong learning is a core responsibility of their vocation. Stop ignoring the correlations between concentrated poverty and pupil underachievement, and *develop an interwoven network of strategies merging bottom-up community organizing with top-down antipoverty programs* to clear away the multiple barriers that impede the learning of children from poor and working-class families. Finally, infuse these changes with an awareness that dissonance and conflict are inevitable components of educational change and public engagement for school improvement. If we can do these things, and if we truly are determined to succeed, we will indeed begin to move into a new era of post-standardization that advances individual student learning, ongoing teacher professionalism, and the promotion of the public good.

References

Academy for Educational Development. (2006). *Lead teacher report: Second year report submitted to the Community Collaborative to Improve Bronx Schools.* Washington, DC: Academy for Educational Development.

Achinstein, B. (2002). *Community, diversity, and conflict among schoolteachers: The ties that blind.* New York: Teachers College Press.

Aho, E., Pitkanen, K., & Sahlberg, P. (2006). *Policy development and reform principles of basic and secondary education in Finland since 1968.* Washington, DC: World Bank.

Alinsky, S. (1965). The war on poverty—political pornography. *Journal of Social Issues, 11*(1), 41–47.

Barber, M. (2008). *Instruction to deliver: Fighting to transform Britain's public services.* London: Politico.

Berliner, D. (2006). Our impoverished view of educational reform. *Teachers College Record, 108*(6), 949–995.

Booher-Jennings, J. (2005). Below the bubble: Educational triage and the Texas accountability system. *American Educational Research Journal, 42*(2), 231–268.

Bryk, A. S., & Schneider, B. L. (2004). *Trust in schools: A core resource for improvement.* New York: Russell Sage Foundation.

Bryk, A. S., Sebring, P. B., Kerbow, D., Rollow, S., & Easton, J. Q. (1999). *Charting Chicago school reform: Democratic localism as a lever for change.* Boulder, CO: Westview.

Campbell, E. (2005). Challenges in fostering ethical knowledge and professionalism within schools as teaching communities. *Journal of Educational Change, 6*, 207–226.

Carnoy, M., Jacobsen, R., Mishel, L., & Rothstein, R. (2005). *The charter school dust-up: Examining the evidence on enrollment and achievement.* New York: Teachers College Press.

Castells, M. (1996). *The rise of the network society.* Malden, MA: Blackwell.

Castells, M. (1997). *The power of identity.* Malden, MA: Blackwell.

Castells, M. (1998). *End of millennium.* Malden, MA: Blackwell.

Center on Education Policy. (2007a). *Answering the question that matters most: Has student achievement increased since No Child Left Behind?* Washington, DC: Author.

Center on Education Policy. (2007b). *Choices, changes, and challenges: Curriculum and instruction in the NCLB era.* Washington, DC: Author.

Cochran-Smith, M., & Lytle, S. L. (1993). *Inside/outside: Teacher research and knowledge.* New York: Teachers College Press.

Dee, T. S, & Jacob, B. A. (2007). Do high school exit exams influence educational alignment or labor market performance? In A. Gamoran (Ed.), *Standards-based reform and the poverty gap: Lessons for No Child Left Behind* (pp. 154–200). Washington, DC: Brookings.

Elmore, R. (2004). *School reform from the inside out.* Cambridge: Harvard Education Press.

Fauser, P., Prenzel, M., & Schrantz, M. (2007). *Was für schulen! Gute schule in Deutschland*. Seelze-Velber, Germany: Klett.

Fruchter, N. (2007). *Urban schools, public will: Making education work for all our children*. New York: Teachers College Press.

Fullan, M. (1993). *Change forces: Probing the depths of educational reform*. New York: Falmer.

Fullan, M. (2001). *The new meaning of educational change* (3rd ed.). New York: Teachers College Press.

Fullan, M. (2006). *Turnaround leadership*. San Francisco: Jossey-Bass.

Fuller, B., Wright, J., Gesicki, K., & Kang, E. (2007). Gauging growth: How to judge No Child Left Behind? *Educational Researcher, 36*(5), 268–278.

Fung, A., Graham, M., & Weil, D. (2007). *Full disclosure: The perils and promise of transparency*. New York: Cambridge University Press.

Hamilton, L. S., Stecher, B. M., Marsh, J. A., McCombs, J. S., Robyn, A., Russell, J. L., Naftel, S., & Barney, H. (2007). *Standards-based accountability under No Child Left Behind: Experiences of teachers and administrators in three states*. Santa Monica, CA: RAND.

Hargreaves, A. (2004). Inclusive and exclusive educational change: Emotional responses of teachers and implications for leadership. *School Leadership and Management, 24*(2), 287–309.

Hargreaves, A., Halasz, G., & Pont, B. (2007). *Finland: A systemic approach to school leadership*. Paris: Organisation for Economic Co-operation and Development.

Hargreaves, A., & Shirley, D. (2007, December 21). The coming of post-standardization. *EdWeek.org*. Accessed at www.edweek.org/ew/articles/2007/12/21/17hargreaves_web.h27.html on June 6, 2008.

Hargreaves, A., & Shirley, D. (in press). The coming of post-standardization. *Phi Delta Kappan*.

Hargreaves, A., Shirley, D., Evans, M., Stone-Johnson, C., & Riseman, D. (2007). *The long and short of school improvement: Final evaluation of the Raising Achievement, Transforming Learning Programme of the*

Specialist Schools and Academies Trust. London: Specialist Schools and Academies Trust.

Hoff, D. J. (2007, December 19). "Growth models" gaining in accountability debate. *Education Week, 27*(16), 22–25.

Hopkins, D. (2007). *Every school a great school: Realizing the potential of system leadership*. Maidenhead: Open University Press.

Huberman, A. M., Grounauer, M. M., & Marti, J. (1993). *The lives of teachers*. New York: Teachers College Press.

Ingersoll, R. M. (2003). *Who controls teachers' work? Power and accountability in America's schools*. Cambridge: Harvard University Press.

Kohn, A. (1999). *The schools our children deserve: Moving beyond traditional classrooms and "tougher standards."* New York: Houghton Mifflin.

Koretz, D. (2008). *Measuring up: What educational testing really tells us*. Cambridge, MA: Harvard University Press.

Lee, J., Grigg, W., & Dion, G. (2007). *The nation's report card: Mathematics 2007 (NCES 2007–494). National Center for Education Statistics, Institute of Education Sciences, U.S. Department of Education.* Washington, DC: Author.

Levin, B. (2008). Curriculum policy and the politics of what should be learned in schools. In F. M. Connelly, M. F. He, & J. Phillion (Eds.), *The Sage handbook of curriculum and instruction* (pp. 7–24). Los Angeles: SAGE.

Levine, A. (2005). *Educating school leaders*. New York: Education Schools Project.

Lieberman, A., & Miller, L. (2004). *Teacher leadership*. San Francisco: Jossey-Bass.

Lima, J. A. (2001). Forgetting about friendship: Using conflict in teacher communities as a catalyst for school change. *Journal of Educational Change, 2*, 97–122.

MacBeath, J., Gray, J., Cullen, J., Frost, D., Steward, S., & Swaffield, S. (2007). *Schools on the edge: Responding to challenging circumstances.* London: Paul Chapman.

MacDonald, E., & Shirley, D. (2006). Growing teacher leadership in the urban context: The power of partnerships. In K. R. Howey, L. M. Post, & N. L. Zimpher (Eds.), *Recruiting, preparing and retaining teachers for urban schools* (pp. 125–144). Washington, DC: American Association of Colleges for Teacher Education.

MacDonald, E., & Shirley, D. (in press). *The mindful teacher.* New York: Teachers College Press.

Morocco, C. C., Brigham, N., & Aguilar, N. (2006). *Visionary middle schools: Signature practices and the power of local invention.* New York: Teachers College Press.

National Center for Education Statistics. (2005). *Mapping 2005 state proficiency standards onto the NAEP scales: Research and development report.* Washington, DC: Author.

National Center for Education Statistics. (2007). *Highlights from PISA 2006: Performance of 15-year-old US students in science and math literacy in an international context.* Washington, DC: Author.

National Comprehensive Center for Teacher Quality and Public Agenda. (2007). *Lessons learned: New teachers talk about their jobs, challenges, and long-range plans.* Washington, DC: Author.

Neal, D. A., & Schanzenbach, D. W. (2007). *Left behind by design: Proficiency counts and test-based accountability.* NBER Working Paper Number W13293.

New Commission on the Skills of the American Workforce. (2007). *Tough choices or tough times.* San Francisco: Jossey-Bass.

Nieto, S. (2003). *What keeps teachers going?* New York: Teachers College Press.

Oakes, J., & Lipton, M. (2002). Struggling for educational equity in diverse communities: School reform as a social movement. *Journal of Educational Change, 3*(3-4), 383–406.

Oakes, J., & Rogers, J. (2002). Struggling for educational equity in diverse communities: School reform as social movement. *Journal of Educational Change, 3*(3–4), 383–406.

Oakes, J., & Rogers, J. (2006). *Learning power: Organizing for education and justice.* New York: Teachers College Press.

Ohanian, S. (1999). *One size fits few: The folly of educational standards.* Portsmouth, NH: Heinemann.

Pedulla, J. J., Abrams, L. M., Madaus, G. F., Russell, M. K., Ramos, M. A., & Miao, J. (2003). *Perceived effects of state-mandated testing programs on teaching and learning: Findings from a national survey of teachers.* Boston College, Chestnut Hill, MA: National Board on Educational Testing and Public Policy.

Polletta, F. (2002). *Freedom is an endless meeting: Democracy in American social movements.* Chicago: University of Chicago Press.

Power, M. (1997). *The audit society: Rituals of verification.* New York: Oxford University Press.

Public Agenda. (2006). *Reality check 2006; issue no. 3: Is support for standards and testing fading?* New York: Author.

Putnam, R. (1993). *Making democracy work: Civic traditions and modern Italy.* Princeton, NJ: Princeton University Press.

Putnam, R. (2000). *Bowling alone: The collapse and revival of American community.* New York: Simon & Schuster.

Ravitch, D. (2000). *Left back: A century of failed school reforms.* New York: Simon & Schuster.

Rennie Center for Education Research & Policy. (2005). *Reaching capacity: A blueprint for the state role in improving low performing schools and districts.* Boston, MA: Author.

Robert-Bosch-Gesamtschule. (2008). *Bausteine der schulentwicklung: Qualitätsbereiche und Handlungsfelder.* Hildesheim, Germany: Author.

Rothstein, R. (2007, December 17). Leaving "No Child Left Behind" behind. *The American Prospect.* Accessed at www.prospect.org//cs/articles?article=leaving_nclb_behind on June 6, 2008.

Sahlberg, P. (2006). Education reform for raising economic competitiveness. *Journal of Educational Change, 7*(4), 259–287.

Sahlberg, P. (2007). Education policies for raising student learning: The Finnish approach. *Journal of Education Policy, 22*(2), 147–171.

Sarason, S. B. (1995). *School change: The personal development of a point of view.* New York: Teachers College Press.

Schlömerkemper, J. (2007). Das allgemeine in der empirie und das empirische im allgemeine. In K. H. Arnold, S. Blömeke, R. Messner, & J. Schlömerkemper (Eds.), *Allgemeine Didaktik und lehr-lernforschung: Kontroversen und entwicklungsperspektiven einer wissenschaft von unterricht.* Bad Heilbrunn, Germany: Verlag Klinkhardt.

Shah, S., & Mediratta, K. (in press). Negotiating reform: Young people's leadership in the educational arena. *New Directions in Youth Development.*

Shirley, D. (1997). *Community organizing for urban school reform.* Austin: University of Texas Press.

Shirley, D. (2002). *Valley Interfaith and school reform: Organizing for power in South Texas.* Austin: University of Texas Press.

Shirley, D., & Evans, M. (2007). Community organizing and No Child Left Behind. In M. Orr (Ed.), *Transforming the city: Community organizing and the challenge of political change* (pp. 109–133). Lawrence: University Press of Kansas.

Skocpol, T. (2004). *Diminished democracy: From membership to management in American civic life.* Norman: University of Oklahoma Press.

Springer, M. G. (in press). The influence of an NCLB accountability plan on the distribution of student test score gains. *Economics of Education Review.*

Stigler, J. W., & Hiebert, J. (1999). *The teaching gap: Best ideas from the world's teachers for improving education in the classroom.* New York: Free Press.

Stone, C. N., Henig, J. R., Jones, B. D., & Pierannunzi, C. (2001). *Building civic capacity: The politics of reforming urban schools.* Lawrence: University Press of Kansas.

Tung, R., & Ouimette, M. (2007). *Strong results, high demand: A four-year study of Boston's pilot high schools.* Boston: Center for Collaborative Education.

Tyack, D., & Tobin, W. (1994). The "grammar" of schooling: Why has it been so hard to change? *American Educational Research Journal, 31*(3), 453–479.

UNICEF. (2007). *Child poverty in perspective: An overview of child well-being in rich countries, Innocenti Report Card 7.* Florence: UNICEF Innocenti Research Centre.

Usdan, M. D., & Cuban, L. (2003). *Powerful reforms with shallow roots: Improving America's urban schools.* New York: Teachers College Press.

Warren, M. R. (2005). Communities and schools: A new view of urban education reform. *Harvard Educational Review, 75,* 133–173.

Waters, T., Marzano, R. J., & McNulty, B. (2003). *Balanced leadership: What 30 years of research tells us about the effect of leadership on student achievement.* Denver, CO: Mid-continent Research for Education and Learning.

Weber, M. (1918/1946). Politics as a vocation. In H. H. Gerth & C. W. Mills, *From Max Weber: Essays in sociology* (pp. 77–128). New York: Oxford University Press.

Welner, K. G. (2001). *Legal rights, local wrongs: When community control collides with educational equity.* Albany: State University of New York Press.

Wilkinson, R. (2005). *The impact of inequality.* London: New Press.

Pedro A. Noguera

Dr. Pedro Noguera is a professor in the Steinhardt School of Education and the director of the Metropolitan Center for Urban Education at New York University. An urban sociologist, Dr. Noguera's scholarship and research focus on the ways in which schools are influenced by social and economic conditions in the urban environment. He has held tenured faculty appointments at the Harvard Graduate School of Education and the University of California, Berkeley. He has published more than 150 research articles, monographs, and research reports on topics such as urban school reform, conditions that promote student achievement, youth violence, the potential impact of school choice and vouchers on urban public schools, and race and ethnic relations in America. His work has appeared in several major research journals. He is the author of *The Imperatives of Power: Political Change and the Social Basis of Regime Support in Grenada from 1951–1991* (1997), *City Schools and the American Dream: Reclaiming the Promise of Public Education* (2003), and his most recent book, *Unfinished Business: Closing the Racial Achievement Gap in Our Schools* (2006). Dr. Noguera is the recipient of the Wellness Foundation Award for research on youth violence (1997), University of California's Distinguished Teaching Award (1997), the Centennial Medal from Philadelphia University (2001), the Whitney Young Award for Leadership in Education (2005), and the Eugene Carothers Award for Public Service (2006).

In this chapter, the author describes the challenges immigrant students face and offers strategies for addressing their needs in our school systems. The author contends that educational theories that presume to be color-blind, theories of school change that are devoid of reference to immigration or race, and theories that are oblivious to cultural and transnational differences create barriers to achievement. He provides concrete recommendations to educational leaders about what they can do to play a positive and supportive role in helping their schools and the larger society adjust to inevitable demographic change. Dr. Pedro Noguera can be reached at pan6@nyu.edu.

Chapter 7

Preparing for the New Majority: How Schools Can Respond to Immigration and Demographic Change

Pedro A. Noguera

Although the United States is a nation of immigrants, having been populated largely through waves of migration by people from nations and territories throughout the world, immigration has historically been a source of controversy and conflict. Throughout American history, each wave of immigration has been greeted by hostility, discrimination, and in some cases, fierce opposition from groups that arrived not long before. In each case, the right of new migrants to settle and reside in the United States has been challenged both on the basis of the perceived threat they posed to the economic security and well-being of those who came before and on their presumed cultural incompatibility with American social norms (Roediger, 1991). Ironically, even groups that today seem to be completely accepted and integrated within the social fabric of American society—Germans, Italians, the Irish, and Jews—were once subjected to attacks and concerted opposition to their entry and settlement by groups that charged they were unwanted and "unassimilable" (Brodkin, 1999; Takaki, 1989).

For example, Irish immigration was vigorously opposed in the early 19th century by so-called Yankee nativists who felt so threatened by the presence of the Irish that some went so far as to create a political party—the No Nothings—to organize opposition to their presence (Roediger, 1991). The Irish gradually overcame opposition to their presence, particularly as they organized and began to exercise political power in several American cities. Not long after, the Irish became some of the most prominent proponents of the call to ban Asian immigration, and they ultimately succeeded in getting the United States Congress to adopt laws that made Chinese (and later Japanese and Filipino) immigration to the United States illegal.[1] The Irish were by no means the only group that went from being victimized and targeted to leading the charge against the next wave of "foreigners." Throughout American history, xenophobic reactions to foreigners and anti-immigrant hostility have followed each wave of immigrants, almost as predictably as night follows day.

Since 1990, the United States has experienced the greatest influx of immigrants in its history (Suárez-Orozco & Suárez-Orozco, 2001), and once again, it finds itself embroiled in a bitter conflict over whether or not the new arrivals, particularly the undocumented, have a right to remain. Public schools find themselves at the center of the nation's controversy over the rights of immigrant children because unlike other institutions that can deny undocumented immigrants access to services, the Supreme Court has repeatedly ruled that public schools cannot (Fass, 2007; Rothstein, 1994).

Historically, public schools in the United States have served as the primary institution responsible for integrating and assimilating waves of immigrant children (Fass, 1989; Olsen, 2000). Today,

---

[1] For a historical discussion of anti-immigrant political expressions in the United States, see Katznelson and Weir (1994) and Ronald Takaki (1989).

public schools have been called upon again to carry out this important task, particularly with respect to ensuring that immigrant children learn the English language. Schools must now determine how best to serve the needs of immigrant children within an increasingly hostile political climate. In such a context, educating a new generation of immigrant children has become a highly politicized project in many communities, and not surprisingly, many schools find themselves at a loss for how best to meet the educational needs of the immigrant children they serve.

This chapter examines the factors influencing how schools are responding to the demographic changes brought about by immigration and the educational controversies accompanying them. I will show that while many of the controversies schools now confront are framed by questions related to language acquisition (English immersion versus bilingual education) and to a lesser degree tracking (because of the tendency to place English language learners in non–college-prep classes) and student achievement, concerns related to the changing nature of the American population are often at the root of these conflicts. Current trends suggest that as immigrants settle in communities throughout the United States and begin to transform the social landscape of American society, change wars over what role schools should play in integrating the children of immigrants and shaping the future of American society will become increasingly intense.

Many of the approaches described in this chapter for addressing the needs of immigrant students are entirely unaddressed by the predominant theories of educational change that are promulgated by mainstream educational researchers. Instead, the ideas presented here are part of a growing body of theories-in-action literature that advocates narrowing of achievement gaps, examination of achievement data, structured literacy strategies, and various combinations of pressure and support that take into account the dynamic nature of change in the social context that impacts schools and student learning (Bryk, & Schneider, 2003; Lipman, 1998; Noguera, 2006). Unlike educational theories that presume to be color-blind, theories of school change that are devoid of reference to immigration or race, and theories that are oblivious to the cultural and transnational differences that create barriers to achievement in schools, this chapter was written with the explicit purpose of providing concrete recommendations to educational leaders regarding what they can do to play a positive and supportive role in helping their schools and the larger society adjust to inevitable demographic change.

Understanding the New Immigration

Most demographers and economists predict that no matter how many guards are deployed at the southern border or how high the fences are erected, immigrants, both legal and undocumented, will continue to find ways to enter the United States.[2] As my colleague Marcelo Suárez-Orozco put it, "Immigration is not only our past, it is our destiny."[3]

Economic forces are largely responsible for driving the current influx of immigrants, and these forces work in two different directions. South of the border, there is an ongoing reality of widespread poverty, gross inequity, unemployment, and underdevelopment in the Caribbean, Latin America, and, most especially, in Mexico that serves as the primary *push* factor prompting migration. Liberalized trade policies, such as the North American Free Trade Agreement (NAFTA), have in some cases contributed to economic hardships in the region and prompted large numbers of displaced farmers to migrate north.[4] Others have been prompted to leave their home

---

[2] For an example of such a prediction, see Clark (1998).

[3] Marcelo and Carola Suárez-Orozco (2001) are leading scholars on the education of immigrant children. For a discussion of how immigrant children are faring in the nation's public schools, see Kao and Tienda (1998) and Olsen (2000).

[4] For a discussion of how liberal trade policies such as NAFTA have contributed to migration from Latin America to the United States, see Hightower (2008).

countries by war, natural disasters, and political unrest. Even in nations like Mexico, Columbia, Peru, and Trinidad where economic growth has occurred, the inequitable distribution of resources and wealth has driven the poor to find ways to migrate to the United States in pursuit of economic opportunity. Undoubtedly, as long as imbalances in wealth, economic opportunity, and living standards between rich and poor regions of the world remain unaddressed, it appears unlikely that current trends will reverse.

On the other side of the immigration equation are the *pull* factors that draw immigrants to the United States and other wealthy nations. First and foremost among these are the insatiable demands of the U.S. economy for cheap labor. Several sectors of the economy, including agriculture, construction, food processing, hotels and restaurants, and healthcare, are highly dependent upon legal and undocumented immigrant labor. The unwillingness of the U.S. Congress to adopt laws that would legalize the movement of labor across borders has not prevented foreign workers from finding ways to secure jobs in industries desperate for their services. It is for this reason that some of the strongest proponents of a more liberal immigration policy have come from business organizations in the private sector.

Once immigrants settle in an area, their presence creates additional pull factors. Family unification is major factor prompting immigration, as is news of the opportunities available in a new land in immigrants' communities of origin (Valdez, 1999). The settlement of immigrants is never a random process. When immigrants move into a community, it is almost always because they have followed a path—a network or channel created by those who arrived first or the employers who have drawn them there.

The current backlash against immigrants ignores the push/pull factors that drive demographic change. Instead, it appears that much of the opposition to immigration is due to two other significant considerations: 1) The greatest number of immigrants coming to the United States today are nonwhite, and their presence is transforming the racial and ethnic makeup of communities (Suárez-Orozco & Suárez-Orozco, 2001), and 2) in some sectors, immigrant labor is being used to displace American workers because they can be paid substantially less (Valenzuela, 1999).

Television commentator Lou Dobbs has emerged as one of the leading spokespersons of the backlash against immigration, and though the other opponents of immigration often claim their hostility is directed at illegal immigration and not immigrants generally, they typically refuse to acknowledge that the hostility is increasingly directed at foreigners generally. In fact, many of the punitive laws adopted by local governments and much of the harassment and even overt violence carried out by vigilantes have been directed at Latinos.[5] In an act of remarkable hypocrisy, several prominent figures in both major political parties have attempted to curry favor among anti-immigration groups and have used rhetoric that has contributed to the attacks on immigrants, even as they have also courted Latino voters. Similarly, no one within the federal government has publicly acknowledged the duplicity of the preoccupation with border security as it proceeds with the construction of a fence on the Mexican border while the longer Canadian border remains largely open and unobstructed.

Lurking in the background of the political debate over immigration is the growing awareness that by the year 2050 whites will no longer constitute the majority of the U.S. population.[6] While a small number of racist organizations openly express alarm over this impending transformation, most mainstream politicians and civic

---

[5]For a discussion of some of the attacks against new immigrants, legal and undocumented, by local governments and vigilante groups such as the Minutemen, see Cornelius (2002).

[6]For a discussion of demographic trends and the emerging nonwhite majority, see Clark (1998).

groups generally do not. Instead, leaders like congressman Tom Tancredo, former Massachusetts Governor Mitt Romney, and Lou Dobbs frame their opposition to illegal immigration as a matter of national security, as a concern that immigrants are taking jobs from American citizens, and as an alarm that American identity and the English language are threatened by immigrants who refuse to assimilate.

While some of those expressing such concerns may legitimately fear the changes brought about by immigration, it is also true that the new immigration has evoked a backlash because it differs from previous patterns in two important respects. First, prior to the Immigration Act of 1965, the majority of immigrants settling in the United States came from Europe, and while many European immigrants experienced hostility and discrimination, today their claims to U.S. citizenship are unquestioned. Since 1965, the overwhelming majority of new immigrants have been from Latin America and Asia, and though many Asians and Latinos have resided in the United States for generations, it is not uncommon for their citizenship to be questioned. As historian Ron Takaki has said with reference to Asian Americans, many are treated as though they are "forever foreign" (Takaki, 1989). A similar argument could be made regarding dark-skinned Latinos who report an increase in harassment and even illegal deportations for those who cannot produce documentation of citizenship or legal residence at the time of an Immigration and Naturalization Service (INS) raid (Chavez, 2001).

Secondly, whereas the settlement of new immigrants was once largely confined to the major cities on the East and West Coasts, today immigrants are settling throughout the nation, in small towns, suburbs, and rural areas—wherever the demand for their labor is greatest. As they arrive in large numbers, immigrants invariably change the character of the communities, schools, churches, and workplaces where they reside. Even when they settle in communities where their labor is needed, in many cases they still generate conflict and tension with those who feel threatened or displaced by their presence. In many communities, long-time residents resent the changes that occur as immigrants who speak different languages and practice different customs transform the environment and local institutions. Even though there is considerable evidence that immigrants generally contribute more to local economies than they take and have been responsible for revitalizing a number of depressed cities and towns, many Americans still state they do not want them here.[7]

Though it is rarely discussed publicly, much of this backlash appears to be related to race, or more precisely, racism. Though there is ample evidence that many undocumented immigrants from Ireland and Canada reside in the United States, there have been no reports of immigration raids targeting these groups. It should be added that while much of the hostility toward immigrants has been expressed in white communities, there have also been sporadic acts of violence directed at immigrants in several historically African-American communities. Particularly in Los Angeles and other communities throughout southern California, there has been a significant increase in violence and tension between recent Latino immigrants and older African-American residents.[8] Though both groups share a history of experiencing discrimination and racial injustice, in many communities they find themselves competing for jobs, services, political office, and control over the public schools.

Today, U.S. immigration policy, or more precisely, the question of how to control the borders and what to do about the estimated 12 million undocumented immigrants who now reside in the United States, has emerged as one of the most potent political issues of the

---

[7]For a discussion on how immigrants contribute to local economies, see Portes and Rumbaut (2002) and Reich (1992).

[8]For a discussion of the factors influencing racial conflict between African-Americans and Latino immigrants in southern California, see Fabienke (2007).

2008 elections. Against this backdrop, how public schools will be affected and respond to the changes brought about by immigration and the backlash to it will increasingly be a subject that educational leaders will not be able to avoid.

What Schools Can Do

Just as they have in the past with other immigrant groups, public schools will continue to serve as the primary institutions of socialization and support for immigrant children today (Katznelson & Weir, 1994). Given the growing hostility toward immigrants and their families (particularly the undocumented) and given the vast array of needs poor immigrant children bring with them (for example, they are more likely than other children to lack health insurance),[9] providing immigrant students with a quality education that prepares them for life in this country will require an expansive vision and commitment to enacting policies and programs that support the education and well-being of immigrant youth. The following is a brief overview of some of the strategies schools can adopt to meet the needs of the immigrant students they serve.

Provide Support as Students Acculturate

Unlike their parents who arrived in the United States with their identities intact, immigrant youth often find themselves caught between two worlds, neither fully American nor fully part of their country of origin (Jiobu, 1988). Many also arrive without having received formal education. Such children are often not literate in their native language, and consequently, they experience greater difficulty learning academic English (August & Shanahan, 2006; García, Wilkinson, & Ortiz, 1995). As they go through this difficult acculturation process, immigrant youth are often susceptible

---

[9]For a discussion of the health challenges confronting immigrant children and their families, see Guendelman, Halpin, Schauffler, and Pearl (2001) and Capps, Fix, Ost, Reardon-Anderson, & Passel (2004).

to a variety of hardships and pressures that many adults, including their parents, do not fully understand. Some of these pressures include a tendency to become alienated from adults and to be drawn toward gangs or groups involved with criminal activity, teen pregnancy, or dropping out of school altogether (Garcia, 2001; Zentella, 2002). Certainly, there are many immigrant youth who manage to avoid these pressures. In fact, in some schools, immigrant students are among the highest achievers, especially if they come to the United States literate, have several years of education in their previous country, or have highly educated parents (August & Hakuta, 1997; Cummins, 1981; Kao & Tienda, 1998). However, for children whose parents are struggling financially, and particularly for children of undocumented parents, the challenges they encounter both within and outside of school can be quite formidable.

Educators can respond to these challenges and mitigate the effects of hostility in the external environment in a variety of ways. For example, research has shown that one of the most effective means to counter the influence of gangs is to provide young people who may be susceptible to recruitment with a variety of extracurricular activities that appeal to their interests (Coltin, 1999). Additionally, scholars such as Ricardo Stanton-Salazar (2001) and Angela Valenzuela (1999) have shown that when schools hire caring adults as teachers, counselors, and administrators—at least some of whom are from backgrounds that are similar to those of their students—it can have a positive effect on students' achievement, graduation rates, and college attendance. Such individuals can help generate the kinds of social capital that middle-class students typically have access to by opening doors to internships, jobs, various social services, and by writing students recommendations for admission to college (Bryk & Schneider, 2003).

Address the Needs of Transnational Families

Immigration often compels families to make tough choices about who will leave and who will remain, and these choices often take a toll on families. When the decision to leave is made, some families are forced to separate and leave children or even a parent behind, often with the hope that in time reunification will be possible. The development of transnational families—families separated by borders and thousands of miles—often results in children experiencing disruptions in school attendance (Ada, 1988). To ensure that relationships are maintained, it is not uncommon for immigrant parents to send a child to their country of origin for 6 weeks during the middle of the school year. For educators who are concerned with academic progress, such a choice might seem nonsensical and even negligent, but to a family coping with the hardships caused by separation, such choices may be the only way to maintain the bonds of family.

Migrant workers often return to Mexico for several weeks during the winter because there is no work available during the nongrowing season. Although they generally return to their jobs, it is often the case that their children lose instruction and may even lose their seats in classrooms because of adjustments made during their absence. Those interested in supporting immigrant youth and their families must at the minimum demonstrate a capacity to understand the difficult choices transnational families face (Olsen, 2000). Finding ways to help reduce the strains caused by separation while minimizing the losses in learning associated with extended absences is an important pedagogical consideration for schools that serve large populations of Latino immigrant youth.

A growing number of schools have adopted strategies to support Latino youth who miss extended amounts of school because they are part of transnational families. For example, one elementary school in Los Angeles modified the academic year so that students could take off for 4 weeks at the end of December and beginning of January. An additional 2 weeks of school was added to the end of the year to ensure that students would not miss out on instruction (Gullatt & Lofton, 1996). A school in Texas near the Mexican border established a cooperative relationship with a Mexican school to ensure that its students received similar instruction in school while in Mexico. Finally, several schools in Miami and New York that serve immigrant youth whose parents reside in the Caribbean have hired social workers who are familiar with students' living arrangements and can provide additional social and emotional support to youth in need (Ada, 1988). Such measures do not eliminate the difficulties experienced by immigrant youth who are separated from their families, but they do help to lessen the hardships students endure, and they demonstrate that the school is not interested in punishing students for a situation they cannot control. Employing staff with language and cultural skills to work effectively with immigrant youth and their families is also of vital importance if trust and respect between home and school are to be established (Fix & Zimmerman, 2001; Valdez, 1999).

A Community-School Approach

Several schools that serve low-income immigrant students have adopted a "community-school approach" to meeting student needs. The community-school approach can be traced back to the early writings of John Dewey. It is premised on the notion that the conditions for academic learning must include attention to the cognitive, emotional, social, physical, and moral development of children (Bronfenbrenner, 1979, 1988). The current movement of community schools began in the late 1980s when various organizations (such as the Children's Aid Society, Communities in Schools, and Beacon Schools) embarked on a reform strategy aimed at forming concrete relationships between schools and nonprofit service organizations in school districts throughout the country. The initial rationale for these community-school partnerships was based on the recognition that the nutritional, mental health, and physical needs of low-income children are primary developmental issues that impact learning. In most cases, schools cannot respond to this broad array of needs without additional support (Dryfoos, 1999). During the late 1980s and throughout the 1990s, the unmet social needs of poor children were exacerbated by changes in state and federal policy (such as Welfare to Work) that compounded many of the difficulties poor children and their families faced and overwhelmed community and school-based resources (Hayes-Bautista, 2002). The combination of these trends has made it increasingly clear that high-poverty schools are in need of assistance.

A number of schools serving low-income immigrant children have adopted the community-school approach, sometimes called the "full-service school." Schools such as Edison Elementary in Port Chester, New York, and Henshaw Middle School in Modesto, California, have shown that when immigrant children are provided with access to social services, schools can do a better job of meeting their academic needs (Hall, Yohalem, Tolman, & Wilson, 2003). Many community schools maintain a full-time licensed social worker, and for some community schools, like the ones operated by the Children's Aid Society, mental health services or wellness centers are staffed by two to four social workers and a part-time psychologist. Community schools also enlist health professionals, such as dentists, optometrists, and nurse practitioners, which allows students to receive their annual physicals and get prescriptions on the school site. Additionally, community schools provide extensive after-school programs that include academic enrichment and recreation. Many community schools also attempt to extend their services to parents and families by providing adult-education classes in the evening and on weekends. All of these services occur in schools that typically operate 10–12 hours per day and 6 or 7 days a week. While the overall number of community schools is quite low, recognition of the need to address the developmental domains of children (the cognitive, social, emotional, moral, and physical) in the social institution in which they are most influenced and spend the majority of their developing years continues (Epstein et al., 2002). There is also evidence that addressing the social, emotional, and health needs of children has a positive impact on their academic performance (Coltin, 1999).

Creating a community school generally requires resourcefulness and creativity on the part of staff and administration. Principals who are entrepreneurial generally take the lead in establishing partnerships with nonprofits, local government agencies, and community groups to meet the needs of the students and families they serve. Additionally, community schools focus on building a sense of community by engaging parents as partners and providing workshops for them on topics that address their needs.

Immigration and America's Future

Like many immigrants today, earlier generations of European immigrants encountered hardships and discrimination. Despite this hostility, these groups gradually improved their social conditions and experienced the social mobility promised by the American dream. Schools played a major role in facilitating immigrants' social mobility by imparting the academic skills and cultural competence needed to climb the economic ladder. Of course, social mobility often came with a price and some sacrifice. Many European immigrants found it necessary to abandon their native languages, give up their cultures, and in many cases, Anglicize their names (Fass, 1989; Jiobu, 1988). For these groups, assimilation made social mobility possible, and over time, they overcame their early stigmas and hardships (Glazer & Moynihan, 1963). Unlike many European countries where immigrants have never been fully accepted, in the United States, groups that were once perceived as ethnically inferior were gradually accepted as full-fledged white Americans (Brodkin, 1999; Roediger, 1991).

The situation is very different, however, for Latino immigrants and their children. Although Latinos represent the fastest growing segment of the United States population and are now the largest minority group, it is not clear that the future will be as bright and promising for them as it was for European immigrants of the past. Globalization and de-industrialization have contributed to a worsening of circumstances for low-skilled Latino immigrants. Ironically, Latinos now constitute the ethnic group least likely to be unemployed, but most likely to be impoverished (Smith, 2002). This is because Latinos are concentrated in the lowest paying jobs, and many lack the skills and education needed to seek better paying alternatives (Smith, 2002). Unlike European immigrants whose offspring reaped the rewards from the sacrifices of earlier generations, Latino immigrants are not experiencing a similar degree of success (Portes & Rumbaut, 2002).

Despite being present in the United States for centuries, Latinos are over-represented among the poor and low-income population at least in part because of the pervasiveness of racialized inequalities, particularly within education. Today, Latino youth are more likely than any other ethnic group to be enrolled in schools that are not only segregated by race, but by class as well (Orfield & Eaton, 1996). In cities such as New York, Los Angeles, and Chicago, where Latino youth comprise the majority of the school-age population, they are disproportionately assigned to schools that are overcrowded, under-funded, and woefully inadequate in terms of educational quality (Garcia, 2001; Noguera, 2003, 2004; Oakes, 2002). Latino youth also have the highest high-school dropout rates and the lowest rates for college attendance (Garcia, 2001). In general, they are over-represented in most categories of crisis and failure, such as in suspensions and expulsions and special-education placements, and underrepresented in categories of success, such as honors and gifted-and-talented classes (Meier, Steward, & England, 1990).

Yet in my work with schools,[10] I often hear from administrators who speak favorably of the conduct of Latino immigrant students. Though not all are described as studious, most are characterized as well-behaved, courteous, and deferential toward adults. Beyond focusing on their behavior, educators must make sure that Latino immigrant students are not over-represented in remedial classes and special education or trapped in English as a Second Language (ESL) classes that keep them from courses that prepare students for college.

Like their parents, many immigrant youth have the drive, work ethic, and persistence to take advantage of opportunities that come their way (Kao & Tienda, 1998). Of course, it is risky to generalize or to overstate the importance of will and work ethic. For immigrant youth who live in communities where economic and social opportunities are limited and who have no ability to control basic circumstances that shape the opportunities available to them— namely, the schools they attend, the neighborhoods where they live, or the hostility of others to their presence—will and determination may not suffice. In fact, research on the socialization of immigrant youth shows that in a reversal of past patterns, assimilation no longer serves as the pathway into mainstream American culture and middle-class status as it once did for European immigrants (Portes & Rumbaut, 2002). Instead, the evidence suggests that the socialization associated with acculturation and assimilation often results in a lowering of the academic achievement and performance of Latino students (Suárez-Orozco & Suárez-Orozco, 2001).[11]

Theoretically, education should serve as the means for immigrant children to escape poverty. For this to happen, education must

---

[10]As a researcher and the director of the Metro Center at New York University, I work with many schools throughout the United States. For a description of my research, see Noguera (2003).

[11]In much of the sociological literature on immigration, it has been held that assimilation would lead to social mobility for immigrants. Second- and third-generation immigrants have generally fared better than new arrivals. For Latinos, available research suggests the opposite may be true.

serve as a source of opportunity and a pathway to a better life, just as it has for other groups in the past. For this to happen, schools must not treat immigrant children as though their inability to speak fluent English is a sign of cognitive or cultural deficit. They must reach out to parents and work with them, and they must find partners who can provide the resources and support that children need.

The children of new immigrants will eventually end up in America's public schools. How educators, parents, and policymakers respond to their growing presence and the controversies that result will ultimately determine whether or not immigration will be a source of strength or lead to greater polarization and conflict in the years ahead.

References

Ada, A. F. (1988). The Pajaro Valley experience: Working with Spanish speaking parents to develop children's reading and writing skills through the use of children's literature. In T. Skutnabb-Kangas & J. Cummins (Eds.), *Minority education: From shame to struggle* (pp. 223–238). London: Multilingual Matters.

August, D., & Hakuta, K. (1997). *Improving schooling for language-minority children: A research agenda*. Washington, DC: United States Department of Education.

August, D., & Shanahan, T. (2006). *Developing literacy in second-language learners: Report of the national literacy panel on language-minority children and youth*. Mahwah, NJ: Lawrence Erlbaum.

Berger, P., & Huntington, S. (2002). *Many globalizations: Cultural diversity in the contemporary world*. London: Oxford University Press.

Brodkin, K. (1999). *How Jews became white folk and what that says about race in America*. New Brunswick, NJ: Rutgers University Press.

Bronfenbrenner, U. (1979). *The ecology of human development: Experiments by nature and design*. Cambridge, MA: Harvard University Press.

Bronfenbrenner, U. (1988). Foreword. In R. Pence (Ed.), *Ecological research with children and families: Concepts to methodology* (pp. ix–xix). New York: Teachers College Press.

Bryk, A., & Schneider, B. (2003). Trust in schools: A core resource for school reform. *Educational Leadership, 60*(6), 40–45.

Capps, R., Fix, M., Ost, J., Reardon-Anderson, J., & Passel, J. S. (2004). *The health and well-being of young children of immigrants.* Washington, DC: Urban Institute.

Chavez, L. (2001). *Covering immigration.* Berkeley: University of California Press.

Clark, W. A. V. (1998). *The California cauldron: Immigration and the fortunes of local communities.* New York: The Guilford Press.

Coltin, L. (1999). *Enriching children's out-of-school time.* Accessed at http://www.eric.ed.gov/ERICWebPortal/contentdelivery/servlet/ERICServlet?accno=ED429737 on May 20, 2008. (ERIC Documentation Reproduction Service No. ED429737)

Cornelius, W. (2002). Ambivalent reception: Mass public responses to the new Latino immigration to the United States. In M. Suárez-Orozco and M. M. Páez (Eds.), *Latinos: Remaking America* (pp. 169–189). Berkeley: University of California Press.

Cummins, J. (1981). Age on arrival and immigrant second language acquisition in Canada: A reassessment. *Applied Linguistics, 2,* 132–149.

Dryfoos, J. G. (1999). The role of the school in children's out-of-school time. *The Future of Children, 9*(2), 117–134.

Eaton, S., & Orfield, G. (2003). Rededication not celebration. *College Board Review, 200,* 28–33.

Epstein, J. L., Sanders, M. G., Simon, B. S., Salinas, K. C., Joanshorn, N. R., & Van Voorhis, F. L. (2002). *School, family and community partnerships: Your handbook for action* (2nd ed.). Thousand Oaks, CA: Corwin Press.

Fabienke, D. (2007, June). Beyond the racial divide: Perceptions of minority residents on coalition building in South Los Angeles. *TRPI Policy Brief.*

Fass, P. S. (1989). *Outside in: Minorities and the transformation of American education.* New York: Oxford University Press.

Fass, P. S. (2007). *Children of a new world: Society, culture, and globalization.* New York: New York University Press.

Fix, M., & Zimmerman, W. (2001). All under one roof: Mixed-status families in an era of reform. *International Migration Review, 35*(2), 397–341.

Fleming, G., & Leo, T. (1999). Principals and teachers: Continuous learners. *Issues . . . About Change, 7*(2). Accessed at http://www.sedl.org/change/issues/issues72/ on May 20, 2008.

Gans, H. (1967). *The Levittowners.* New York: Pantheon Books.

Garcia, E. (2001). *Hispanic education in the United States.* New York: Rowman & Littlefield.

García, S. B., Wilksinson, C. Y., & Ortiz, A. A. (1995). Enhancing achievement for language minority students: Classroom, school, and family contexts. *Education and Urban Society, 27*(4), 441–462.

Glazer, N., & Moynihan, D. (1963). *Beyond the melting pot: The Negroes, Puerto Ricans, Jews, Italians, and Irish of New York City.* Cambridge, MA: MIT Press.

Guendelman, S., Halpin Schauffler, H., & Pearl, M. (2001). Unfriendly shores: How immigrant children fare in the U.S. health system. *Health Affairs, 20*(1), 257–266.

Gullatt, D., & Lofton, B. (1996). The principal's role in promoting academic gain. Accessed at http://www.eric.ed.gov/ERICWebPortal/contentdelivery/servlet/ERICServlet?accno=ED403227 on May 20, 2008. (ERIC Document Reproduction Service No. ED403227)

Hall, G., Yohalem, N., Tolman, J., & Wilson, A. (2003). *How afterschool programs can most effectively promote positive youth development as a support to academic achievement: A report commissioned by the Boston after-school for all partnership.* Wellesley, MA: National Institute on Out-of-School Time.

Halpern, R. (1999). After-school programs for low-income children: Promises and challenges. *Future of Children, 9*(3), 81–95.

Hayes-Bautista, D. (2002). The Latino health research agenda for the twenty-first century. In M. M. Suárez-Orozco & M. M. Páez. (Eds.), *Latinos: Remaking America* (pp. 215–235). Berkeley, CA : University of California Press.

Hightower, J. (2008, February 7). Immigrants come here because globalization took their jobs back there. *Lowdown.* Accessed at http://www.alternet.org/story/76076 on May 20, 2008.

Hofferth, S. L., & Jankuniene, Z. (2001). Life after school. *Educational Leadership, 58*(7), 19–23.

Jiobu, R. (1988). *Ethnicity and assimilation.* Albany: State University of New York Press.

Kao, G., & Tienda, M. (1998). Educational aspirations among minority youth. *American Journal of Education, 106*(3), 349–384.

Katznelson, I., & Weir, M. (1994). *Schooling for all: Class, race, and the decline of the Democratic ideal.* Berkeley: University of California Press.

Lipman, P. (1998). *Race, class, and power in school restructuring.* Albany: State University of New York Press.

Meier, K., & Stewart, J. (1991). *The politics of Hispanic education.* Albany: State University of New York Press.

Meier, K. J., Stewart, J., & England, R. E. (1990). *Race, class and education: The politics of second generation discrimination.* Madison: University of Wisconsin Press.

Mendel, C., Watson, R., & MacGregor, C. (2002). A study of leadership behaviors of elementary principals compared with school climate. Kansas City, MO: Southern Regional Council on Educational Administration.

Noguera, P. A. (2003). *City schools and the American dream: Reclaiming the promise of public education.* New York: Teachers College Press.

Noguera, P. A. (2004, April). Social capital and the education of immigrant students: Categories and generalizations. *Sociology of Education, 77*(2), 180–183.

Noguera, P. (2006). Education, immigration and the future of Latinos in the United States. *Journal of Latino Studies, 5*(2).

Oakes, J. (2002). Adequate and equitable access to education's basic tools in a standards-based educational system. *Teachers College Record,* special issue.

Ogbu, J. (1988). Variability in minority student performance: A problem in search of an explanation. *Anthropology and Education Quarterly, 18*(4), 312–334.

Olsen, L. (2000). *Made in America: Immigrant students in our public schools.* New York: New Press.

Orfield, G., & Eaton, S. (1996). *Dismantling desegregation: The quiet reversal of* Brown v. Board of Education. New York: New Press.

Portes, A., & Rumbaut, R. (2002). *Legacies: The story of the immigrant second generation.* Berkeley: University of California Press.

Reich, R. B. (1992). *The work of nations: Preparing ourselves for 21st century capitalism.* New York: First Vintage Books.

Roediger, D. (Ed.). (1991). *The wages of whiteness: Race and the making of the American working class.* New York: Verso Press.

Rothstein, R. (1994). Immigration dilemmas. In N. Mills (Ed.), *Arguing immigration: The debate over the changing face of America* (pp. 48–66). New York: Simon & Schuster.

Rothstein, R. (2002). *Out of balance: Our understanding of how schools affect society and how society affects schools, The Spencer Foundation 30th Anniversary Essay.* Chicago: The Spencer Foundation.

Ruiz-de-Valasco, J., Fix, M., & Clewell, B. C. (2001). *Overlooked and underserved: Immigrant students in U.S. secondary schools.* Washington, DC: The Urban Institute.

Stanton-Salazar, R. (2001). *Manufacturing hope and despair: The school and kin support networks of U.S.-Mexican youth.* New York: Teachers College Press.

Smith, R. (2002). Gender, ethnicity, and race in school and work: Outcomes of second-generation Mexican Americans. In M. M. Suárez-Orozco & M. M. Páez (Eds.), *Latinos: Remaking America* (pp. 110–125). Berkeley: University of California Press.

Suárez-Orozco, M., & Qin-Hilliard, D. (2004). *Globalization: Culture and education in the new millennium.* Berkeley: University of California Press.

Suárez-Orozco, M., & Suárez-Orozco, C. (2001). *Children of immigration.* Cambridge, MA: Harvard University Press.

Takaki, R. (1989). *Strangers from a different shore: A history of Asian Americans.* New York: Penguin.

Valdez, G. (1999). *Con respeto.* Stanford, CA: Stanford University Press.

Valenzuela, A. (1999). *Subtractive schooling.* Albany: State University of New York Press.

Zentella, A. C. (2002). Latinos @ languages and identities. In M. M. Suárez-Orozco & M. M. Páez (Eds.), *Latinos: Remaking America* (pp. 321–338). Berkeley: University of California Press.

Jonathan D. Jansen

Dr. Jonathan Jansen is honorary professor of education at the University of the Witwatersrand in Johannesburg, South Africa, and visiting fellow at the National Research Foundation, South Africa. His most recent books are *Knowledge in the Blood: How White Students Remember and Enact the Past* (2009) and his coauthored book *Diversity High: Class, Color, Culture, and Character in a South African High School* (2008). In these and related works, he examines the ways in which leadership for social justice works against the grain of biography. In particular, he studies how education leaders balance the dual imperatives of reparation and reconciliation in their leadership practice.

Dr. Jansen is a recent Fulbright Scholar to Stanford University (2007–2008), former dean of education at the University of Pretoria (2001–2007), and he received an Honorary Doctor of Education from the University of Edinburgh. He is a former high school biology teacher and achieved his undergraduate education at University of the Western Cape (BSc), his teaching credentials at University of South Africa (HED, BEd), and his senior postgraduate education at Cornell (MS) and Stanford (PhD).

In this chapter, the author, the first black dean of education at the former all-white University of Pretoria, uses examples from post-apartheid South Africa to underscore the complexity and contours of change and the roles of leaders within racially polarized institutions. He gives a brief overview of the change literature on emotion and explores the link between emotion and educational change. He then examines the challenges for leadership in divided societies and looks at how emotions configure within leadership that operates in a racial minefield. He offers seven platforms for thinking about a new politics of emotion in pursuing educational change in divided societies.

Dr. Jonathan Jansen can be reached at jdjansen@telkomsa.net.

Chapter 8

When Politics and Emotion Meet: Educational Change in Racially Divided Communities

Jonathan D. Jansen

In a relatively short period of time, there has been an explosion of research and writing on the link between emotion and decision-making in general, and between emotion and educational change in particular. Emotion was once the missing dimension in research on educational change. We knew that schools, as with any organization, are emotionally charged spaces, but the dominant literature on educational change continued to ignore the emotional dimensions of educational organizations. The dominant approaches to educational change have previously been behavioristic (focused on external behaviors rather than on inward emotions), rationalistic (focusing on reason over feeling), and instrumentalist in orientation (seeking the "What?" rather than the "Why?"). The common treatment of emotion when it did surface in the literature was as an impediment or a deviance (the result of deficiency) that must be brought under control. In addition, emotions have been viewed as having a distinctly gendered expression within organizations such as schools. But the manifestation and treatment of emotion in educational and other organizations is intimately related to the cultural context; organizations, not just individuals, have emotional dispositions. Leaders are themselves emotional subjects with the authority to shape the emotional disposition of an organization, and the emotional disposition of an organization and of the leaders within an organization have direct consequences for the health of followers. Indeed, ignoring emotional constitution of organizations significantly reduces the chance of achieving deep change. (For discussion on these points from various disciplinary perspectives, see Jansen, 2005; Kristjansson, 2007; Leithwood & Beatty, 2007; Schutz, Pekrun, & Phye, 2007; Tamboukou, 2006; Thagard, 2006; and Zembylas, 2007.)

Now that emotion is no longer treated as a nuisance variable to be ignored (rational organization), an outcome of traumatic experiences to be healed (psychotherapeutic intervention), or as an interfering factor to be controlled (corporate management), we are free to regard emotion as a crucial determinant of educational outcomes. And we know that ignoring its elephantal presence in our classrooms will further constrain enduring change.

Nowhere is the emotional dimension of educational change more tangibly felt than in societies emerging from centuries of conflict where divisions of race and ethnicity still define human interaction. One such place is in South Africa in the aftermath of apartheid.

Emerging From the Aftermath

From 2000 until 2007, I was the first black dean of education at the formerly all-white University of Pretoria in the capital city of South Africa. Most of the staff was white, most students were white, the institutional culture was unmistakably white, and the curriculum contained distinctively white knowledge. The country had changed as it emerged from the 5-year presidency of Nelson Mandela, but institutions do not change as quickly as the political systems around them, and so my unwritten responsibility was to contribute to the transformation of a 100-year-old white university into a racially and culturally inclusive environment that reflected the democratic values embedded in the country's brand new constitution. I faced the challenge of leading in a time when black and white academics and students suddenly found themselves in the same halls and classrooms for the first time. Still more challenging, I faced the task of identifying the *role* of leadership within deeply divided communities and determining how emotions and politics shape the terms (and outcomes) of interpersonal and curricular engagement within post-conflict settings. To say that change is complex, challenging, and contested within recently deracialized and deracializing institutions is to almost understate the dilemma. It is emotionally, spiritually, and psychologically taxing and transformational at the same time.

Change is especially taxing when those leading the change are a minority within a large organization—in this case, an organization of more than 40,000 students and more than 2,000 staff on seven campuses. Pushing change in this context meant altering the racial demographics of the academic and administrative staff, the racial profile of the student body, the racial character of curricular knowledge, and the essentially white core of the institutional culture. But since the institution existed within a societal envelope where reparation (distributing social benefits disproportionately to the black majority) and reconciliation (retaining the social support of the white minority) were understood among leaders to be simultaneous commitments, the emotional burden was enormous.

Despite this stress, change is also transformational. Intense engagement between white and black staff and students, and between black leaders and white followers, transforms the ways in which those occupying the same learning and living spaces begin to encounter each other around critical issues of race, identity, history, and cultures. These critical dialogues, organized through what I have elsewhere called a *post-conflict pedagogy* (see Jansen, in press), begin to chip away at racial certainties and cultural dogmas. The process transforms blacks and whites alike in a context in which common citizens are compelled to learn and live—and remember the past—together.

Even with the recent explosion in literature on the link between emotion and educational change, literature on the emotion of leadership in divided societies remains sparse, and with few exceptions, it dwells endlessly on the positive worth of emotions and not with emotion as a political subject; there is no sense of emotion as both potentially destructive and constructive in the life of an organization. Even in those instances when the relationship between emotions and power is recognized, such as in the work of Megan Boler (1999), the research is more likely to deal with the gendered nature of the subject rather than its racialized expressions within institutions. The literature might deal, for example, with the notion of emotion as a challenge involving balancing for leaders, which makes a lot of sense—except that the content, costs, and consequences of balancing are seldom described in this line of inquiry. In general, the literature on politics and the literature on emotion travel in opposite directions in the vast and still largely technicist literature on change. It is therefore the purpose of this essay to work within these lacunae of change research on emotion.

The Challenges of Change

A white undergraduate student returns from a field trip to the Apartheid Museum and is filled with anger as she challenges the professor for what she feels is a lack of balance in dealing with the pain of loss among whites. A newly arrived black professor flies into a rage when he is instructed by an unwitting white campus manager to move his car from parking reserved for academics. During a casual lunch conversation, a white professor breaks down and sobs as she recognizes, for the first time, the complicity of whites in the oppression of her black colleagues. White students protest furiously at the university's plan to integrate the student residences for the first time in almost 100 years. Black students submit a letter to the dean of their school complaining about deliberate racist jibes from a professor in the course of her teaching. Black administrators send a delegation to the university authorities claiming that the promotions policies of the institution favor white administrators even when they have less experience and knowledge. And a poor white parent confesses tearfully to the black dean that he does not have any money to fund his daughter's university education and that she might have to give up on her dream of becoming a teacher. I experienced events like these every day during my leadership at a former white university that had committed to physical desegregation, but which faced enormous hurdles with respect to social integration among black and white academics, administrators, and students.

What do challenges of integration such as these mean for leaders in divided societies, and how do emotions figure within leadership that operates in a racial minefield where even the slightest action can be read as favoring one side over another? Based on our recorded experiences and ongoing research on leadership in such contexts, I offer the following seven theses as a platform for thinking about a new politics of emotions in pursuing educational change (Jansen, 2006, 2007).

Thesis 1: We Must Recognize the Politics of Emotions That Energize Behaviors

A complaint, an aggressive act, or a quiet withdrawal in racially divided communities cannot be resolved through organizational alterations, policy reform, or curricular change only. Such expressions of pain, anxiety, or pressure are human problems that must be approached directly. In the case of outright aggression or racial insult, the direct approach must name the act in order to resolve it.

Once that is done, the challenge is to address underlying causes. The young white woman who returned from the Apartheid Museum had just had a terrifying experience. Until that day, her belief system rendered blacks as the aggressive enemy and whites as decent and civilized. Everything she was told about her people fell apart as she encountered, for the first time, the racial oppression and economic exploitation of whites upon blacks. To simply dismiss this young woman as an incorrigible racist is to incite racial anger and conflict on both sides of the divide.

Once her hostility is rendered unacceptable, her humanity must be accessed. As white students recognize evil in what they have lost, the task of the leader is to engage their fears and anxieties, their sense of loss and defeat, and the unbearable burden of whiteness. In short, the emotions expressed are not irrational, nor do they show a lack of interest; rather, they are, inescapably, political expressions.

This example raises challenging questions for teaching and teacher preparation, for it takes incredible skill and the capacity for empathy to even begin to engage students in ways that lead to productive dialogues about difficult subjects like race and representation. It is even rarer for teachers to be able to recognize the underlying politics of emotion at play.

Thesis 2: The Change Strategy Cannot Create Victims

It is easy in a divided society like South Africa to take the side of the black person; historically it is true, black people were victims of apartheid in every sense—economically, educationally, physically, and psychologically. But change does not happen when the other side—the second generation of whites (young people born after apartheid)—are treated as the oppressors. They too are victims. They are victims of a deficient education system based on white supremacy. They are the victims of lies and deceit that will trouble their lives for years to come. They are victims who have to come to terms with the reality of their parents as part of the oppressive classes that ruled with impunity for so long. They lack access to the cultures and languages of their fellow black citizens. They are the first generation of white South Africans to come into a democracy with racial knowledge handed down to them from past generations, but without the racial power of the past, which has been taken away from them.

There is another dimension to this sense of white victimhood: When white—especially Afrikaner—students talk about the distant past, they speak of their own oppression in the concentration camps of the British during the South African Wars at the turn of the previous century. They speak of white poverty in the early part of the 20th century and the accompanying sense of desperation that fuelled Afrikaner nationalism. They speak of tribal heroes who trekked across the vast plains of South Africa, overcoming the elements and the natives to establish new towns and cities. When white and black students therefore confront each other in the university classroom, "the clash of martyrological memories" is on display (Hoffman, 2004, p. 140–141).

Leaders must take both sides into account without slipping into the dangerous terrain of moral relativism. The atrocities of apartheid as a crime against humanity demand that white South Africans concede and recognize their role in the perpetration of that horror. But in doing so, the change leader nevertheless accepts that there is hurt on both sides, and moves with empathy rather than condemnation to enable a critical dialogue to take place.

Thesis 3: The Problem Must Be Named and Confronted

The post-conflict pedagogy being proposed here could be misread as a superficial healing process in which victims and villains are "recognized" without the need to confront and overcome the real problems of racism, tribalism, sexism, and classism that persist in any society; however, quite the contrary is true. What makes educational change possible is that the expressed and the underlying problems that bedevil human relationships are confronted directly. The question is not *whether* this must be done, but rather *how,* for the approach is absolutely crucial in resolving conflict within divided societies.

In the case of the lecturer who intersperses her teaching with snide racial comments about the capabilities of black students, a leader must make it clear that racism is unacceptable, that a higher standard of behavior is required, and that the continuation of such acts of racial insult will lead to dismissal. This must happen regardless of the personal trauma or ethnic history of the group with which this white academic associates. The confrontation is not about the lecturer, per se; it is about broader communication to the watchful audience of campus dwellers and surrounding communities for whom taking a stand is an indication of what is acceptable and what is not, and of the position of leadership on this potentially explosive matter. Everyone appreciates a firm and open position on controversial matters. Ambivalence, however, virtually guarantees the continuation of such destructive behavior.

There are politics at stake here, so approach matters. It matters who speaks, how, and what is said. It matters that the response to the situation is consistent with what is said everywhere else in the organization. It matters that the party charged with this behavior is presumed innocent and given a chance to defend herself. It matters that there is follow up by leadership. It matters that there is a clear indication of support to the teacher to enable her to change her language, attitudes, and beliefs, and it matters greatly that there are consequences for such behavior.

Thesis 4: Leaders Must Exemplify the Expected Standard of Behavior

This seemingly old-fashioned point is vitally important in divided communities. Leaders are watched for their affiliations; a leader whose circle of friends and associates are only white or only black cannot speak with any moral authority about the need for social and cultural integration among teachers and students. Leaders who compose their leadership teams of those who belong to the same racial or religious affiliation are unable to demand respect and attention when urging others to pursue social justice.

Those who observe leadership behavior, especially students, take their cues from their leaders. Their leaders must show the moral standard they seek to instill in their followers if they are to gain their trust. The same is true of staff at all levels of an organization. A head of department is unlikely to move firmly toward greater racial inclusiveness in staff appointments within his or her realm of authority if the principal or dean of his school or university does not lead the way in making such affirming appointments.

The problem, of course, is that making positive choices often involves considerable emotional risk. Our research has shown consistently that white principals who open their schools deliberately to children and teachers from other races risk alienation from within their own group. For example, they are called names, their children no longer get invited to family parties, and they are ignored in public spaces by long-time friends and associates. These consequences are real and could cut off leaders from warm and familiar emotional networks. This is even more difficult for students, of course, who are at an age when the need for affirmation and acceptance is intense. Still, our research shows that leaders who lead through the power of demonstration open up broader, more inclusive and enriching networks of friends and colleagues that liberate them from their own prejudices. Without such leadership, educational change in hostile environments simply cannot happen.

Thesis 5: We Must Engage Emotionally With Students in Their World

It is impossible to change students' deep knowledge and emotions about the past by simply treating the subject as a cognitive or intellectual problem. That is, the assumption that by introducing new knowledge in the curriculum that is logical and rational, one can change the minds of those in divided communities (staff or students) is quite simply wrong. The much more complex problem here is what I call *knowledge in the blood*—the complex spiritual, emotional, psychological, and political learnings that together constitute knowledge, which comes from the heart as much as from the head.

To shift this knowledge in the blood, or understandings of the heart, requires emotional engagement with the subject. In my work, this meant visiting students in their homes, engaging them in student residences, conversing with them on campus grounds, observing them in the classroom, making contact with their parents, and showing interest in their extracurricular endeavors. There is no simple pedagogy here, for the delivery of an erudite lecture to hundreds of students on emotional topics like race and privilege and then withdrawing into professorial seclusion is to create a distance that cuts off opportunities for deeper engagement.

This strategy does not simply involve the changing of the student; it also involves the changing of the teacher, for by entering these different realms of student life, it is possible to understand the ways in which they come to gain emotional knowledge, and why the simplistic retreat into academic training as the solution does not make any sense. The complexity here must therefore be understood so that attitudes can be changed; there are no shortcuts outside of deep involvement with students. Only in this way is it possible, for example, to understand the repulsion felt by white students about living with black students in the same room. Recognizing and coming to grips with the fact that all socializing agencies—the family, the school, the church, cultural associations, and peer groups—together emphasized the same message of racial exclusivism and race supremacy over and over again aids in the understanding of why it is so difficult to change hearts.

Thesis 6: Teachers and Principals Are Themselves Emotional Actors

The idea that the student is the target of change is commonplace in the educational change literature. But what about those who teach? Have they somehow come to terms with the politics of emotions in their own lives, and can they therefore be trusted to engage young people in this most troubling of subjects—race, emotions, and change? In divided communities, as elsewhere, teachers and principals come into schools and universities with personal histories that have shaped their understandings of other people, and they do not simply shake off those emotional and political influences in their own lives when they teach a more inclusive curriculum. Often unconsciously, teachers and leaders make choices, dispense attention, assess literature and tools, organize seating patterns, allocate praise, withdraw support, and associate themselves with other teachers and students on the basis of race.

Consider Max, a teacher of South African history to students in grade 11 for more than 25 years. As a white South African reared in the political vortex of the apartheid years, Max came to understand deeply that the history of white settlement was one of triumph over adversity, of civilization over backwardness, of Calvinist faith against atheistic communism, of freedom against tyranny. He lost members of his family in the border wars, and he witnessed the struggles of his parents against white poverty and their gradual rise, through the discipline of hard work, to a comfortable though not extravagant middle-class lifestyle. Then Nelson Mandela was elected in 1994, and a new history was suddenly to be taught with very different narratives from the ones he had come to believe and thus relied upon to make his choices in life. For him, the teaching of history is emotional knowledge, even though he accepts, in his mind, the inevitability of a new official knowledge.

Thesis 7: The Environment Must Accommodate Risk

White students do not rush into pedagogic spaces confessing guilt or acknowledging racism, nor do white parents suddenly own up to years of privilege at the expense of black citizens. Even when such compulsion is felt, it is extremely difficult for human beings to unburden themselves in private or public spaces. This was the most important mistake of the Truth and Reconciliation Commission (TRC) in South Africa: the assumption that whites, given the platform, would stream forward to tell the truth about their complicity in and their benefiting from apartheid. Archbishop Desmond Tutu, the chairperson of the TRC, was adamant that whites should use this invitation not only to speak the truth, but also to advance reconciliation. This of course did not happen, and it was for a very good reason: Human beings do not willingly release painful memories, especially not on a public platform, that could draw the ire of victims and impose shame by association.

When I do workshops on risk accommodation within the classroom, invariably a teacher or professor becomes adamant that there can be no reconciliation without truth; they believe people need to acknowledge their racism and their privilege as a very first step, or there is nothing to talk about. This is a particularly Western way of thinking—to "fess up," as if this is an involuntary reflex to some central command. The explosion of talk shows in American public culture in which the most personal and the most bizarre behaviors are displayed without restraint to live audiences on national television strikes many in the third world as disgusting. Guilt and shame are more common responses to burdensome knowledge than the apparent reveling in extreme and obnoxious behavior.

Nevertheless, when I sense the adamant position that whites must simply step forward and acknowledge their racism, I ask a simple question: "Do any of you here have a memory of something so painful that you have not shared that memory with anyone, even those closest to you?" As the thud of this unexpected question takes hold in the room, I scan the faces of the participants as they struggle for a few seconds to process what was just asked. Slowly, most of the hands in the room go up, acknowledging that they possess information known only to them that cannot be spoken. Nothing demonstrates this point more powerfully than the acknowledgment of Nobel Laureate Günter Grass that he had actually been a youthful member of Hitler's notorious Waffen-SS during World War II. For half a century, the author of *The Tin Drum* (first published in 1959) was the moral conscience of post-war Germany, urging his fellow citizens to own up to their terrible knowledge about the Holocaust and their role in that horrendous conflict. But he harbored secret knowledge, which he revealed when he said, "What I had accepted with the stupid pride of youth I wanted to conceal after the war out of a recurrent sense of shame" (Isaacson, 2007, p. 13).

It is crucial in a post-conflict pedagogy that the teacher creates an atmosphere and structures teaching-learning episodes in ways that reduce the risk of speaking openly about direct and indirect knowledge. Students must be able to speak without feeling that they will be judged or despised for what they believe. They must know that in a divided classroom, there will be an attempt to "hear them out" even if their ideas are outrageous or offensive. Students must be reassured through the example of the teacher-leader that teachers and leaders can be trusted with such personal knowledge. Clearly, what is true for white students in this example is true also for black students, especially when the latter group is a minority within the classroom. This creation of risk-accommodating environments certainly does not mean that "anything goes" and that a student can spout offensive words about another group without consequences. Long before the pedagogic encounter, the teacher should have set the atmosphere by explaining the terms of engagement and sharing the rules for dialogue. Such difficult dialogues can only take place if students have trust in the teacher-leader and see the example of reconciliation he or she sets both inside and outside of the classroom.

Nonetheless, such encounters remain risky. I used to speak about risk-removing classroom climates; that is clearly impossible. At best, the teacher will work towards a risk-accommodating environment in which students, in taking risks, are assured that they will be treated fairly and their positions given serious consideration irrespective of what they believe. It is only when students trust the teacher-leader, however, that the ability to speak honestly is made possible. Then the teacher can take what is said and steer students toward a dialogue that counters racism, sexism, and classism (among other things that divide) and demonstrates the harmfulness and the offensiveness of bigotry in school and society.

Bridging the Divide

Educational change is combustible at the point where politics and emotions meet. Such is the case in post-conflict societies where educational leaders face special challenges in bridging divides among teachers, staff, and students from rival communities that in the recent past were at war with each other, either literally or figuratively. My research and experience and that of my colleagues points to a post-conflict pedagogy that recognizes, responds to, and works inside the emotional contexts within which the micropolitics of change unfold. But we are only beginning to understand what kinds of leadership and change are possible in the aftermath of conflict. This essay offers a modest contribution that, while located within post-apartheid South Africa, holds lessons for racially divided communities everywhere.

References

Boler, M. (1999). *Feeling power: Emotions and education.* New York: Routledge.

Grass, G. (1962). *The tin drum.* New York: Pantheon Books.

Grass, G. (2007). *Peeling the onion.* London: Harvill Secker.

Hoffman, E. (2004). *After such knowledge: Memory, history, and the legacy of the Holocaust.* London: Secker & Warburg.

Isaacson, M. (2007, July 15). A brave and riveting confession. *Sunday Independent,* p. 13.

Jansen, J. D. (2005). Black dean: Race, reconciliation and the emotions of deanship. *Harvard Educational Review, 75*(3), 306–326.

Jansen, J. D. (2006). Leading against the grain: The politics and emotions of leading for social justice in South Africa. *Leadership and Policy in Schools, 5,* 37–51.

Jansen, J. D. (2007). The leadership of transition: Correction, conciliation and change in South African education. *Journal of Educational Change, 8,* 91–103.

Jansen, J. D. (in press). *Knowledge in the blood: How white students remember and enact the past.* Palo Alto, CA: Stanford University Press.

Kristjansson, K. (2007). *Aristotle, emotions, and education.* Aldershot, UK: Ashgate.

Leithwood, K. A., & Beatty, B. (2007). *Leading with teacher emotions in mind.* Thousand Oaks, CA: Corwin Press.

Schutz, P. A., Pekrun, R., & Phye, G. (Eds.). (2007). *Emotion in education.* New York: Academic Press.

Tamboukou, M. (2006). Power, desire and emotions in education: Revisiting the epistolary narratives of three women in apartheid South Africa. *Gender and Education, 18*(3), 233–252.

Thagard, P. (2006). *Hot thought: Mechanisms and applications of emotional cognition.* Cambridge, MA: MIT Press.

Zembylas, M. (2007). Theory and methodology in researching emotions in education. *International Journal of Research and Method in Education, 30*(1), 57–72.

James P. Spillane

James P. Spillane is the Spencer T. and Ann W. Olin Chair in Learning and Organizational Change at Northwestern University, where he is a professor of Human Development and Social Policy, Learning Sciences, and Management and Organizations. Dr. Spillane is a faculty fellow at Northwestern University's Institute for Policy Research and is a senior research fellow with the Consortium for Policy Research in Education (CPRE). With funding from the National Science Foundation, Spencer Foundation, and Institute of Education Sciences, Dr. Spillane's work explores the policy implementation process at the state, district, school, and classroom levels, and school leadership and management. He is the author of *Standards Deviation: How Schools Misunderstand Education Policy* (2004), *Distributed Leadership* (2006), and numerous journal articles and book chapters, and coeditor of *Distributed Leadership in Practice* (2007).

In this chapter, the author argues that in order to make a substantial contribution to school improvement, research and development efforts must focus on the day-to-day *practice* of leadership and management, a focus that has been largely neglected in the field of school administration. The author claims that if leadership and management research and development are to make a substantial difference in further educational reform, then the study and development of practice must be a central concern in the work. Efforts to understand and develop practice must involve the twin processes of diagnosis and design, and a distributed perspective offers a rich framing for these processes.

Dr. James Spillane can be reached at j-spillane@northwestern.edu.

Chapter 9

Engaging Practice: School Leadership and Management From a Distributed Perspective

James P. Spillane

School leadership and management play a pivotal role in education reform. Various lines of scholarship, from the effective schools research (Purkey & Smith, 1985) to research on the school as a professional community (Louis & Kruse, 1995; McLaughlin & Talbert, 2006; Rosenholtz, 1989), capture the importance of school leadership and management in reform efforts (Leithwood et al., 2007). And it is known that the successful local implementation of external reforms—from federal policy initiatives to school district improvement efforts—depends in good measure on school leadership and management (Berman & McLaughlin, 1977; Fullan, 2007).

Policymakers appear to agree with local, state, and federal policies holding school leaders—almost exclusively the school principal—responsible for school improvement. Indeed, in some jurisdictions, school principals can lose their positions if their schools do not show adequate improvement in student achievement. By decree, school principals are to become masters of leading and managing instruction and its improvement. Some philanthropic organizations also concur and have invested considerable resources in the research and development of school leadership and management.

Strategies for improving school leadership and management are plentiful. Some focus on leadership styles—democratic versus autocratic, transformational versus transactional, the value of shared leadership, and so on. Others focus on behaviors of effective and not-so-effective school leaders, identifying those behaviors that appear to make a difference on the job. Some strategies rely on the knowledge and expertise in a school. Still others focus on culture and other aspects or conditions of the organization, arguing for the creation or cultivation of particular types of professional or workplace cultures that promote innovation. Although diverse, these perspectives share a commitment to improving our understanding of school leadership and management.

Another thing these perspectives share is an inattention to practice. They skirt the practice of leading and managing, working around it rather than working to understand it. Certainly, culture, individual behaviors, leadership styles, and so on are relevant considerations when it comes to the practice of leading and managing a school—or any other organization for that matter. But studying culture, individual behaviors, and styles of leadership does not necessarily further our understanding of the *practice* of leading and managing.

If we are to realize and marshal school leadership and management in the cause of furthering educational reform, we have to engage the practice of leading and managing. To make a substantial contribution, research and development efforts have to focus on the day-to-day practice of leadership and management, a focus that has been mostly neglected in the field of school administration and in administration in general.

Based on the available evidence, the success or failure of educational reforms, from standards and accountability policies to efforts to improve teacher quality, will depend in important part on school leadership and management. Hence, tapping and developing school leadership and management is critical for furthering educational reform, especially reforms that aim to improve the quality of classroom teaching and student learning. If leadership and management research and development are to make a substantial difference in furthering education reform, then the following circumstances are essential:

- Research and development must focus on the *practice* of leading and managing.

- School leaders, the key agents in efforts to improve leadership and management practice, must be central players in the work.

- Efforts to understand and develop leading and managing practice, both inside and outside schools, must involve the twin processes of diagnosis and design.

- Research and development can benefit from taking a distributed perspective, which provides a framework for focusing and centering diagnoses and design work on practice.

- Diagnosing the practice of leading and managing, and designing for its improvement, should be a central pursuit not only for school leaders, but also for those outside the schoolhouse whose aim is improvement.

Making the Case for Practice

Scholars in education and beyond bemoan the inattention to practice in leadership and management and argue for an action or activity perspective (Eccles & Nohria, 1992; Heck & Hallinger, 1999; Heifetz, 1994). Considering that "the strength of leadership as an influencing relation rests upon its effectiveness as activity," a focus on practice seems especially important (Tucker, 1981, p. 25). Some readers may find claims about the inattention to practice somewhat exaggerated and point to the sizable literature on leadership styles and leadership behaviors. Part of the problem here is that the term *practice* is used to refer to various phenomena, including the counterpart of theory, the comprehensive enactment of a profession, a set of specific behaviors, and leading and managing in particular places and times.

By *practice*, I mean the real-time unfolding of the work of leadership and management in schools; I distinguish the practice of leading and managing from leadership and management practices (Pickering, 1995). With respect to the latter, we might, for example, identify a set of practices in a school system for evaluating teachers that might include the following sequence of activities: a preconference between the teacher and the principal, the principal observing the teacher teaching a lesson, and a postconference, with each component more or less specified. Indeed, some professions, such as medicine and law, have relatively well-specified sequences of activities for their professional or social practices. While these sequences of activities are critical in understanding practice, they are not what I mean by practice. Practice cannot be reduced to a set of behaviors or activities that can be extracted from the place and time in which they are embedded (Bourdieu, 1990). When we disconnect practice from place and time, we lose its urgency—the immediacy of the interactions (Bourdieu, 1981, p. 310). Practice is emergent— someone acts or makes a move in relation to someone or something else, and it is in these interactions that practice takes form. The best-laid plans and well-honed social practices can have unexpected outcomes in practice, even in fields such as medicine. My argument for attention to the practice of leading and managing should *not* be misconstrued as a suggestion that the work of leading and managing schools is such that it defies any sort of codification. I will return to the discussion of practice later when I explore the distributed perspective.

Before proceeding, I will clarify several other terms used in this chapter. The term *management* refers to the maintenance of current arrangements and ways of doing business; leadership, in contrast, focuses on transforming these existing ways of doing things to achieve new ends (Burns, 1978; Cuban, 1988). Leadership refers to activity that is designed by organizational members, or understood by them, to influence the motivation, knowledge, affect, or practice of other organizational members to initiate and bring about change in the organization's core work (Spillane, 2006). Though leadership is often defined in terms of individuals who influence others—for better or worse—to do things differently, it will become clear later why I focus on the practice of leadership rather than on the leaders themselves.

Contrary to some accounts, leadership and management work in tandem (Cuban, 1988). School leaders, once having successfully implemented a change in some aspect of their school, must then manage or maintain the fruits of their labor lest they disappear. Moreover, school leaders cannot change everything at once; some aspects of the organization have to be maintained so that other aspects can be changed. Indeed, in the day-to-day work of the schoolhouse, distinguishing management from leadership activities is often difficult as they are closely intertwined in the same activities (Spillane & Diamond, 2007). Still, the analytical distinction between management and leadership is helpful for engaging in the work of diagnosis and design.

Diagnosis and Design

Diagnosis and design are essential components of school improvement and critical in any effort to better understand and improve the practice of leading and managing (Spillane, 2006; Spillane & Coldren, in press). Diagnosis is an essential component of most work—from the doctor's office to the principal's office—though in some jobs the work is more codified into social practices than others. Diagnosis involves determining the nature or cause of a situation. For example, increased teacher absenteeism or turnover may prompt school leaders to gather information about various aspects of school life both inside and outside the classroom to investigate whether or not there is a problem. Likewise, students' declining comprehension skills in the upper primary grades may prompt school leaders to gather data by analyzing test scores and samples of classroom work in an effort to find the cause of the decline. Of course, while diagnosis seems clear-cut—collect data to determine the cause of the problem—school leaders can disagree even when they have used the same data or information; they might construct different definitions of the problem and propose different solutions for solving it. Data are not evidence; rather, we use data to build evidence of a problem.

We often reserve the term *design* for the work of architects, engineers, and fashion designers, but design is often an ordinary and rather mundane activity that most of us engage in, often without thinking of it as design. Design is about shaping things for an intended purpose (Perkins, 1986). While school leaders as middle managers are often cast as implementers of the designs of higher-ups, in reality, design is often a key component of the job. Moreover, the grand designs of school district officials and external school-improvement providers often have to be redesigned so that they fit and work better in a particular school. School leaders design and redesign key aspects of the infrastructure, from organizational routines to key tools central for doing the work of leading and managing.

Adams Elementary on Chicago's South Side provides an example of the importance of design in school leadership and management. Adams' principal and her leadership team designed and implemented various organizational routines, including the monthly Breakfast Club and the 5-week assessment routine in an effort to build a professional community among staff that centered on improving instruction (Halverson, 2007; Sherer, 2007). On Chicago's North Side, the principal of Baxter Elementary worked to create an infrastructure that would actively engage teachers in decision-making about instruction. In an interview, he explained, "Our biggest challenge had been developing an organizational infrastructure that could be relied upon to deliver quality services to faculty members, who could in turn provide better services in turn to the kids." To build this infrastructure, Baxter's principal designed and implemented a set of interdependent organizational routines, including a faculty leadership group, grade-level cycles, and subject-specific committees (Burch, 2007). Of course, in the busy daily life of the schoolhouse, a lot of design and redesign work is done on the hoof.

Diagnosis and design go hand-in-hand in the work of school leadership and management. Diagnostic work forms the basis for design work. In turn, the implementation of new designs or the redesign of existing ones set the stage for more diagnostic work.

It is important to note that diagnosis and design for improvement must be anchored in student learning and classroom teaching. Determining whether and how our design and redesign efforts connect with teaching and learning is a key component of our diagnostic challenge. These connections can be either direct or indirect. The Breakfast Club routine at Adams Elementary, for example, involved both direct and indirect connections to instruction. By providing opportunities for teachers to discuss research on teaching and learning, the team forged a direct link to classroom teaching. Their routine was also designed to forge indirect connections to instruction by creating opportunities for staff to collaborate around their teaching, so as to build and sustain a professional community. Of course organizational routines do not always work as intended. Hence, we have to attend to both the *intended* connections as captured in the designers' espoused theories of action and the *actual* connections as captured in their theories in use.

While the work of diagnosis and design has to be anchored in instruction, it is also essential that it reaches outside the classroom. School leaders increasingly urge teachers to study and reflect on their classroom practice through video clubs, lesson study, and other strategies, but they are often taken aback when reflection and analysis of leadership and management practice—where they are often the primary "movers and shakers"—are brought to the table. Diagnostic and design work must focus on the practice of leading and managing instruction at all levels, and this focus needs a framework.

A Distributed Perspective

School leaders, developers, and researchers need a set of analytic tools that focus their work—a framework for diagnosis and design. This is especially critical if the work involves two or more people. Without a shared framework, people can work together on the same issue, but talk past one another—especially if they have different perspectives on an issue, even when they share a common vocabulary. A distributed perspective is an analytic framework for focusing diagnostic and design work. Like any analytic framework, the distributed perspective foregrounds some features of school leadership and management and in the process backgrounds others.

A distributed perspective involves two core aspects: the *leader plus aspect* and the *practice aspect* (Spillane, 2006; Spillane & Diamond, 2007). The leader plus aspect, which has received most of the attention in the research, recognizes that leading and managing school improvement involves more than what individuals with formally designated leadership positions do. Both people with formally designated leadership positions (such as principals, assistant principals, and subject specialists) and those without such designations (such as classroom teachers, parents, and students) can and do take responsibility for leadership and management work. The distributed perspective then presses us to move beyond an exclusive focus on formally designated leadership positions to consider other sources of leadership and management.

A word of caution is in order: Contrary to the beliefs of some in education, the leader plus aspect does *not* argue that everyone in the schoolhouse has—or even should have—responsibility for leading and managing improvement. Further, the leader plus aspect in no way assumes that the more people involved in the work of leading and managing, the more effective that work will be in improving teaching and learning. More is not always better.

The second aspect of a distributed perspective puts the practice of leading and managing front and center in diagnosis and design work. The practice of leading and managing, as opposed to the more traditional practice of leadership with designated leaders, is at the core of the perspective. Rather than viewing practice as equivalent to the actions of an individual leader, formally designated or not, the practice of leading and managing is *distributed* in the interactions among school leaders and followers as mediated by aspects of their situation, including tools, organizational routines, culture, and so on (Gronn, 2002; Spillane, Halverson, & Diamond, 2004). Practice emerges from the *interactions* among people and their situation, rather than as a function of the *actions* of any one individual leader. In this way, practice is not about isolating and naming actions or behaviors, but instead it is about understanding how these actions are embedded in a system of practice. As Dewey and Bateson note, it is essential to see an "action as *part* of the ecological system called context and not as the product or effect of what remains of the context after the piece which we want to explain has been cut out from it" (1972, p. 338, cited in Cole, 1996, p. 142). Practice in a particular place and at a particular time is part of a system of practice, or activity system (Engeström, 1999; Gronn, 2003).

Some readers may be skeptical, thinking that the distinction between "actions" and "interactions" is purely semantic. But there is more than semantics at play here. Let us consider the performance of a two-step in dancing. (If you are ambitious, consider a four hand reel or a square dance). Though the actions of each partner in the performance of the two-step are important, the actual practice of the two-step is in the interactions of the two partners. The performance (their practice) of the dance is what happens *between* them. Diagnosing the actions of either partner—or even both—does not necessarily diagnose the practice of the two-step. The same holds for everyday work practice in organizations such as the schoolhouse. Indeed, it is even more significant because such practice often lacks the level of scripting that is common in dancing.

Situation is a key consideration in this way of thinking about practice. People do not interact directly with one another—their actions are mediated by situational elements. In the example of the two-step, the dancers' interactions are mediated by the music that provides the important rhythm for their performance. The same holds true in our everyday practice where our interactions with others are mediated by such things as language, routines, available tools, and so on. We take these situational elements for granted, or if we do acknowledge them, we most likely credit them for allowing us to do things more or less efficiently. But these situational elements have a greater impact than simply making practice more or less efficient; they enable and constrain practice and thereby define it. Compare the practice of buying a book a decade ago, prior to the introduction of the Internet, with the practice of book buying today. The introduction of the Internet, a key situational element, has fundamentally changed the practice of purchasing a book. It has impacted much more than the ease and efficiency with which we can buy books; the Internet has fundamentally transformed the practice of book buying. As educators, we take many situational elements for granted, casting them as accessories or aids to our individual practice, things that let us execute our plans more or less efficiently. A distributed perspective, however, considers these aspects of the environment in a different light by framing them as defining aspects of practice. By framing and focusing interactions among school staff in this way—on some aspects of the environment rather than on others—the situation defines practice.

The framework provided by the distributed perspective gives school practitioners a set of diagnostic and design tools for the work of improvement. Like any analytical tool, it frames leadership and management in a particular manner, focusing our attention on some dimensions and downplaying or obscuring others. A distributed perspective is useful for centering diagnosis and design work on the *practice* of leadership and management. What is important in adopting a frame, such as the distributed frame, is that we keep in mind the dimensions of the phenomena that the frame foregrounds and backgrounds: While a more conventional psychological frame would foreground the personality traits, knowledge, skill, and behavior of individual leaders, for example, a distributed frame foregrounds the interactions among leaders and followers as framed by aspects of their situation.

A distributed perspective casts a broad net in diagnosing leadership and management, attending to both the formal and informal organization (Meyer & Rowan, 1977). The formal or designed organization refers to leadership and management work as captured in formal accounts—organizational charts, formally designated leaders' accounts of what they do, and so on. The informal or "lived" organization refers to the organization as it is experienced in the day-to-day life of organizational members, not only those with formal leadership designations, but also those individuals with no such designations. A distributed perspective provides a frame that compels us to look at the designed and lived organization in tandem. Both are key because you cannot have one without the other. The designed and lived organization must be understood in interaction. You must understand one to understand the other. Formal organizational routines structure practice, but because of the emergent nature of practice, they cannot script it as the designers intended.

Thus, a distributed perspective offers a way of framing relations between the designed organization and the lived organization. Aspects of the designed organization, such as formally designated leadership positions and organizational routines as instantiated in day-to-day practice, structure the practice of leading and managing. In turn, these same structures are produced and potentially reproduced in day-to-day practice.

Practice and Its Improvement

One challenge in adopting a distributed perspective is that while practice is central, we cannot design practice—we can only design for it. Practice, as distinct from practices, is emergent. While research and diagnostic work can focus on practice, design work has to focus on the people performing the practice and those situational aspects that enable and constrain practice. To illustrate what is involved in a diagnostic and design agenda centered on leadership and management practice, I offer the example of organizational routines. In this example, I consider the role that school leaders, as well as individuals outside the school, such as school-improvement providers, district policymakers, and universities, might play in this research and development agenda on practice.

Like most organizations, schools work through a set of interconnected organizational routines. Organizational routines, as distinct from personal routines, are "repetitive, recognizable patterns of interdependent actions, involving multiple actors" (Feldman & Pentland, 2003, p. 111). They include teacher hiring and evaluation routines, grade- and cycle-level meetings, school-improvement planning, and so on. Organizational routines are critical for a school to function more or less efficiently, provide stability and continuity over time, and socialize new school staff (Cohen & Bacdayan, 1994; Feldman, 2000; Feldman & Pentland, 2003; March, 1981; March &

Simon, 1958). Organizational routines can also contribute to inertia by inhibiting innovation (Hannan & Freeman, 1984).

Organizational routines are both a product of leadership and management practice and a vehicle for that practice. Organizational routines mediate interactions among school staff (who talks to whom and the focus of these conversations), and the practice of leading and managing emerges in these interactions. For example, Hillside School in Chicago, Illinois, developed a writing folder review routine in which the principal reviewed students' writing folders monthly, including teachers' grading of student work. This focused principal-teacher and principal-student interactions on the quality of students' actual writing. At Hillside, the principal and school staff could describe the key components and sequencing of the writing folder review routine—its idealized form; they had a rather broad script that guided their participation in the routine. Similarly, when school principals conduct a teacher evaluation or hire a teacher, they draw on a more or less explicit script, which is sometimes detailed by regulations. This script or schematic form of the routine is its "*ostensive aspect*," which structures the routine in practice in a particular place, at a particular time—the "*performative aspect*" (Feldman & Pentland, 2003, p. 101; Pentland & Rueter, 1994).

Serving as a script, the ostensive aspect of an organizational routine enables and constrains interactions. It defines leadership and management practice in particular places at particular times. Still, because these scripts are relatively loose, the performance of a routine at any particular time involves improvisation and the choices, intentional or otherwise, of the individuals responsible for the routine, which can transform practice (Feldman & Pentland, 2003). Further, routines are created in and through practice. In response to external pressure or to meet some locally defined need, school leaders design or redesign organizational routines. The Breakfast Club and the 5-week assessment routine at Adams Elementary and the Faculty Leadership Group and the grade-level cycles at Baxter Elementary were designed by school leaders to meet particular needs and address particular organizational functions, such as teacher development (Burch, 2007; Halverson, 2007; Sherer, 2007). Similarly, the writing folder review routine at Hillside School was designed to get teachers to teach writing and to improve the quality of their writing instruction (Coldren, 2007). Hence, many aspects of the situation that contribute to defining leadership and management practice are themselves products of that practice—designed or redesigned in the interactions among school leaders and followers. Further, school leaders redesign organizational routines so that they better meet their goals when responding on the fly to changing circumstances or based on a diagnosis of existing practice (Sherer & Spillane, 2008).

The discussion to this point highlights the centrality of diagnosis and design in improving the practice of leading and managing in schools; that is, diagnosing practice and designing for its improvement. I have intentionally drawn my examples from inside schools to underscore the importance of engaging school leaders in a research and development agenda that is centered on the practice of leading and managing. In foregrounding school leaders, however, my intention is not to underplay the potential critical role of agents and agencies outside the school—policymakers, research funding agencies, school-improvement providers, professional associations, and so forth. These external and extra-system providers can and should play a role in a research and development agenda focused on the practice of leading and managing schools. Some already do, but more involvement is needed.

Many school districts mandate particular organizational routines, such as school-improvement planning, and provide varying levels of support for the performance of these routines. Unfortunately, the mandates tend to surpass the support. Some comprehensive school reform models train school leaders to perform organizational routines designed to improve instruction and monitor these performances for some period of time. School leaders' professional associations could engage in diagnosing leadership and management practice in an effort to identify promising social practices. And with the support of research funding agencies, researchers might be able to generate some credible data about the promise of the social practices they document.

External agents and agencies might, for example, develop and support schools in the implementation and institutionalization of *kernel routines*; that is, organizational routines that are designed to transform school practice by seeding and propagating new forms of practice in schools (Resnick & Spillane, 2006). The core idea here is to introduce into a school or school system a routine that, because of its specificity and support with well-defined tools and social practices, can be implemented quickly at a reasonable level of quality under the guidance of local leaders and with external support. Kernel routines anchor school practice in instruction and connect other existing organizational routines in the school to more fully focus the organization's attention on instruction. School districts, school-improvement providers, and professional associations could work to support the identification, development, and implementation of these kernel routines in schools.

Keeping the Focus on Practice

Increasingly, federal, state, and local government policies hold school leaders, typically the school principal, accountable for student performance. We expect our school leaders to manage and lead improvement in teaching and learning so that student achievement increases and the achievement gap narrows. The pressure is on. While pressure is necessary, it is unlikely a sufficient strategy for reform. School leaders, and not just school principals, need support. That support needs to be firmly anchored in understanding and developing the *practice* of leading and managing. We can continue to tinker around the edges of leadership and management practice as we engage in loose talk about school culture, styles, behaviors, and so on, but if we do not engage the practice of leading and managing, we are unlikely to provide the necessary support for school leaders to diagnose practice and design for its improvement. And as a result, we will fail to realize the full potential of school leadership and management in furthering educational reform. Improving school leadership and management professionwide, as opposed to just a school here and a school there, is difficult, and it will ultimately come down to improving day-to-day practice in the schoolhouse. While we cannot design that practice, we can diagnose and design for its improvement.

References

Berman, P., & McLaughlin, M. W. (1977). *Federal programs supporting educational change, volume 7: Factors affecting implementation and continuation.* Santa Monica, CA: RAND.

Bourdieu, P. (1981). Men and machines. In K. Knorr-Cetina & A. V. Cicourel (Eds.), *Advances in social theory and methodology* (pp. 304–317). London: Routledge.

Bourdieu, P. (1990). *The logic of practice* (R. Nice, Trans.). Stanford, CA: Stanford University Press. (Original work published in 1980)

Burch, P. (2007). School leadership practice and the school subject: The Baxter case. In J. P. Spillane & J. B. Diamond (Eds.), *Distributed leadership in practice* (pp. 129–145). New York: Teachers College Press.

Burns, J. M. (1978). *Leadership.* New York: Harper & Row.

Cohen, M. D., & Bacdayan, P. (1994). Organizational routines are stored as procedural memory. *Organizational Science, 5*(4), 554–568.

Cole, M. (1996). *Cultural psychology: A once and future discipline.* Cambridge, MA: Belknap Press.

Coldren, A. (2007). Spanning the boundary between school leadership and classroom instruction at Hillside Elementary School. In J. P. Spillane & J. B. Diamond, (Eds.), *Distributed leadership in practice* (pp. 16–34). New York: Teachers College Press.

Cuban, L. (1988). *The managerial imperative and the practice of leadership in schools.* Albany: State University of New York Press.

Eccles, R. G., & Nohria, N. (1992). *Beyond the hype: Rediscovering the essence of management.* Boston: Harvard Business School.

Engeström, Y. (1999). Activity theory and individual and social transformation. In Y. Engeström, R. Miettinen, & R.-L. Punamäki (Eds.), *Perspectives on activity theory* (pp. 19–38). Cambridge: Cambridge University Press.

Feldman, M. S. (2000). Organizational routines as a source of continuous change. *Organizational Science, 11*(6), 611–629.

Feldman, M. S., & Pentland, B. T. (2003). Reconceptualizing organizational routines as a source of flexibility and change. *Administrative Science Quarterly, 48*(1), 94–118.

Fullan, M. (2007). *The new meaning of educational change* (4th ed.). New York: Teachers College Press.

Gronn, P. (2002). Distributed leadership as a unit of analysis. *Leadership Quarterly, 13*(4), 423–451.

Gronn, P. (2003). *The new work of educational leaders: Changing leadership practice in an era of school reform.* London: Paul Chapman.

Halverson, R. R. (2007). Systems of practice and professional community: The Addams Case. In J. P. Spillane & J. B. Diamond (Eds.), *Distributed leadership in practice* (pp. 35–63). New York: Teachers College Press.

Hannan, M. T., & Freeman, J. (1984). Structural inertia and organizational change. *American Sociological Review, 49*(2), 149–164.

Heck, R. H., & Hallinger, P. (1999). Next generation methods for the study of leadership and school improvement. In Murphy, J. & Louis, K. (Eds.), *Handbook of educational administration* (pp. 141–162). New York: Longman.

Heifetz, R. A. (1994). *Leadership without easy answers.* Cambridge, MA: Belknap Press.

Leithwood, K., Mascall, B., Strauss, T., Sacks, R., Memon, N., & Yashkina, A. (2007). Distributing leadership to make schools smarter: Taking the ego out of the system. *Leadership and Policy in Schools, 6*(1), 37–67.

Louis, S., & Kruse, S. (Eds.). (1995). *Professionalism and community: Perspectives on reforming urban schools.* Thousand Oaks, CA: Corwin Press.

March, J. G. (1981). Footnotes to organizational change. *Administrative Science Quarterly, 26,* 563–577.

March, J. G., & Simon, H. A. (1958). *Organizations.* New York: Wiley.

Meyer, J. W., & Rowan, B. (1977, September). Institutionalized organizations: Formal structure as myth and ceremony. *American Journal of Sociology, 83,* 340–363.

McLaughlin, M. W. (1987). Learning from experience: Lessons from policy implementation. *Educational Evaluation and Policy Analysis, 9,* 171–178.

McLaughlin, M. W. (1990). The RAND change agent study revisited: Macro perspectives and micro realities. *Educational Researcher, 19*(9), 11–16.

McLaughlin, M. W. (1991). Enabling professional development: What have we learned? In A. Lieberman & L. Miller (Eds.), *Staff development for education in the '90s: New demands, new realities, new perspectives* (2nd ed., pp. 61–82). New York: Teachers College Press.

McLaughlin, M. W., & Talbert, J. E. (1993). How the world of students and teachers challenges policy coherence. In S. H. Fuhrman (Ed.), *Designing coherent education policy: Improving the system* (pp. 220–249). San Francisco: Jossey-Bass.

McLaughlin, M. W., & Talbert, J. E. (2006). *Building school-based teacher learning communities: Professional strategies to improve student achievement.* New York: Teachers College Press.

Pentland, B., & Rueter, H. (1994). Organizational routines as grammars of action. *Administrative Science Quarterly, 39*(3), 484–510.

Perkins, D. N. (1986). *Knowledge as design.* Hillsdale, NJ: Erlbaum.

Pickering, A. (1995). *The mangle of practice: Time, agency, and science.* Chicago: University of Chicago Press.

Purkey S., & Smith, M. (1985). School reform: The district policy implications of the effective schools literature. *Elementary School Journal, 85*(3), 352–389.

Resnick, L. B., & Spillane, J. P. (2006). From individual learning to organizational designs for learning. In L. Verschaffel, F. Dochy, M. Boekaerts, & S. Vosniadou (Eds.), *Instructional psychology: Past, present and future trends. Sixteen essays in honor of Erik De Corte* (pp. 259–276). Oxford: Pergamon.

Rosenholtz, S. (1989). *Teachers' workplace: The social organization of schools.* New York: Longman.

Sherer, J. Z. (2007). The practice of leadership in mathematics and language arts: The Addams case. In J. P. Spillane & J. B. Diamond (Eds.), *Distributed leadership in practice* (pp. 106–128). New York: Teachers College Press.

Sherer, J. Z., & Spillane, J. P. (2008). *A constancy and change in work practice in schools: The role of organizational routines.* Manuscript submitted for publication.

Spillane, J. P. (2006). *Distributed leadership.* San Francisco, CA: Jossey-Bass.

Spillane, J. P., & Coldren, A. (2008). *Leadership practice: Taking a distributed perspective in practice.* Manuscript submitted for publication.

Spillane, J. P., & Diamond, J. (Eds.). (2007). *Distributed leadership in practice.* New York: Teachers College Press.

Spillane, J., Halverson, R., & Diamond, J. (2004). Towards a theory of school leadership practice: Implications of a distributed perspective. *Journal of Curriculum Studies, 36*(1), 3–34.

Tucker, D. J. (1981). Voluntary auspices and the behavior of social service organizations. *Social Science Review, 55*(3), 603–627.

Richard F. Elmore

Dr. Richard Elmore is Gregory R. Anrig Professor of Educational Leadership at Harvard University and the director of the Consortium for Policy Research in Education (CPRE), a group of universities engaged in research on state and local education policy, funded by the U.S. Department of Education. He teaches regularly in programs for public-sector executives. Dr. Elmore has held positions with the Department of Health, Education, and Welfare and the U.S. Office of Education (1969–1971), as well as several government advisory positions at the city, state, and national levels. His research focuses on the effects of federal, state, and local education policy on schools and classrooms. He is currently exploring how schools of different types and in different policy contexts develop a sense of accountability and a capacity to deliver high-quality instruction. He has also researched educational choice, school restructuring, and how changes in teaching and learning affect school organization.

The author examines the relationship between research and practice. He uses the example of his work in an urban school district characterized by all the issues of instructional quality and student performance that plague most urban school systems. He explores the deep disconnect between research and practice embedded in the culture of American schooling. He then explores the pathologies of "nested" systems and relates them to his own research and practice in an urban setting.

Dr. Richard Elmore can be reached at richard_elmore@harvard.edu.

Chapter 10

Institutions, Improvement, and Practice

Richard F. Elmore

In recent years, my work on school improvement has shifted gradually and perceptibly away from a primary interest in research *on* policy and practice toward what I would call research *in the service of* practice. I am spending much more time working with practitioners at various levels—primarily in schools and local school districts—on issues of improvement, and less time treating practitioners as the objects of study. This transition has occurred for a variety of reasons, most notably, however, is that my views on the relationship between policy, research, and practice have changed as I have gotten closer to, and become more involved in, the work of school improvement.

I used to believe that research could inform policy and practice, that practitioners and policymakers could benefit from good research, and that, at the very least, research and policy had a connection to practice that was seldom direct or influential, but over time, modestly positive. I subscribed to the "climate view" of policy, practice, and research: Research affects the general flow of ideas around social and institutional problems, and while it might not have a direct, traceable effect on specific decisions, over time, it has a generally informative effect (see Cohen, Fuhrman, & Mosher, 2007; Cohen & Hill, 2001; Klemperer, Theisens, & Kaiser, 2001; Weiss, 1977). I have now come to think of research, policy, and practice as highly *self-interested enterprises*, in the most straightforward political sense of that term. I have moved from what I would characterize as a kind of benign, instrumental view of the relationship between policy and practice to a much more harshly skeptical, adversarial, and institutional view.

Research occurs in a highly circumscribed institutional environment in which the range of topics deemed to be legitimate subjects for inquiry and the ways in which they may be studied are determined largely, if not entirely, by the institutional interests of government agencies, foundations, universities, and individual researchers working in mutually supportive and largely self-interested relationships. Policymaking occurs in a similar institutional environment and is driven largely by the electoral incentives of public officials, by the institutional interests of public agencies, and by the desire for access and influence on the part of organized interest groups, one of which is the research community. Likewise, practice occurs in institutional settings that are, first and foremost, concerned about their own survival and their position relative to other institutions in a harshly competitive battle for resources, visibility, and influence. Connections among research, policy, and practice in this environment are highly opportunistic and interest-driven, highly stylized and often superficial, and, not surprisingly, mostly counterproductive at the level of the core functions of schooling.

I used to believe that over the long run, we could sort out the seeming conflicts between research, policy, and practice in a kind of long, civil conversation. I now believe that these conflicts are deeply rooted in the institutional structures in which we do research, make policy, and govern and manage public institutions (see Meyer

& Rowan, 1977; Moe, 1989; Rowan, 1982). Relationships among policy, research, and practice are fractious and often counterproductive because they are deeply rooted in the institutional and individual interests of the actors in these relationships. They operate not by principles of rational discourse, but by the disjointed logic of the "garbage can model"—problems in search of solutions, solutions in search of problems, and solutions and problems paired in opportunistic ways in response to windows of opportunity (see Cobb & Ross, 1997; Kingdon, 2003). There is no positive, or even benignly neutral, relationship among institutions and interests in this model, and I think my work suggests that there is often a pathological and highly destructive relationship.

School Improvement in an Urban Context

Let me put this general argument in a more specific context: My work takes me into many schools and school systems. I spend a large portion of my time either observing teachers teach or working with educators to develop their practice around how to identify high-quality instruction when they see it, and how to create conditions for high-quality instruction when they do not. I try to provide useful advice to practitioners about how to organize and manage schools and school systems in ways that make it more likely that students will have access to high-quality teaching and will be able to learn at high levels. I have been working in one setting in particular that I would like to use as an example. It is a medium-sized urban school system—fewer than 150 schools at all levels—and it is characterized by all the issues of instructional quality and student performance that plague most urban school systems. I spent most of 2007 developing a diagnostic process for helping low-performing schools in this system to create a common plan of action around a set of instructional problems that would lead them to improve their performance. We gave them data from this diagnostic process designed to help them understand how their organization worked, and provided them with support in using the data to focus their improvement efforts at the level of instructional practice.

We focused our attention on the very lowest performing schools—those that are profoundly and chronically low performing (see Elmore & Skogvold Isaksen, 2007, for research details). Somewhere between two-thirds and three-quarters of their students score below proficient on the state accountability test, and most of them have been stuck at that level of performance more or less indefinitely. They are highly atomized and dysfunctional organizations in which teachers work largely in isolation from each other and in which relations among adults, and among adults and students, are characterized by distance, relative distrust, and sometimes outright hostility. These schools have all been the object of several generations of reform and improvement efforts, originating in policies at the federal, state, and local levels. They have all made major internal structural changes designed to provide common planning time for teachers to work together. They have all had large amounts of targeted professional development, focused on teacher collaboration around specific instructional improvements. All of them have access to sophisticated data-management systems that allow them to track student performance over time on a number of measures. Many of them have had specialized training in how to use data on student performance to identify and address issues of student learning. The lead administrators in these schools have all had access to professional development on instructional leadership, and they all receive some level of supervision and support from the system level from administrators who were themselves successful heads of high-poverty schools. There is, in my view, *nothing* one could recommend by way of a "treatment" for a low-performing school that these schools have not already been exposed to in one way or another. They have shown negligible to no sign of improvement.

So what is the problem? All of these schools share a common pattern of extremely low coherence in adult expectations, an extremely low sense of efficacy and agency among adults, and extremely high levels of atomization in instructional practice. Moving from classroom to classroom, one sees a range of expectations for student engagement in learning, from students sitting in orderly rows staring silently at the teacher's back as she writes on the blackboard, to students working in pairs or small groups on common problems, to teachers teaching a half-dozen students in the front of the class while the rest of the students are completely disengaged or working on tasks unrelated to what the teacher is teaching. Asked to identify factors that are most influential in determining student learning and performance on tests, teachers in these buildings typically choose factors outside the school (peer culture, family background, students' socioeconomic status, for example) or factors inside the school but outside the classroom (the discipline policy, for example) rather than factors inside the classroom (adult expectations, teachers' knowledge of content and pedagogy, for example). But while the schools are similar in these respects, they differ quite a lot by context.

These differences remind one of Tolstoy's opening lines in *Anna Karenina:* "All happy families are the same. Each unhappy family is unhappy in its own way." The schools vary remarkably in the diversity of their student bodies—home languages, racial and ethnic backgrounds, proportions of special education students, and so on. They also vary a lot in the way administrators and teachers behave toward students—from a kind of benign and caring, but largely ineffective concern, to a harsh and dictatorial posture. The composition of teaching force also varies somewhat; most have large proportions of new teachers, but a number also have a core of very experienced teachers who have been in the same school for most of their careers.

While these schools share a core of common characteristics, they are sufficiently different so that any practice of improvement has to be tailored to the particular features of the setting. It is not hard to define a few elements of clinical practice from the research that could be tailored to address the fundamental problems of instructional and organizational coherence in these schools that would probably lead to improvement in instructional practice and student performance, but we needed to also address implementation of these practices.

Our work focused on demonstrating in grade-level, content, and schoolwide team meetings how teachers and administrators might approach an agreed-upon set of instructional problems with specific practices. We asked them to make a binding commitment to each other to try these practices in their own classrooms and bring the results of their work back, over several cycles, for discussion, analysis, and re-commitment.[1] Our theory was fairly straightforward: You build coherence in an organization by putting people in situations where they can collaborate and build trust around strategies that show relatively clear and relatively immediate results, and then you use these successes to build progressively higher levels of trust and collaboration. There is nothing especially original or unique in this conceptualization, but the practice is somewhat more specific and focused than most school improvement work. For the most part, the educators we worked with engaged in these practices with some fidelity and commitment. For the most part, in 1 year, the group-work practices were positively received by teachers, and they had relatively modest effects on teaching practice in the classroom. But despite this, there was no discernible impact on student performance. Thus, the work continues.

---

[1] Our work grew out of our prior study of internal accountability (Elmore, 2004), Anthony Bryk and Barbara Schneider's work on organizational trust (2002), and James Spillane's work on distributed leadership (2006).

Clearly, the problems in these schools are deeply rooted, and we could not fix them with a year's work with the practice we developed. My purpose here, though, is not to talk about the development of the practice, which is an unfinished story. Rather, I will reflect on the relationship between our practice—and the practice of school improvement more generally—and the institutional setting in which we were working. I will group my reflections in two categories: research into practice, and the pathologies of "nested" systems.

Research Into Practice

There is a deep disconnect between research and practice embedded in the default culture of American schooling. Our work was informed by research—by our previous research on internal accountability and by the research of others on leadership and organizational trust and coherence. But one thing became clear as we began our work: The research is largely based on cross-sectional studies that measure and describe the status of an organization at a given point in time, while the problems of improvement are longitudinal and require a view of how organizations develop over time. Developmental theories of organizational improvement in schools are largely normative and prescriptive, not empirical in any rigorous sense. They are drawn largely from looking cross-sectionally at a number of cases (organizations) at different stages of development, or retelling the stories of practitioners who are reflecting retrospectively (with limited reliability) on their recollections of what happened. These theories, if they can be called that, do not help answer the "What next?" questions that are actually involved in translating broad prescriptions into concrete settings. Developmental practice requires developmental theory that looks beyond the "What happened then?" to the "What happens next?" which is where our current education research is weakest.

A brief example will illustrate: We asked teachers and administrators to analyze the evidence from our diagnostic survey, interviews, and observations in their school. We asked them to work in groups, looking at their performance data, to identify promising practices they might pursue together. Most of the groups chose very specific issues. A common issue was students' answers to open-response questions on the state test. The open-response questions are the highest level questions on the test, and in the teachers' view, they raise the most challenging instructional issues. It was clear, for example, that a substantial number of students were not even attempting to respond to the questions, which would signal that work on how to approach an open-response question might yield a significant gain in improvement. In addition, the open-response issue dovetailed nicely with the district's focus on "workshop instruction," in which teachers were expected to engage students in writing and responding to each others' written work. As we worked with teachers over the course of the year in grade-level teams, it became clear to us that they did not have an instructional theory about how students moved from one level of performance to another on open-response questions. We had many interesting and engaging discussions about student work, spanning a massive range of student performance. Teachers were—somewhat surprisingly to us—more than willing to share the full range of student work in their classes. But for the most part, these were discussions of a given student's performance at a given time and whether it was "better" or "worse" than the last time. Exactly *how* one got from worse to better seemed to elude everyone. The teachers who seemed to have some success in this regard found it difficult to explain how they did it. And in the absence of specific guidance on the question of how to get from a grade of B to a grade of A, it was extremely difficult to answer the "What next?" question at the classroom, grade, and organizational levels. It is, in other words, impossible to have a developmental theory of improvement at the organizational level without a corresponding developmental theory at the individual and group level concerned with how new knowledge of practice gets into the heads and hands of teachers working in real time. It is one thing to set up the organizational structures and processes by which schools will be expected to improve, but it is quite another to get the right knowledge deployed in the right place at the right time so that the work of improvement actually results in improvement.

In a perfect world, there would be a body of research that could be used to answer the "What next?" question. It would be in a form that teachers would find accessible and useable, and it would be factored into discussions in a just-in-time manner. This is not how research works, however. Research gets done on topics that concern researchers, and gets funded by agencies and foundations that in some sense *know* what the important problems are before they start studying them (and often the answers they will get), based on their own organizational interests at a particular moment in time. Sometimes the knowledge produced through these relationships happens to match the problems that practitioners are dealing with; however, more often than not, the connections are, at best, distant and problematical. So practitioners, and the people who try to help them, end up fabricating theories and ideas to guide their work—theories that are often schematic and not very well-informed.

The Pathologies of "Nested" Systems

It has now become commonplace to refer to system-level improvement strategies as "nested." That is, classrooms are nested within schools, which are in turn nested within local systems, which are in turn nested within a broader policy and governance system. This idea of "nestedness" is influenced heavily by the norms of the system. Systemic improvement is possible only when the major features of the system are aligned around a common set of goals, and actors at each level have the knowledge, skill, and competence to execute their part of the strategy. As a policy metaphor, this idea has certain value, and it is one that I find appealing in some ways;

however, when you stand in the corridors and classrooms of failing schools, you see the pathologies of nestedness.

For the most part, the students and teachers in the lowest performing urban schools are the "unchosen." Student assignment systems in large urban districts are designed to reward "active choosers"—parents who have the time and material resources to decode and manipulate the elaborate rules of assignment to higher-level options. The same might be said of teachers. Union contracts and system-level teacher assignment practices disproportionately allocate less experienced teachers toward the lowest perform-ing schools, and they provide opportunities for more experienced teachers to opt out of those schools, but only if they are "chosen" by another school. If they are not chosen, they stay where they are. This produces a bimodal distribution of teachers in the lowest perform-ing schools with the least experienced, least prepared teachers at one end of the spectrum and the most experienced, least chosen teach-ers at the other. Over time, then, the nested system of district-level policies, union contracts, and student and personnel assignment practices produces a model of almost perfect adverse selection. The students and teachers who end up in the lowest performing schools are the ones that have the fewest options to improve their status in the system. And then we wonder why it is that low-performing schools are generally characterized by cultures with a low internal locus of control and agency.

In one school where I worked last year, the principal spent a large percentage of her time from February through June trying to figure out how to pass off two or three of her lowest perform-ing teachers onto another low-performing school to clear positions that she could use to recruit younger, more promising teachers. At the same time, she was trying to figure out how to keep one of her most gifted teachers—a visual artist with unconventional training—who did not meet the federal and state requirements for a "highly qualified teacher" and therefore was slated for dismissal at the end of the year. Her efforts to stay in touch with classroom practice while she was managing these personnel issues were undermined by the fact that her assistant principal, who was assigned to her school without her concurrence, was unable to help her with either instructional or managerial issues. He made no bones about the fact that his expertise was student discipline, which teachers complained he did not do very well. The principal said that she had a "supportive" relationship with her system-level supervisor, but she received no help from that level with the personnel issues in her school over the course of the year.

Nested systems operate predictably to push problems down until they come to rest at a place where they cannot move any further. Accountability systems require schools to meet performance targets. Failure to meet these targets activates sanctions, and the sanctions require someone to do something about the problem. The story of accountability in the U.S. has been one of the federal government and the states gradually and appreciably withdrawing over time from the direct administration of sanctions and the direct provision of supports to schools, while at the same time pushing responsibilities for enforcement and remediation down to the local level. The state of Massachusetts, for example, started out in the immediate aftermath of No Child Left Behind with an aggressive, hands-on intervention strategy in the state's lowest performing schools, sending state-sponsored intervention specialists directly into failing schools, overriding local responsibility. As the number of failing schools multiplied, the state began a not-so-graceful retreat. First, it sent teams of investigators into schools using a structured protocol that resulted in voluminous improvement plans that schools and districts were expected to implement. Now, it labels schools as failing and turns the problem of how to fix them over to local districts, which are, of course, required to have a plan.

But the process of passing down the problem does not stop there. System-level administrators in urban districts usually have very large caseloads of schools to supervise, and an increasingly large portion of those schools are classified as failing under the accountability system. The remedies urban districts have available for supporting failing schools are, as we have seen, highly sensitive to the *internal* workings of schools. But the system-level administrators have limited capacity to work with schools in a planful way on their internal operations, because they are responsible for many schools. So the responsibility for creating and managing an improvement strategy for the system as a whole devolves downward to the schools, without regard to the actual capacity of those schools to do the work, and without regard for the system-level consequences of school-level decisions. And when schools are atomized, they cannot operate as organizations in any meaningful sense, so the responsibility devolves further to the classroom.

It is important to understand that this set of relationships is dysfunctional only if you believe that the system is designed to improve schools. In its manifest functions, however, the system is primarily designed to serve the interests of the actors and agencies that make it up. The federal and state governments have discharged their responsibility for oversight by labeling schools and shipping the responsibility for fixing them off to the districts. The districts have discharged their responsibility by creating a system in which schools are accountable for their performance, but the people who work in the system have little or no capacity to actually support the lowest performing schools in the kind of work that will actually improve their performance. And the schools have essentially chosen *not* to organize themselves for collective action in order to preserve a culture of teacher autonomy and atomization of practice. Everyone's interest is served in these transactions, with the possible exception of the students. Once you reach the student, there is nowhere else for the responsibility to go.

I have been in a number of system-level discussions of these pathologies in urban districts, including the one where I have worked in schools. In these discussions, I have observed a common pattern for how the problems of nestedness are handled in the system. Someone will propose an alternative staffing plan for low-performing schools, for example, and everyone around the table will agree that the system is broken and needs to be fixed. Then the discussion begins to unpack the broad array of district policies, union contract provisions, and special side deals that are implicated in the existing staffing model, and gradually the discussion recedes into a morass of technicalities—away from the problem of hard-to-staff schools into the chaos of institutional politics. People begin to use phrases like, "You don't want to go there." Each technicality, of course, is not *just* a technicality; it is a specific expression of an interest for some key institutional actor, and when it is challenged, it propels that actor into a defensive maneuver. As people strategize, they gradually come to recognize that the nestedness of the system is an artifact of a complex web of organized, interest-based actors, each of whom thinks he or she represents the general interests and purposes of the system, but, in fact, mainly represents him or herself.

A Practice of Improvement

I continue to believe that the improvement of schools depends on the development of a *practice*—a shared set of understandings, a body of knowledge, and a set of protocols that can be used to develop a broad network of practitioners within schools and across professional networks that support schools engaged in continuous work aimed at improving the learning of students. I also believe that "change" is not the right metaphor to describe the work of school improvement. In fact, I avoid using the term *change* in anything other than a transitive sense, such as, "changing structures to achieve . . . ," not change as the object of reform. My definition of the object of reform is *improvement*, not change, simply defined as increases in quality of practice and performance over time. A central part of the pathology of institutionalized relations in the education sector is a preoccupation with change and a failure to improve. Being associated with change creates political and institutional credit, the more so if it does not actually require the system to improve its core functions. Sponsorship of change allows individuals and institutions to accumulate all the credit for the entrepreneurship of big ideas with none of the messiness of having actually to connect them to practice and then to learning.

I do not think that improvement can occur without conflict—the kind of conflict that is precipitated when individual and institutional interests are disclosed, challenged, and subjected to open debate. Nor do I think that schools will improve without fundamentally challenging the culture that creates atomized practice and the institutional surround that supports and reinforces that culture. It is important to have a clinical practice of improvement to be able to do the work that needs to be done at the school and classroom level. But a clinical practice is a lost cause without a corresponding theory of how to challenge the basic structures of convenience that keep the surrounding system from improving. We cannot answer the question of "What next?" if we continue to examine only the "What has happened?"

References and Resources

Bryk, A., & Schneider, B. (2002). *Trust in schools: A core resource for improvement.* New York: Russell Sage Foundation.

Cobb, R., & Ross, M. C. (1997). *Cultural strategies of agenda denial: Avoidance, attack, and redefinition.* Lawrence: University of Kansas Press.

Cohen, D., Fuhrman, S., & Mosher, F. (2007). *The state of education policy research.* Mahwah, NJ: Lawrence Erlbaum Associates.

Cohen, D., & Hill, H. (2001). *Learning policy: When state education reform works*. New Haven, CT: Yale University Press.

Elmore, R. F. (2004). *School reform from the inside out: Policy, practice, and performance*. Cambridge, MA: Harvard Education Press.

Elmore, R. F, & Skogvold Isaksen, L. (2007). *How accountability fails schools*. Strategic Education Research Project, Graduate School of Education, Harvard University.

Kingdon, J. (2003). *Agendas, alternatives and public policies* (2nd ed.). New York: Longman.

Klemperer, A., Theisens, H., & Kaiser, F. (2001). Dancing in the dark: The relationship between policy research and policy making in Dutch higher education. *Comparative Education Review, 45*(2), 197–219.

Meyer, J., & Rowan, B. (1977). The institutionalized organization: Formal structure as myth and ceremony. *American Journal of Sociology, 83*, 340–363.

Moe, T. (1989). The politics of bureaucratic structure. In J. Chubb & P. Peterson (Eds.), *Can the government govern?* (pp. 267–329). Washington, DC: Brookings Institution.

Rowan, B. (1982). Organizational structure and the institutional environment: The case of public schools. *Administrative Science Quarterly, 27*(2), 259–279.

Spillane, J. (2006). *Distributed leadership*. San Francisco, CA: Jossey-Bass.

Weiss, C. (1977). *Using policy research in public policy*. Lexington, MA: Lexington Books.

Douglas Reeves

Dr. Douglas Reeves is the founder of The Leadership and Learning Center. He has worked with education, business, nonprofit, and government organizations throughout the world. The author of more than 20 books and many articles on leadership and organizational effectiveness, he has twice been named to the Harvard University Distinguished Authors Series. His monthly column on change leadership appears in *Educational Leadership.* Dr. Reeves was named the Brock International Laureate for his contributions to education. He also received the Distinguished Service Award from the National Association of Secondary School Principals and the Parents' Choice Award for his writing for children and parents. Free downloads of research, presentations, and articles by Dr. Reeves are available at www.LeadandLearn.com.

The author begins with a discussion of what we know but too rarely admit: Traditional change strategies are failing. First, he considers the elements of change: direction, speed, and scope. He then considers the essential balance between hierarchy and networks. Next, he presents the five levels of networks, giving examples of each level. Finally, he explores multidisciplinary examples of dynamic level-five change networks in action to learn what a school system, a global multibillion-dollar organization, and remarkable public health systems all have in common.

To learn more about Dr. Douglas Reeves and his work, visit www.LeadandLearn.com. He can be reached at dreeves@leadandlearn.com.

Chapter 11

Level-Five Networks: Making Significant Change in Complex Organizations

Douglas Reeves

The term *change leadership* yields more than 12,200,000 hits on Google. Amazon.com will happily sell you more than 7,000 books with the words *change leadership* in the title. So with all the information available on change leadership, why is effective organizational change still so elusive?

Effective organizational change remains elusive because too many leaders substitute labels for substance. Much of what is labeled a "change initiative" is little more than window dressing on a crumbling foundation. For example, consider the school with a new mission, vision, and strategic plan, but little or no change in schedule, teacher assignment, professional collaboration, student expectations, feedback systems, or intervention systems for students in need. So what can organizations do to create changes that are both significant and profound—changes that not only meet the immediate priorities of the moment, but also energize everyone in the organization to seek a greater good? To make these changes, organizations must develop *level-five networks*—the focus of this chapter.

I will begin with a discussion of what we know but too rarely admit: Traditional change strategies are failing. Next, I will consider the elements of change: direction, speed, and scope. The third section of the chapter considers the essential balance between hierarchy and networks. Fourth is an examination of the different levels of networks that distinguishes contrived networks from organic networks. Fifth and finally, I explore multidisciplinary examples of dynamic change networks in action using examples from a school system, a global multibillion-dollar organization, and remarkable public health systems. If a theory of change is to be credible, it must be robust. Therefore, I consider evidence not only from education, but also from health care, business, the military, and nonprofit organizations.

Why Traditional Change Strategies Are Failing

Hargreaves and Fink begin their important book *Sustainable Leadership* (2006) with the compelling words, "Change in education is easy to propose, hard to implement, and extraordinarily difficult to sustain" (p. 1). Educational leaders and policymakers have embraced the traditional change strategy of "command and control," a strategy borrowed from business management. But this strategy, as well as most other commonly-used strategies, employs techniques distinguished more by popularity than by effectiveness. Leaders and authors of the 21st century continue to enthuse about these failed leadership methods that emerged from the 19th century. In 1963, Alfred Sloan, the creator not only of General Motors but of the modern practice of hierarchical management, wrote, "Two events occurred in 1908 that were to be of lasting significance. . . . William C. Durant formed the General Motors Company and Henry Ford announced the Model T. . . . Mr. Durant's work has yet to receive the recognition it deserves" (p. 1). Perhaps this anecdote strikes the modern reader as quaint and anachronistic, or, if you are one of the tens of thousands of people who lost a job due to the inability of the automobile industry to change effectively, it might strike you as patently offensive. Nevertheless, contemporary leadership literature hails as genius hierarchical practices that, after decades of failure, deserve reconsideration (Freeman, 2005).

Consider two radically different but equally compelling examples of failed change initiatives: grading policies in education and the process of water purification. What both of these examples have in common is strong and authoritative people—think of the portrait of Alfred Sloan hanging in the board room of General Motors—who consistently support ineffective, counterproductive, and dangerous policies. In other words, these are case studies of smart people making bad decisions.

The Case of Grading Policies

There is a century of consistent evidence that makes the need for change in grading policies obvious. Guskey (2000a, 2000b, 2002, 2005a, 2005b), Guskey and Bailey (2001), Marzano (2006), O'Connor (2007a), O'Connor (2007b), and Reeves (2004b, 2008) present just some of the available evidence that many common grading practices are ineffective and counterproductive. I recently conducted a simple experiment with more than 10,000 teachers and administrators in Canada, the United States, and South America. Specifically, I asked participants to calculate the final grade for a student in grade 8 who earned the following grades throughout the term: C, C, MA (missing assignment), D, C, B, MA, MA, B, A. Participants had one simple task, a task that literally millions of teachers around the world must do all the time: Take the scores earned during a term and calculate a final letter grade. Each time I have done this experiment, the results are the same: Teachers and administrators conclude that the final grade is everything from an A to an F. To make matters worse, it makes no difference whether the participants in the experiment are assigned a grading policy with a 100-point system, a 4-point system, or no policy at all. The power of their individual discretion undermines the policy at every turn. The more than 10,000 participants in this experiment are neither malevolent nor incompetent—they are our friends and colleagues, professionals who genuinely love and care about students. Nevertheless, they have provided clear evidence that their grading policies are deeply flawed—in fact, that their policies are profoundly unfair. How can thoughtful and intelligent professionals look at the same work from the same student and evaluate it so differently? How can any sane person continue to engage in a flawed grading system given what we know from experiments such as this and the weight of almost a century of evidence that the present system is in error? We might as well ask why almost half of people who have received heart bypass surgery soon return to the habits that led to their life-threatening heart disease in the first place (Deutschman, 2005). The only conceivable answer is that typical strategies—from insights by Mr. Sloan in 1908 to paeans to his genius a century later—are impotent compared to the pervasive resistance to change.

The Case of Water Purification

Second, consider the example of water purification in developing countries. From Guinea worm disease (Patterson, Grenny, Maxfield, McMillan, & Switzler, 2007) to dysentery and cholera (Kidder, 2004), the persistent use of impure water sources is the single greatest threat to health in the developing world. Millions of dollars of aid, exemplary humanitarian efforts by international organizations, and intense political pressure from the most authoritarian of regimes have all proven remarkably unable to overcome the resistance of cultures to change. To the well-intentioned person from the industrialized world, the answers are obvious—purify the drinking water and educate the populace to continue life-saving practices. Were the solution this simple, the world would not lose almost 40,000 people every day because of impure water (Global Water, 2007). Threats of death and disease, however, are frequently insufficiently powerful to overcome centuries of tradition. Even when water purification systems have been imposed by dictatorial regimes, traditions such as using a common water container result in the reintroduction of contaminants that the purification initiatives had removed (Patterson et al., 2007).

These examples of grading policies and water purification are hardly isolated. In areas ranging from systemic school reform to international economic policy, tradition and personal beliefs trump evidence on a regular basis. Thus, the power of change resistance creates a significant challenge for leaders who are used to fixing problems. They want to read a book, get a new strategy, order its implementation, and move on to the next challenge; however, change leadership is not so easy.

Now that we have acknowledged that past strategies have not been effective, let us consider the elements of effective change.

Elements of Effective Change: Direction, Speed, and Scope

Imagine you are the sailor on the bridge of the Titanic who, through the fog, sees the precursor to your own demise and that of your shipmates and passengers. You yell, "Iceberg dead ahead!" The implication of your warning is that a change is needed; indeed, your warning requires a 180-degree change because beneath the visible tip of the iceberg lies a deadly mountain of ice stretching in all directions. Moreover, because the Titanic already has significant forward momentum, your warning requires a change that is quick. Finally, it requires a change that is large in scope—it must include all of the crew and passengers. Now put that unpleasant image aside, and imagine that you are in somewhat more congenial circumstances—in a two-person kayak approaching the same iceberg. After the briefest of conversations with your fellow passenger, you execute a 180-degree turn in less than 3 seconds, and then you relax and snap some photographs of the beautiful mountain of ice.

The lesson is not that if the passengers on the Titanic had crossed the Atlantic in a kayak rather than an ocean liner, they would have been better off. In fact, the seas that rocked the passengers of the Titanic to sleep at night would have capsized even the most skilled of kayakers. Rather, the lesson to be learned is that change strategies must be adapted to the scope of the challenge at hand. For example, the kayak is quickly turned not only because of its small size, but because of the immediacy of the communication among the crew. The same lesson can be applied to systems of much larger complexity.

Contrary to the mythology of change theory metaphors, a modern aircraft carrier can execute a 180-degree turn in about 10 minutes (Retired Commander C. Cutshall, personal communication, January 2, 2008)—a surprisingly rapid maneuver given the scope (almost 6,000 passengers) and complexity of the challenge (about 150 sailors directly involved in executing the maneuver). In fact, the act of turning around an aircraft carrier should be a metaphor for rapid change in complex organizations. When making a 180-degree turn, there are four to six levels that separate the leader who issued the command from the lowest level of the organization that executed it. But if there are any problems in operations or safety in executing the turn, then the number of communication channels that separate the lowest-ranking sailor in the engine room from the highest-ranking officer on the deck shrinks to two. In other words, the pace of change that is safe and effective is related not only to communication *from the leader* in executing the change, but particularly in communication *to the leader* from throughout the organization when things do not go as planned. In other words, you do not turn an aircraft carrier by virtue of an inspirational speech from an admiral or a PowerPoint™ presentation from the staff. When complex systems change, there are at most two strategic priorities:

executing the present move, or getting ready to execute the next move at precisely the right time. As we will see later, complex organizations that create meaningful change in a short period of time are not weighed down by voluminous strategic plans; they have absolute clarity about a very few things that must be done immediately.

The final lesson from these examples is that the selective application of authority does not negate the continued invitation from all those involved for input, ideas, innovation, and leadership. When the lone kayaker makes a bad move, there is no one else to suggest alternative maneuvers. While larger and more complex organizations have greater challenges, they also have more sources for creativity, ingenuity, and when necessary, challenges to authority—provided that there are networks in place so the leader can hear these challenges.

Balancing Hierarchy With Networks

Leadership makes a difference. This is not only a feel-good statement heard at leadership conferences, but a demonstrable fact from extensive leadership research. John Goodlad (1984, 1990, 1994) demonstrated with thousands of schools the singular influence that leadership makes. Tom Peters (Peters, 2003; Peters & Austin, 1985; Peters & Waterman, 1982) came to a similar conclusion in the business world, and Frances Hesselbein (Hesselbein, 2002; Hesselbein & Goldsmith, 2006) applied the same research to nonprofit and governmental organizations. Synthesizing the research from every discipline, the conclusion is inescapable: Even when organizations have the same budget, clientele, regulatory environment, physical facilities, infrastructure, and, in economic terms, "externalities," leadership makes a profound difference in organizational performance. Nevertheless, the definition of leadership must be adjusted from the singular charismatic authority figure to the "architects of improved individual and organizational performance" (Reeves, 2002, p. 12). Architects provide blueprints that communicate, in clear and explicit language, the vision in a way that every brick-layer and executive, plumber and financier, mason and manager can translate into practical day-to-day actions.

The myth of hierarchy suggests that the leader creates the vision, and then the vision is mystically transmitted throughout the organization. But a wealth of leadership research suggests that the charismatic leader is not only ineffective, but also counterproductive. Collins (2001) found that the most effective leaders were self-effacing, not particularly articulate, never self-aggrandizing, and more likely to let the power of ideas exceed the power of personality. Ideas persist and spread because the ideas have value, not because an authority figure gave a speech. Leaders who give profound and powerful speeches issuing directives to senior leaders, and those who call on outside consultants to provide inspirational seminars in the hopes that participants will share the message with the next level of the organization are engaged in delusional behavior that approximates the children's game of "telephone." Children know that with each repetition of the message, the chances for distortion grow to the point that subsequent messages bear little resemblance to the original. In the organizational context, this is worse than a waste of time. It makes every member cynical as he or she recalls having been down the same path many times before; and no one is eager to endure the refrain from colleagues that "this too shall pass."

Fortunately, there is a better way. The answer is not the abdication of leadership, nor is it the conclusion that vision and mission are without value. Rather, the conclusion is that *networks are more effective than hierarchy* when the organization requires significant and profound change. Networks are, in the elegant metaphor of University of Notre Dame network theorist A.-L. Barabási (2003), a "web without a spider" (p. 219). While Barabási has many complex mathematical formulae to demonstrate the power of networks, a simpler analysis will suffice: If you are the leader of an organization of 50 people, what is the probability that you can spend quality time, one on one, with each of your colleagues? Kim Marshall, one of the most remarkably effective educational leaders I have known, was able to do this five or six times per year with his staff of more than 50 teachers, and he engaged in extraordinary effort to do so (Marshall, 2005). Indeed, many leaders with fewer than 50 people directly reporting to them cannot boast of five or six one-to-one interactions per person during a year. But using Marshall as our benchmark, the math becomes compelling quickly. The leader in a system of 500 persons who has Marshall's energy and vigor will have perhaps .5 meaningful contacts per year; the leader with 5,000 persons with the same level of commitment will have .05 contacts per year per person. It is worth noting that well-intended inspirational speeches, mass emails, web casts, and announcements dutifully repeated by cynical and uninspired subordinates during meetings do not count. Either the message is conveyed in a meaningful encounter, or it is not. The only possible alternative is the effective employment of networks—the use of person-to-person contacts within an organization of any size. Networks supplant speeches and commands with personal experience, what Patterson and colleagues (2007) call "the mother of all cognitive maps" (p. 51). In the next section, I will consider five levels of networks with surprising implications for organizations of every size and level of complexity. The goal in any organization is the formation of level-five networks, which provide the best hope for initiating, implementing, and sustaining change.

The Five Levels of Network Effectiveness

Networks are hardly a novel concept in education. Sizer (2004), and Hargreaves, Lieberman, Fullan, and Hopkins (2004) are among many who have suggested the importance of networks. Indeed, Hargreaves and Fink (2006) suggest that "networks need to be alternate structures of improvement; not additions to those that already exist. Networks require resource shifts, not resource additions, otherwise they will prosper only in optimistic eras of economic expansion and atrophy whenever times get tough" (p. 189). The latter assumption, particularly in education, is more likely to be true than the former. Therefore, the question at hand is not whether to engage in effective educational networks, but how leaders can best nurture them.

Level One: Contrived Networks

In contrived networks, leaders want to encourage communication among multiple levels of an organization. They create "matrix management" (Bartlett & Ghoshal, 1990), multidivisional task forces, and global working groups. With technology making inaptly named "work groups" more prolific, email volume has expanded exponentially, and meeting time—particularly virtual meeting time—has increased as well. The latter, unfortunately, invites multi-tasking by the participants who are engaging in the same behavior that is evident in many live meetings: incessant text messaging, cell phone interruptions, and other preoccupations. Contrived networks create the illusion of communication without the reality. As Rick DuFour has noted, these new ways of organizing are "new labels for old meetings" (DuFour, 2007). Gresham's law of meetings (Kaplan & Norton, 2008) holds that "discussions about bad operations inevitably drive out discussions about good strategy implementation" (p. 64). Therefore, repackaging existing communication patterns as a "network" is an exercise in illusion.

Level Two: Spontaneous Networks

Every organization has networks that were designed to provide communication in a simple and direct manner to those who most need the information, without any bureaucratic filters. The best contemporary example of this spontaneous internal network is CompanyCommand.com, a site created by unit commanders in the Persian Gulf War for front-line commanders (Allison, 2006;

Wheatley, 2007a, 2007b; M. J. Wheatley, E. Allison, & D. B. Reeves, personal communication, November 21, 2007). The questions on the forum are profoundly practical, such as, "I've never had to write to a family on the death of a soldier before. What do I say?" or "I'm really having trouble with a couple of my subordinates, but I need them for this next mission. What do I do?"

The soldiers who use CompanyCommand.com are young people dealing with life and death issues, yet I can imagine school principals, department heads, nonprofit directors, and leaders in every walk of life dealing with the same issues—challenges that are safe only to raise in the anonymous environment of a global community that excludes hierarchy, evaluation, and judgment. For quite some time, the United States Army hierarchy was only vaguely aware of CompanyCommand.com and wisely allowed it to continue while it pondered what to do with this information source that operated outside of established boundaries of command and control. School systems have created the same informal networks; we will meet the creators of Focus Schools later in this chapter, a group whose members do not wait for instructions from the central office or superintendent, but rather do what they can do *right now* to improve student achievement by learning from colleagues. Will Fitzhugh created *The Concord Review* (www.tcr.org), a reservoir of the best high-school writing in the world, with students from public, private, and international schools contributing their best efforts, resulting in a remarkable exposition of sophisticated, challenging, and first-rate research and writing. The social network phenomenon offers a cacophony of spontaneous networks.

Level Three: Co-Opted Networks

Ultimately, the United States Army brought CompanyCommand. com in house, and it became an officially supported website of the larger institution—a co-opted network. Rather than restrict its members to current military employees, the site welcomes participation by "current, future, and past company commanders." Likewise, Focus Schools is now an official part of the agenda of several high-achieving, high-challenge urban systems. The danger in co-optation is that networks will revert to level-one status, losing their entrepreneurial character. Therefore, senior leaders must weigh the benefits of the spirit and risk that created level-two networks against the rewards of expanding those networks to level-three status. The risk is that because network members are volunteers, they can easily migrate from a level-three network to a level-two network, seeking anonymity and freedom, but losing organizational support. The potential reward of a level-three network comes when the voluntary spirit of the network is combined with the informational and technological resources of the entire organization. The central purpose of level-three networks is to focus participants' time on sharing effective practice, rather than on becoming amateur web masters.

Level Four: Nurtured Networks

At this level, leaders do not contrive networks, as in level one, nor do they co-opt existing networks, as in level three. Rather, they create the freedom and space for individuals and groups to create their own networks. Historical examples of this level of freedom include 3M, the innovation machine that allows each employee to take time for personal invention and exploration, and Google, which attracts new employees with the promise that they will have the opportunity to dream, explore, think, and create (Patterson et al., 2007). Ainsworth and Viegut (2006) demonstrate the power of nurtured networks among teachers who share classroom assessments that are engaging, creative, and effective. A growing number of noncommercial web sites, such as www.AllThingsPLC.info, provide a global network of educators and school leaders who share promising practices beyond geographic or political boundaries.

Level Five: Value-Driven Networks

Level four may seem as good as it gets when it comes to organizational support for networks. The critical distinction of level-five networks is their purpose and orientation. The focus is not merely an organizational objective, but the greater good (Allison, 2006)—an orientation that transcends financial objectives, test scores, and quarterly goals. This transforms the network to a "community of practice" (Wenger, McDermott, & Snyder, 2002; Wheatley 2003, 2007a, 2007b). Hargreaves and Fink (2006) make clear that it is the moral imperative—not merely technical competence—that distinguishes sustainable change from ephemeral change. Value-driven networks transcend the performance objectives that demand the attention of most organizations and ask the broader question, "What is the moral imperative?"

This is the question Paul Rusesabagina faced as genocidal maniacs from the Rwandan army descended on his hotel. He could hide, surrender, or engage. The last strategy—the one he chose—saved thousands of lives. Many professionals confront this same question at work every day. For example, Pfeffer (2007) discusses how nurses might willingly confront unsafe practices by physicians, their hierarchical superiors. This insubordination can save patients' lives. This is the question the accountants at Enron faced when they foresaw the demise of their employer and the loss of the retirement funds of their coworkers (McLean & Elkind, 2003). This is the question faced by principals, teachers, bank tellers, accountants, construction managers, and many others who ask, "What is the greater good?"

These value-driven level-five networks are boundary-defying entities that are unthreatened and uncontrolled by bureaucracies. As a result, level-five networks can become the most enduring and meaningful networks within any organization. Because they pursue objectives beyond those of their participants or the organization, their "greater good" criteria for exploration and communication propels them to new levels of innovation and effectiveness. They communicate not only the "what" and "how" of the typical message, but a sense of meaning that makes level-five network communication rise above the chaos of overwhelmed communication channels.

We will now consider three powerful level-five networks in practice.

Level-Five Networks in Practice

We see examples of level-five networks in the real world in education, the military, and health care. When Norfolk Public Schools wanted to create models for effective practice in high-poverty environments, it looked inward, creating Focus Schools. As the name implies, these are schools that need an improved focus on student achievement. The genius of Norfolk's system is that rather than delivering mandatory solutions to the schools, leaders created the environment for the emergence of a network. Each Focus School is paired with a school that is demographically similar but achieving superior results. Schools hold joint faculty meetings and exchange visits. What is particularly important is that without the central office hosting meetings or issuing instructions, Focus Schools now voluntarily meet, exchange ideas, and provide mutual encouragement more than 5 years after the model was introduced. Changes in leadership in the board and central office have not stopped the persistence of these remarkable level-five networks. The results speak for themselves: Not only did Norfolk dramatically improve student achievement and educational equity with the creation of Focus Schools (Reeves, 2002, 2004a, 2006), but the system continues to create benchmarks that are far beyond merely meeting standards.

The Department of Defense Joint Program Executive Office for Chemical and Biological Defense is a global organization responsible for billions of dollars and, most importantly, the lives of soldiers and civilians throughout the world. The timeframe from conception to implementation for major defense programs was typically 7 to 10 years as a result of the need for multiple levels of approval, Congressional oversight, and the vast complexity of projects. Then came September 11, 2001, and, a week after that, the first of several anonymous anthrax attacks. "We went from a dead stop to implementing a biological and chemical defense system in less than 45 days, and simultaneously to creating a billion-dollar system for protection, preparing the fighting forces for deployment to Afghanistan and, the following year, to Iraq," said the leader of the project (and my brother), Major General Stephen Reeves (personal communication, December 31, 2007). The immediate sense of urgency when the nation was under attack was palpable. But as General Reeves noted, the burnout pace of the post-9/11 days could not be sustained indefinitely. The question was, "How do we institutionalize the lessons of those frenetic and successful days in a way that is sustainable over the long term?" Among the answers was an astonishing move to flexibility and adaptability with rarely more than two levels of communication between any team and the global commander. General Reeves explained, "We got rid of a lot of the recipe cards and insisted that people take responsibility and authority for immediate action. Feeling empowered is the opposite of being in day-long meetings with the boss." The results are difficult to measure, because there are no newspaper headlines about attacks that did not happen due to the success of chemical and biological defense systems. The organization has, however, twice been awarded the prestigious Packard Award for its significant contributions and exemplary innovations.

The final examples of level-five networks in action come from the field of healthcare. The American Association of Critical-Care Nurses found that improved communication patterns among nurses and physicians reduced patient deaths associated with hospital-borne infections by approximately 122,000 in more than 3,000 hospitals over an 18-month period (Patterson et al., 2007). These hospitals already had procedures, inspections, and, to be sure, hierarchies. The basis for change was not new rules within the hierarchy, but new patterns of communication and mutual encouragement among informal networks of healthcare workers (Maxfield, Grenny, McMillan, Patterson, & Switzler, 2005). In fact, it was not a stronger hierarchy that saved lives, but the leveraging of the 5 to 15% of opinion leaders in the organization who not only saved lives with their professional practices, but influenced others *over whom they had no authority* to do the same. In the developing world, the Carter Center's success in attacking the scourge of Guinea worm disease speaks for itself: The disease has been reduced by 99.7%, "completely eradicating the disease from 11 of the 20 endemic countries it originally targeted" (Patterson, et al., 2007, p. 255). A report from the Centers for Disease Control concludes, "Global eradication of Dracunculiasis [Guinea worm disease] will mark the first worldwide elimination of a parasitic disease and the first time a disease has been eradicated without benefit of a vaccine" ("Progress toward global eradication," 2007). Indeed, behavior, communication, and the networks that sustain them change the world.

This chapter began with despair over the intractable resistance of organizations to change. It concludes with evidence that meaningful, lasting, and profound change can occur. We should resist the siren calls for autonomy—the typical reaction to bureaucracy gone wrong—as much as we resist demands for authoritarianism—the typical reaction to change that is stalled. Change is most likely to occur not within the realms of the extremes of organizational fads, but with the "permeable connectivity" (Fullan, 2006, p. 96) that is the hallmark of level-five networks. While clearly not a panacea for organizational change, level-five networks provide the best hope for initiating, implementing, and sustaining change.

References

Ainsworth, L., & Viegut, D. (2006). *Common formative assessments: How to connect standards-based instruction and assessment.* Thousand Oaks, CA: Corwin Press.

Allison, E. (2006). *Schools in trouble: The wisdom of educational leaders who transform adversity into positive growth.* Accessed at http://www.wisdomout.com/PDF/article.WisdomSchoolLeaders.pdf on May 20, 2008.

Barabási, A.-L. (2003). *Linked: How everything is connected to everything else and what it means.* New York: Plume.

Bartlett, C. A., & Ghoshal, S. (1990). Matrix management: Not a structure, a frame of mind. *Harvard Business Review, 68*(4), 138–145.

Collins, J. C. (2001). *Good to great: Why some companies make the leap . . . and others don't.* New York: HarperCollins.

Deutschman, A. (2005, May). Change or die. *Fast Company, 94,* 53.

DuFour, R. (2007). In praise of top-down leadership. *The School Administrator, 10*(64), 38–42.

Freeman, A. (2005). *The leadership genius of Alfred P. Sloan: Invaluable lessons in business, management, and leadership for today's manager.* New York: McGraw-Hill.

Fullan, M. (2006). *Turnaround leadership.* San Francisco: Jossey-Bass.

Global Water. (2007). *The problem.* Accessed at http://www.globalwater.org/background.htm on December 28, 2007.

Goodlad, J. I. (1984). *A place called school: Prospects for the future.* New York: McGraw-Hill.

Goodlad, J. I. (1990). *Teachers for our nation's schools.* San Francisco: Jossey-Bass.

Goodlad, J. I. (1994). *Educational renewal: Better teachers, better schools.* San Francisco: Jossey-Bass.

Guskey, T. R. (2000a). Grading policies that work against standards . . . and how to fix them. *NASSP Bulletin, 84*(620), 20–29.

Guskey, T. R. (2000b). *Evaluating professional development*. Thousand Oaks, CA: Corwin Press.

Guskey, T. R. (2002). *How's my kid doing? A parents' guide to grades, marks, and report cards*. San Francisco: Jossey-Bass.

Guskey, T. R. (2005a). Five key concepts kick off the process. *Journal of Staff Development, 26*(1), 36–40.

Guskey, T. R. (2005b). *Benjamin S. Bloom: Portraits of an educator*. Lanham, MD: Rowman & Littlefield.

Guskey, T. R., & Bailey, J. M. (2001). *Developing grading and reporting systems for student learning*. Thousand Oaks, CA: Corwin Press.

Hargreaves, A., & Fink, D. (2006). *Sustainable leadership*. San Francisco: Jossey-Bass.

Hargreaves, A., Lieberman, A., Fullan, F., & Hopkins, D. (2004). *International handbook of educational change*. The Netherlands: Kluwer Academic Publishers.

Hesselbein, F. (2002). *Hesselbein on leadership*. San Francisco: Jossey-Bass.

Hesselbein, F., & Goldsmith, M. (Eds.). (2006). *The leader of the future 2: Visions, strategies, and practices for the new era*. San Francisco: Jossey-Bass.

Kaplan, R. S., & Norton, D. P. (2008, January). Mastering the management system. *Harvard Business Review, 86*(1), 62–80.

Kidder, T. (2004). *Mountains beyond mountains: The quest of Dr. Paul Farmer, a man who would cure the world*. New York: Random House.

Kotter, J. P. (2007, January). Leading change: Why transformation efforts fail. *Harvard Business Review, 85*(1), 96–103.

Marzano, R. J. (2006). *Classroom assessment and grading that work*. Alexandria, VA: Association for Supervision and Curriculum Development.

Marshall, K. (2005, June). It's time to rethink teacher supervision and evaluation. *Phi Delta Kappan, 86*(10), 727–735.

Maxfield, D., Grenny, J., McMillan, R., Patterson, K., & Switzler, A. (2005). *Silence kills. The seven crucial conversations for healthcare.* Accessed at http://www.aacn.org/aacn/pubpolcy.nsf/Files/SilenceKills/$file/SilenceKills.pdf on January 2, 2008.

McLean, B., & Elkind, P. (2003). *The smartest guys in the room: The amazing rise and scandalous fall of Enron.* New York: Portfolio.

O'Connor, K. (2007a). *A repair kit for grading: 15 fixes for broken grades.* Portland, OR: Educational Testing Service.

O'Connor, K. (2007b). The last frontier: Tackling the grading dilemma. In D. B. Reeves (Ed.), *Ahead of the curve: The power of assessment to transform teaching and learning* (pp. 127–145). Bloomington, IN: Solution Tree.

Patterson, K., Grenny, J., Maxfield, D., McMillan, R., & Switzler, A. (2007). *Influencer: The power to change anything.* New York: McGraw-Hill.

Peters, T. (2003). *Re-imagine! Business excellence in a disruptive age.* London: Dorling Kindersley Limited.

Peters, T. J., & Austin, N. (1985). *A passion for excellence: The leadership difference.* New York: Warner Books.

Peters, T. J., & Waterman, Jr., R. H. (1982). *In search of excellence: Lessons from America's best-run companies.* New York: Warner Books.

Pfeffer, J. (2007). *What were they thinking?: Unconventional wisdom about management.* Boston: Harvard Business School.

"Progress toward global eradication of drancunculiasis, January 2005–May 2007." (2007, August 17). *Morbidity and Mortality Weekly Report.* Accessed at http://www.cdc.gov/mmwR/preview/mmwrhtml/mm5632a1.htm on January 2, 2008.

Reeves, D. B. (2002). *The daily disciplines of leadership: How to improve student achievement, staff motivation, and personal organization.* San Francisco: Jossey-Bass.

Reeves, D. B. (2004a). *Accountability for learning: How teachers and school leaders can take charge.* Alexandria, VA: Association for Supervision and Curriculum Development.

Reeves, D. B. (2004b). *The* case against zero. *Phi Delta Kappan, 86*(4), 324–325.

Reeves, D. B. (2006). *The learning leader: How to focus school improvement for better results.* Alexandria, VA: Association for Supervision and Curriculum Development.

Reeves, D. B. (2008, February). Effective grading practices. *Educational Leadership, 65*(5), 85–87.

Schmoker, M. J. (2004). Tipping point: From feckless reform to substantive instructional improvement. *Phi Delta Kappan, 85*(6), 424–432.

Sizer, T. (2004). *The red pencil: Convictions from experience in education.* New York: R. R. Donnelley.

Sloan, A. P. (1963). *My years with general motors.* New York: Doubleday.

Wenger, E., McDermott, R., & Snyder, W. (2002). *Cultivating communities of practice: A guide to managing knowledge.* Boston: Harvard Business School.

Wheatley, M. J. (2003, February 15). When change is out of our control. *Link&Learn eNewsletter.* Accessed at http://www.linkageinc.com/company/news_events/link_learn_enewsletter/archive/2003/02_03_wheatley_control_change.aspx on January 2, 2008.

Wheatley, M. J. (2007a). How large-scale change really happens—working with emergence. *The School Administrator, 4*(64). Accessed at http://www.aasa.org/publications/saarticledetail.cfm?ItemNumber=8648&snItemNumber=950&tnItemNumber= on May 20, 2008.

Wheatley, M. J. (2007b). Leadership of self-organized networks: Lessons from the war on terror. *Performance Improvement Quarterly, 20*(2), 59–66.

Ben Levin

Dr. Ben Levin is a professor and Canada Research Chair in Education Leadership and Policy at the Ontario Institute for Studies in Education, University of Toronto. In addition to his academic career, he is author of several books and more than 150 other publications in various languages and countries. He has also served as a senior manager in two Canadian ministries of education, including serving as deputy minister (chief civil servant) for education in Manitoba from 1999 to 2002 and for Ontario from 2004 to 2007.

In this chapter, the author discusses the shortcomings of large-scale reform efforts that are done *to* the system and why they do not have the desired effects. He then poses an alternative approach to generate real improvement in schools, to the benefit of students, that also creates greater energy and motivation among educators and support for students, parents, and the broader community. The strategy he describes has been implemented in Ontario, Canada, and has four key elements.

Dr. Ben Levin can be reached at blevin@oise.utoronto.ca.

Chapter 12

Reform Without (Much) Rancor

Ben Levin

If we have learned anything about large-scale improvement in education since the 1980s, it is that reforms that are done *to* the system do not have the desired effects. These imposed solutions from outside the system have many motivating factors: It may be seen as "good politics" to talk tough about schools. It may be that people do not see how else to drive change in large and complex systems. Or directive reform may be seen as the only way to respond in any reasonable period of time to the urgent need of many children to get a better education. But whatever the motivation, imposed solutions do not work. In the short term, they produce frustration and resistance from educators—often from the best educators—and equally as often from students. In the long term, because they do not generate motivation within schools, they do not last. Instead, they join in oblivion the myriad of other reforms that, as an American colleague once said to me, "are washed up to litter the beaches of California."

Is there an alternative to these imposed solutions? Is there a way to generate real improvements in schools, to the benefit of students, in ways that also create greater energy and motivation among educators and garner the support of students, parents, and the broader community? I suggest there is an approach to accomplish just that.

This chapter describes the theory of action behind this approach. Moreover, the strategy described here is not just theoretical; it has been implemented to a large degree in Ontario, Canada, since 2003 (see Levin, 2007, and Levin, Fullan, & Glaze, in press).

What distinguishes this approach from most of those described in the education literature is its explicit attention to the politics of change, both small and large scale. Because so much of my career has been spent in government, I am keenly aware of the politics that surround any change, whether in a school, a district, or a country. I take the view that politics determine, for better or worse, the reforms that are adopted and the ways in which they are implemented, but the politics of education reform have largely been left aside in the literature on change.

There are four key elements to this approach:

1. Have a plan that focuses on improved student outcomes and is founded on the best available evidence.

2. Implement that plan in a careful but relentless way.

3. Create real buy-in by paying careful attention to two-way communications and taking very seriously the views and ideas of stakeholders.

4. Manage inevitable distractions and competing pressures so that there can be a sustained focus on a small number of key goals.

In this chapter, I pay more attention to steps three and four because they relate most directly to the politics of change.

An Approach for Effective Change

Effective change is a matter of both *will* and *skill*. People have to want to do it, and they have to know how to do it. Both are necessary; will without skill produces effort but no results, while skill without will produces no effort. In the case of educational change, we are talking about will and skill on the part of teachers, administrators, school board members, and—a crucial addition—students, their parents, and the broader public, although for the latter groups the kinds of skills are quite different. This four-step approach for effective change addresses the need for both will and skill and involves all key stakeholders.

Have a Plan Focused on Improved Student Outcomes and Founded on the Best Available Evidence

It seems unnecessary to say that a plan for improving schools should focus on outcomes and be based on evidence, but it is clear from experience that many plans do not have these characteristics, or only partially so. For example, many reforms have focused on changing governance structures (changing the roles of school boards, introducing more choice, forming charter schools, using collective bargaining arrangements, and so on), yet we know that governance changes do not themselves bring about improvements in teaching and learning or in student outcomes. Changes in governance systems may need to be addressed as part of a comprehensive strategy, but they cannot themselves generate much improvement.

The same is true of testing and accountability. High-quality evidence on how well students are doing is crucial, but it is misguided to think that more assessment or more punishment for poor results will alone lead to better outcomes, either for students or for schools and educators.

One of the challenges of setting educational goals is that there is so much diversity in what people want schools to achieve. People want students not only to develop their academic and intellectual skills, including gaining all kinds of specific knowledge, but also to develop more universal skills, such as teamwork and problem-solving, and to learn desirable character traits, such as generosity and engagement in the community. In short, we want schools to make every child perfect, or close to it, which is a tall order!

There are some goals, though, on which there is wide agreement. Expecting that all children learn to read, write, and do basic arithmetic is a universally accepted goal. High school graduation with a credential that enables further options in life is another pretty common goal. However, people do not want those goals addressed at the expense of everything else, so goals have to be developed and set in a way that does not exclude attention to the rich array of elements that make up a good education.

To improve student outcomes, improvement plans must address those outcomes specifically. Improvement plans must address the things we know matter to those outcomes: changing teaching and learning (and assessment) practices, improving teachers' skills to do so, strengthening leadership capacity, improving student engagement in learning, and reaching out to parents to support their children's learning.

As the amount and quality of research in education has increased in recent decades, we also have more evidence to guide policy and reform. For example, we now know that early reading instruction should include both specific teaching of phonemic and other skills as well as immersion in a rich and stimulating environment of literacy tasks and resources (Pressley, 2005). We know that we can reduce high school dropout rates if students feel that there is at least one adult in the school who genuinely knows and cares about them. We know that formative assessment without grading generates more learning for students (Black & Wiliam, 1998). We know that retention in grade is useless if not harmful to students' future progress (Hong & Raudenbush, 2005). We know that we can increase parental engagement with children's learning if we have a deliberate and respectful approach to all parents (Jeynes, 2007). This research, along with the research done by the authors in this book, has extended our base of evidence for good policy and practice.

Although our knowledge about effective practice is increasing, practice itself is lagging behind. For example, social promotion continues to be widely advocated and practiced despite abundant evidence that it does not work. Many students still feel lost in our high schools. And assessment continues to be used to punish students for their attitudes or behaviors. The list goes on. But one should not be too discouraged by this gap in knowledge and practice. Our experience in other areas—for example, smoking cessation and use of seat belts in cars—shows that it can take many years to move from clear research findings to common practice. Moreover, there are many areas in which our knowledge is still very limited and cannot guide practice effectively. In those areas of good research evidence, we are seeing a gradual increase in appropriate practice.

Still, there is no excuse for any educational jurisdiction to have an improvement plan that does not use the good evidence that is available.

Implement That Plan in a Thoughtful but Relentless Way

In 1974, Pressman and Wildavsky first drew our attention to the importance of implementation, and many others have followed suit since then. A good plan is nothing without effective implementation. However, the realities of political and organizational life are such that implementation tends to get short shrift in comparison to the time and effort spent developing and announcing a policy or program. Usually there are so many pressures on decision-makers that they just do not have the time, even if they had the inclination, to follow up carefully on all the steps needed for effective implementation.

Let us assume here, too, that implementation does not mean strict adherence to a predetermined policy but instead is the effort to achieve the intended purpose, including adaptations to suit local conditions and circumstances. Mindlessness is antithetical to education under any circumstances, whether it has to do with what we expect from educators or from students. Adopting this more thoughtful view of implementation does not, however, reduce the challenges involved.

Indeed, the requirements of an evidence-informed strategy make implementation more challenging. If the goal of improvement is to change daily teaching and learning practices in large numbers of classrooms in a way that makes sense to all those involved, a colossal amount of learning has to happen. People do not easily change their habits even when they begin with a preference for making the change.

The list of potential difficulties in implementation is long. Fullan (1991) considers the barriers to change in terms of the *characteristics of the change* itself, the *setting* where implementation is to occur, and the wider *context*. The characteristics of change are features such as the clarity, complexity, and degree of difficulty of a proposed change. The setting addresses aspects of the school as an organization, such as the level of commitment by important actors (for example, school principals), the skills of those involved, the resources allocated to support change, and the extent to which a given change fits the existing culture and structure of the system. The wider context includes the various other pressures either supporting or inhibiting implementation. These might include the nature of the support system, competing demands on schools, or levels of community support for change.

In reality, if a change is to have real and lasting impact, all of these elements have to be addressed. Implementation cannot be assumed or left to chance; it must be carefully nurtured. Announcements followed by documents and a few training sessions will not change what happens in a big and complex system.

The first big strategy to recognize the need for real effort on implementation was the National Literacy and Numeracy Strategy in England, which created regional teams and hundreds of teacher-consultant positions to support school change, and provided large amounts of data, resources, and professional development as well as extra money. These efforts made a big difference in the impact of the strategies, but although unprecedented in scale, the efforts were still fairly small relative to the system they were trying to change (Barber, 2007; Earl et al., 2003). In Ontario, the government has recently increased its implementation work even more, which has had a considerable impact (Levin, 2007; Levin, Fullan, & Glaze, in press). However, we do not yet have enough cases or enough evidence to be able to say what level of support is required to create real and lasting change in practice and outcomes in large numbers of schools. How many people, how much time, and how much training is required for lasting change? Almost certainly the answer to that question will depend on local conditions such as the existing levels of skill and morale, the stability of the work force, and competing demands.

Implementation has to be addressed directly. There has to be a real plan for implementation that is shown to have the potential to create and support change across an entire system. This means appropriate infrastructure at all levels of the system; direction and careful attention to other important factors, such as high-quality training with support for ongoing changes in practice; leadership development; support networks for those leading change; clear goals; the provision of useful data; and protecting the core tasks from all the inevitable pressures. Resources must be allocated to achieve those purposes. Few change initiatives are addressed in such a comprehensive way, which brings us to the more political aspects of this chapter.

Create Real Buy-In by Paying Careful Attention to Two-Way Communications and Taking Very Seriously the Views and Ideas of Stakeholders

Education reform often remains something that is done *to* schools and educators. We have learned—often the hard way— that imposed reform is mostly unsuccessful reform. And this is not just a matter of resistance, whether active or passive. Insofar as real change in results depends on people behaving differently—as it must in education—the people involved have to be willing to get on board and stay committed over time.

Building support for change is not just a matter of telling people how important it is or ordering them to do it. As any classroom teacher knows, explaining why something is important does not necessarily result in that thing being done, let alone being done well. Nor do threats of dire consequences necessarily bring the desired result. This is even truer with adults in professional roles.

Leaders of reform must be willing to build support by engaging in real dialogue with all the parties whose understanding and support is vital. In a district, this means principals, teachers, support staff, students, parents, and community groups. At a state or national level, it means engagement with all the groups and bodies that have a real interest in the process. In Ontario, the government created a "Partnership Table," chaired by the Minister of Education, that brought together on a regular basis leaders from more than 20 organizations—school trustees, superintendents, principals, teachers, parents, students, and support staff. Most of the government's plans for education were tabled and discussed there before being implemented. While the process had its limits, and certainly did not create unanimity about change, it did give people a real sense that their views and voices mattered, resulting in considerably smoother change efforts. Just as importantly, the government was given advice that helped make its initiatives and programs both more acceptable and more effective.

One advantage of the Partnership Table was that all groups got to hear each other's positions. Of course one-to-one meetings with various partners continued to be held, and were sometimes more important when it came to difficult issues, but there is no substitute for everyone being in the same room and hearing the same messages at least sometimes.

In fact, ongoing communication is often a neglected aspect of education reform. The leaders are very busy and typically very convinced about what they are doing. They do not take the time to tell people what a reform is about and why it may be desirable. Or there is some communication at the start, and then it is forgotten. Yet we know that ongoing communication, with many repetitions of key messages, is necessary. It is easy to forget that the folks far away from the central office do not see things the same way or have the same understanding. In the absence of real and honest communication, rumors and negative assumptions will take root.

Communication also has to operate in both directions; it has to involve listening as well as telling. Dialogues are important, but so are other tools such as surveys of opinion or practice, provided that the results are shared with all participants in a timely and transparent way. One reason people often do not communicate enough is their fear of revealing imperfections in plans or practices. But these imperfections are likely to be widely known in any case, and in the long run acknowledging problems—which are inevitable in any large scale change—and then remedying them does much more to build trust than does a pretense that all is going exactly according to the plan.

A final point on communications is the importance of dialogue with employee unions. Reformers are sometimes impatient with teacher unions, seeing them as barriers to change. Yet teacher unions are important not only for their ability to block reforms—which they have certainly been able to do in many instances—but also for their potential role as supporters of good practice. A first requirement for effective education is to have high-quality teachers. This is most likely to happen where teachers have reasonable wages and working conditions, which is most likely to occur where there are unions to bargain for those things. Reformers who care about students should be encouraging teacher unions to think hard about professional and public confidence issues, not attacking unions as impediments to improvement.

Manage the Inevitable Distractions and Competing Pressures So There Can Be a Sustained Focus on a Small Number of Key Goals

Effective leaders know that it is essential to have a small number of key goals. No organization can do 50 things well all at the same time. There is a saying in the business literature that "having more than two objectives is like having no objectives at all." Yet all our experience shows that keeping focus over time is perhaps the single hardest thing to do in managing change at any level, from one school to a national education system. When you try to follow the advice and focus your school or system on a few key goals, such as improving early literacy or engaging parents more effectively, something surprising happens: All kinds of pressures surface around things other than the priorities, and leaders find their time taken up with everything but the things they want to focus on.

This happens even when most people in the organization have agreed to focus on the priorities. A careful process of staff and stakeholder engagement leading to agreement on priorities is important, but it is no guarantee that the very same people will not turn around the next day and demand action on a whole list of other issues.

As a result, education leaders at all levels constantly lament that their situations just do not permit them to do the things they know are important. Principals find they do not have time to visit classrooms or talk with teachers. Superintendents have the same problem in their quest to visit schools or reach out to the community. Elected political leaders, even when they have run on a clear set of priorities, find that the main pressures on them are not about those priorities, and they are constantly distracted by other matters.

Inevitably, focus suffers. The truly important is driven out by the urgent. The squeaky wheel gets the grease, even if it is not the wheel that moves the bus. Not only do priorities get inadequate attention, but some of the most important ancillary functions of the organization also tend to get short shrift. A good example is communications, both internal and external, as just discussed.

Managing change means accepting the reality of opposition and distraction. Although it is very tempting for leaders to treat these differences as nuisances—or at best as problems—no amount of arguing or convincing will make them go away. Any plan that assumes "full speed ahead" without disruption is going to result, as my 10th-grade French teacher used to say, in "a rude awakening." The history of education reform is full of such instances.

A second important psychological disposition is to avoid feeling personally aggrieved when things do not go as planned, or when people do not get or stay on our side. Reformers are often completely convinced by their own good intentions, so when others fail to sign on, change leaders can get frustrated. Yet that is just when it is most important to keep one's sense of proportion and direction, and to remain calm and focused. There will be opposition, thoughtful or not, so no point being offended by it. There will be surprises, so no point being stunned by them (although by definition one cannot be prepared for a surprise). There are simply many occasions where the first response to a problem should be something like counting slowly to 10 before saying or doing anything else.

Keeping a positive orientation is important. It is helpful to assume that others are generally acting from some reasonable basis of understanding, or from important pressures, rather than just trying to be obstreperous or negative. As in any conflict, trying to understand another's thinking and see how to respond to their genuine issues is an important step in moving forward.

It should hardly be necessary to say that another disposition must be to maintain one's sense of direction and overall strategy. Yes, all the asides have to be addressed in some way, but if the architects of a vision do not keep to it, nobody else will. Despite all the distractions, the importance of the original goals and strategy must constantly be reinforced in actions, such as budget allocations, as well as in words.

This means ensuring that some key change leaders in the organization are protected from the distractions and can keep much, if not all, of their attention on the core business. It means organizing things so that we do not demand from superintendents or principals that they be change leaders and then insist that they do 20 other things first. It means sharing leadership at all levels so there are more people focused on the main task.

Managing also requires being proactive and anticipating problems that might arise. Leaders who are well attuned to their organizations and communities know what many of the distractions will be. These can and should be anticipated and managed ahead of time so that they do not blow up. The dialogue and communication discussed earlier will provide one important early warning system for such distractions. Some action can be taken to demonstrate an understanding that there are issues important to other people that deserve attention. Often a relatively small step now will head off a much bigger problem later.

Creating Positive Synergy

These four strategic approaches work together. More dialogue builds more trust, which in turn will reduce the number of distractions. Having a clear, well-grounded plan will also help build support.

Effective implementation strategies will generate more motivation and commitment to core goals. It is possible to create a positive synergy.

The challenges of doing so, however, should not be underestimated. The many reform programs that failed to produce real and lasting change were undertaken, often, by smart, well-intentioned people who worked very hard to try and make them successful.

The approaches described in this chapter should be regarded as a set of desirables, not minimum requirements. In any given setting, the advocates of better outcomes for all students have a responsibility to try to do whatever we can, even if that is less than everything and in a way that is imperfect. Waiting for just the right conditions can mean waiting forever, and given the needs of students in our school systems today, we do not have that luxury.

References

Barber, M. (2007). *Instruction to deliver*. London: Politico, Methuen.

Black, P., & Wiliam, D. (1998). Assessment and classroom learning. *Assessment in Education, 5*(1), 71.

Earl, L., Watson, N., Levin, B., Leithwood, K., Fullan, M., & Torrance, N. (2003). *Watching and learning 3: Final report of the OISE/UT evaluation of the implementation of the National Literacy and Numeracy Strategies*. Prepared for the Department for Education and Skills, England: OISE/University of Toronto. Accessed at http://www.standards.dfes.gov.uk/primary/publications/literacy/63525/dfes_watchlearn010103summary.pdf on February 1, 2008.

Fullan, M. (1991). *The new meaning of educational change* (2nd ed.). New York: Teachers College Press/OISE Press.

Hong, G., & Raudenbush, S. (2005). Effects of kindergarten retention policy on children's cognitive growth in reading and mathematics. *Educational Evaluation and Policy Analysis, 27*(3), 205–224.

Jeynes, W. (2007). The relationship between parent involvement and urban secondary school achievement: A meta-analysis. *Urban Education, 42*(1), 82–110.

Levin, B. (2007). Sustainable, large-scale education renewal. *Journal of Educational Change, 8*(4), 323–336.

Levin, B., Fullan, M., & Glaze, A. (in press). Results without rankings or rancor. *Phi Delta Kappan.*

Pressley, M. (2005). Balanced elementary literacy instruction in the United States: A personal perspective. In N. Bascia, A. Cumming, A. Datnow, K. Leithwood, & D. Livingstone (Eds.), *International handbook of educational policy* (pp. 645–660). Dordrecht, The Netherlands: Springer.

Pressman, J., & Wildavsky, A. (1974). *Implementation: How great expectations in Washington are dashed in Oakland; or, why it's amazing that Federal programs work at all, this being a saga of the Economic Development Administration as told by two sympathetic observers who seek to build morals on a foundation of ruined hopes.* Berkeley: University of California Press.

Michael Fullan

Dr. Michael Fullan is professor emeritus at the Ontario Institute for Studies in Education at the University of Toronto and special adviser on education to Dalton McGuinty, the Premier of Ontario. He served as dean of the Faculty of Education at the University of Toronto from 1988 to 2003, leading two major organizational transformations including a merger of two large schools of education. He is currently working as adviser-consultant on several major education reform initiatives around the world.

Michael Fullan bases his work on the moral purpose of education as it is applied in schools and school systems to bring about major improvements. He has written several best sellers that have been translated into many languages. His latest books include *The New Meaning of Educational Change* (4th edition, 2007) and *The Six Secrets of Change: What the Best Leaders Do to Help Their Organizations Survive and Thrive* (2008).

This chapter is about a theory of action for whole system improvement in education. The Theory of Action for System Change (TASC) has six components: direction and sector engagement, capacity-building linked to results, supportive infrastructure and leadership, managing the distractors, continuous evaluation and inquiry, and two-way communication. The author describes the elements and underlying thinking of each component, and then he describes the framework's use since 2003 in the public school system of Ontario, Canada.

Dr. Michael Fullan can be reached at mfullan@oise.utoronto.ca.

Chapter 13

Have Theory, Will Travel: A Theory of Action for System Change

Michael Fullan

A theory is a way of organizing ideas that makes sense of the world. A *theory of action* is a way of understanding the world that identifies insights and ideas for effectively improving it. This chapter is about a theory of action for whole-system improvement in education. There are three conditions a theory must meet to be called a theory of action: First, it must meet the *systemness* criterion. Do the ideas stand a chance of addressing the whole system, not just a few hundred schools here and there? Second, the theory must make a compelling case that using the ideas will result in positive *movement*. We are, after all, talking about improvement—transitioning from one state of being to another. Third, such a theory must demonstrably tap into and stimulate people's *motivation*. I ask the reader to consider these three criteria when assessing the theory I am about to offer, and when comparing it with other competing theories of action: To what extent does this theory meet the systemness, movement, and motivation criteria? To what extent do other theories meet the criteria?

This theory of action—A Theory of Action for System Change, or TASC—has been built by myself and others with attempts at system reform since 1997, first in England, and then, more recently, in Ontario. I have had an opportunity to draw on and test the theory in relation to the research literature on large-scale reform, and in comparison to the best research on successful businesses (Fullan, 2008a). Most significantly, we have had a golden opportunity to apply much of the theory to reform in the public school system in Ontario since 2003 and now heading into 2011 with 2 million students, in 4,900 schools and 72 districts. Improving large systems is a complex task, so I consider these ideas a work in progress—all the more reason to make them clear and up for debate.

In presenting this theory, I will take special care to identify the underlying thinking. In education, there is too much reliance on models, technologies, and strategic plans. These tools can be useful, but they are only tools. The best theories are only as good as the mindset using them. William Duggan's *Strategic Intuition* (2007) makes the same case. Strategic plans, which abound in the business literature, are of limited use, says Duggan, because they do "not tell you how to come up with a strategic idea" in the first place (p. 3). According to Duggan, it is not imagination that counts, but rather it is discovery through cumulative action and insight. Gawande (2007) makes a similar point when he says breakthroughs occur during "the infant science of improving performance" (p. 242). It is learning by doing, but it is really learning by *thinking* in relation to doing.

Experience precedes insight. In cases of innovation, people do not develop a vision and then implement it; instead, they have purposeful experiences and then gain insight that they build upon. Consolidation through reasoning follows experience and insight. Duggan (2007) explains it this way: Step 1 is to look in the laboratories of the other practitioners, step 2 is to examine your own experiences, and step 3 is your reason—action, insight, reason. A theory of action about change, then, depends on insight that derives from experience, purposeful and otherwise.

Because this chapter is about whole system reform, the system leaders (politicians and bureaucrats) responsible for leading reform and the academics working on these issues will be most interested in this theory of action. But the theory is also valuable for practitioners. Superintendents and other district administrators can use the theory as if the system was the district and they are attempting to bring about districtwide reform. Principals and teacher leaders can apply the six components of the theory to changing their own school cultures and for determining how to link to the external infrastructure. Many of the ideas in this chapter furnish practical strategies for school principals as outlined in *What's Worth Fighting for in the Principalship* (Fullan, 2008b).

The theory I will present has come from at least a decade of action-insight-reason. For each component of the theory, I will describe its meaning, discuss the underlying thinking that supports the component, and offer evidence of the theory's validity.

A Theory of Action for System Change (TASC)

Figure 1 shows the six components of TASC: 1) direction and sector engagement, 2) capacity-building with a focus on results, 3) supportive infrastructure and leadership, 4) managing the distractors, 5) continuous evaluation and inquiry, and 6) two-way communication. Each of the six components of the theory has several elements that must be understood. It is easy to get a theory of action wrong as nuanced meaning is everything. Keep in mind that at the outset, all six components are interrelated, and they are all addressed simultaneously.

Direction and Sector Engagement

The first component we will discuss is direction and sector engagement. In this component, direction from the top, in this case

Figure 1: A Theory of Action for System Change (TASC)

the government, is especially important and consists of at least five aspects:

1. An inspirational overall vision

2. A small number of ambitious goals publicly stated

3. A guiding coalition

4. Investment of resources

5. A sense of flexibility and partnership with the field

An Inspirational Overall Vision

An *inspirational vision* means having a clear overall picture of the purpose, nature, and rationale of the reform. The vision must contain both the purpose of the reform *and* how it will be achieved. The vision taps into the moral imperative of educational reform—raising the bar and closing the gap for all children. It articulates why and how education is key to societal prosperity. It calls for and seeks public confidence in the education system. It is invitational rather than narrowly prescriptive, and it invites partnership with the education sector and other elements of society. It combines direction and flexibility. Finally, its essence is non-negotiable. To do all this, leadership at the center has to "get it right"—that is, create a vision that attracts stakeholders to the articulated reform. For a good recent example of an inspirational vision, see *Energizing Ontario Education: Reach Every Student* (Ontario Ministry of Education, 2008).

A Small Number of Ambitious Goals Publicly Stated

Many governments make the mistake of having a large number of equally desirable goals that overwhelm schools and fragment their efforts. Instead, governments need to choose a small number of critical ambitious goals and then stay the course. Ontario, for example, has three core priorities: literacy, numeracy, and high school graduation. It is essential to focus on these goals while not conceiving them narrowly. They can and must be conceived as higher order learning goals, and linked to other parts of the curriculum, such as the arts and character education. A small number of goals can have a significant impact on the well-being of the whole child, and they can be achieved more realistically.

One of the most controversial aspects of central goal-setting concerns whether or not to have targets. Andy Hargreaves and I have an ongoing debate about this. Neither of us is wholly in favor of or wholly against targets. If targets are imposed, we both agree that they will become dysfunctional. My theory of action says that people do better if they have some outcome against which their efforts can be assessed. To me, it is okay to have an umbrella target as long as it is not obsessively pursued. In any case, the most important element in any target is to be able to assess how well you are doing relative to your starting point, to keep track of this on an annual basis, and to determine progress on a 3-year rolling cycle. Doing this serves as both a strategy for improvement (along with daily assessment *for* learning methods) and as an external accountability device. Thus, schools compare themselves 1) to themselves, 2) to other schools in similar circumstances, and 3) to an absolute or external standard. The caution is to not obsess on the target, but rather keep it as a focus of aspiration.

A Guiding Coalition

A guiding coalition is critical to the success of the reform. At first this involves the six or seven key leaders at the center of the reform and their advisers—the Premier, Minister, Deputy Minister, and others, in the Ontario example. They need to meet frequently enough to be clear and consistent about all six elements of the theory of action. As strategy development progresses, the guiding coalition extends to include other leaders at other layers of the system, such as district leaders and school leaders, as well as other vertical leadership such as teacher unions, administrative organizations, and school trustees.

Investment of Resources

Any new system improvement requires investment. It will need funding, reallocation of resources, and the time and expertise of those involved. In one sense, it is a *quid pro quo* proposition—the initial and recurring investment is amplified with greater commitment from other levels of the system. As success evolves, additional resource investment comes to be seen as money well spent.

A Sense of Flexibility and Partnership With the Field

Finally, none of this direction and engagement is unidirectional or simply top-down. It includes clear and firm direction as we have seen, but also a keen sense of partnership with the field, and flexibility according to local needs and variation.

A key part of direction from the center of the reform is to establish engagement with the education sector—schools and districts in particular. Quite often, systems do not function in a way in which teachers, principals, and district educators experience the education of students as the core priority. The goal of the center of the reform should be to identify the small number of ambitious priorities that are likely to resonate with local schools. Part of the solution, then, is to anticipate and capture what is likely to align with local educators. As this is contemplated, it is essential to connect with the field to determine if the identified agenda seems to be on the right track.

Communication, additional new resources, and engagement in capacity-building (element two in Figure 1) all serve to confirm that the selected direction is seen as desirable. We have found that starting with literacy and numeracy at the elementary level is bound to resonate with stakeholders, provided that it is not imposed in a narrow manner. You can predict that going deeper in literacy and numeracy will be a solid start—as long as this is not pursued in a narrow fashion, and as long as the agenda is expansive (such as literacy across the curriculum), there is plenty to do to move literacy and numeracy forward. The idea is to have sufficient two-way communication with the field (districts, schools, and classrooms) so that literacy and numeracy becomes a goal for all.

The test of the theory of action at this stage is whether the center and those in the field generally agree on the path being pursued. The crucial goal of sector engagement is that local educators find the agenda desirable not because it is the government's agenda, but rather because it is also valued locally. No local educator will or should ever be sufficiently motivated to implement a priority just because it is the government's plan—it has to make sense locally as well. Sector engagement means that the center and locals find a common goal worth pursuing jointly. The idea is to pursue an agenda with purpose and with a view to expanding the focus (literacy and numeracy in the Ontario example) across the curriculum, and to connect these developments with the well-being of the whole child.

Underlying Thinking

If we probe the underlying thinking of the direction and sector engagement element of the theory of action, the assumption is that systems will not improve without system leadership of a certain kind—leadership that realizes that top-down reform does not work, nor do decentralized bottom-up strategies. Rather, system leaders strive for a blended model of simultaneous top-down/bottom-up forces: top-down direction and investment coupled with bottom-up capacity-building. In a word, system leaders direct but do not try to micromanage the change. They trust the process and their theory of action embedded across the six elements of the theory.

Sector engagement is key and represents a dilemma: If the government imposes the reform, locals will reject the agenda. If the center is laissez-faire, there will be little direction. The goal of sector engagement is to begin to foster a "we-we" sense of identity: Every effort is extended to show that those in the field and those at the center of the reform have a common interest. The Theory of Action for System Change—all six components—make it much more likely that those involved will find common ground. Take, for example, the evolution of the second component: capacity-building.

Capacity-Building With a Focus on Results

Capacity-building is at the heart of TASC. This component consists of the strategies and actions that mobilize capacity defined as 1) new knowledge, skills, and competencies, 2) additional resources (time, ideas, money, expertise), and 3) new motivation on the part of all to put in the effort to get results.

There are two separate but related dimensions of capacity. One concerns the pedagogical or instructional core of the change, such as effective instructional practices in literacy and numeracy from the Ontario example. The other equally necessary component relates to the management of change—how to build professional learning communities, manage distractors, achieve focus, motivate implementers, link to the various parts of the infrastructure, and so on.

Within capacity, one of the highest yield competencies relates to the deep and frequent use of data. It concerns establishing daily practices of assessment for learning, or, more accurately, assessment *as* learning in which curriculum, instruction, and assessment in relation to individual students' learning are synergized. Instruction and assessment become seamless (see Fullan, Hill, & Crévola, 2006).

Capacity-building with a focus on results also means using assessment of learning simultaneously as an additional strategy for improvement. I have already introduced this element in the first component of our theory. Schools begin to measure and track progress relative to their own starting point and to external standards. The internal accountability within the school or district also serves as external accountability to the state.

Capacity-building itself is promoted directly from the center of the reform with respect to providing training, curriculum resources, and the like, but its most powerful form is *indirect*. By indirect capacity-building, I mean the use of deliberate strategies designed to help peers learn from each other—within schools, across schools, and across districts. We call this *lateral capacity-building*, and it is most powerful because educators are learning from their colleagues. The central leaders have a proactive role in funding and coordinating these activities. They seek best ideas wherever they can be found and use the "wisdom of the crowd" to spread and assess their worth and impact.

This theory of action is proactive but constructive. This is crucial for situations in which there is underperformance or stagnation. Intervention in these situations is necessary, but it must be capacity-driven rather than judgmental. Intervention is judgmental when poor performance is identified in a negative or pejorative way. The question is not whether the judgment is warranted, but rather what will motivate and enable people to make improvements. It is better to assume that lack of capacity is the problem and tackle that first. In Ontario, we have been able to establish a turnaround school program—the Ontario Focused Intervention Partnership (OFIP)—in which more than 1,000 of the 4,000 elementary schools have been involved. The concept is to identify problematic situations in schools, avoid stigmatizing the schools, and then to engage them in turnaround capacity-building. In 2006–2007, these schools gained 10 additional percentage points in literacy and numeracy than the rest of the system (Ontario Ministry of Education, 2008).

Capacity-building, then, encompasses the following:

- Knowledge, resources, and motivation
- Instruction and management of change expertise
- Assessment *for* as well as assessment *of* learning
- Direct and indirect capacity-building
- A link between capacity and results
- Early and continuous intervention in case of need

Underlying Thinking

The neglect of capacity-building has been the fatal weakness of reform policies such as No Child Left Behind. Politicians generally favor more direct external accountability schemes. By contrast, TASC argues that capacity is *sine qua non* of improvement. New capacities *cause* results. Moreover, capacity enhancement is motivational. There is nothing like getting better at something important to want to do more of it. Capacity-building enhances ownership, and capacity-building is empowering. When people become excellent at something, they become experts. They become, for example, more critical of ill-conceived external ideas. Other potentially good but insufficiently developed ideas that might have been started from the center become tempered by the expertise of skilled practitioners. Empowered, competent people also talk back when the situation calls for it.

Finally, internal (within the school) and external (in relation to the public) accountability become interrelated. An effective balance between the two is established as a platform for moving forward. Intervention programs are capacity-driven and seem to serve accountability for the better because they get results with less rancor.

Supportive Infrastructure and Leadership

All of this work requires a strong infrastructure to support and propel it. For this component, we have used the concept of *tri-level reform*: What has to happen at the government, district, and school/community levels to engage in the depth of change required.

At the government level, most state departments and ministries of education do not have the culture and capacity to lead the work. Thus, new structural and cultural arrangements are required. It need not and should not result in new layers of bureaucracy, but rather it should involve reconfiguring and adding to existing resources. But beware of the folly of doing yet another reorganization, as my colleague Ben Levin (twice Deputy Minister) warns. Reorganizations are distractors and thus should be kept to a minimum.

Ontario created a Literacy and Numeracy Secretariat (as did England) staffed by some existing ministry personnel, but significantly strengthened by respected practitioners from schools and districts. The goal of this project at the government level is to work on changing the internal culture of the ministry, and to establish a new two-way partnership with the other levels, district and school. Needless to say, capacity-building is required at the department of education level.

We are all learning more about the characteristics of effective districts, and they are congruent with the theory of action espoused in this chapter: focus on instruction, use data, develop capacity, foster leadership, build learning communities, link to results, and so on (see, for example, Childress, Elmore, Grossman, & Johnson, 2007). Near the beginning of a new change process, some districts will be ahead of the government, so to speak, and others will be behind. The goal, then, is to develop the capacity of school districts so that they can lead in two directions—one as an effective infrastructure to their schools (with all the simultaneous top-down/bottom-up strategies that this implies), and the other as a proactive agent vis-à-vis the government. Districts need to become semi-autonomous but engaged players vertically and laterally with other districts. At the school and community level, the new capacities of leading collaborative cultures need to be firmly embraced. Principal and teacher leadership is required for this task.

It is obvious that new forms of leadership are required at all three levels. We need leaders who can focus on details and look at the bigger picture simultaneously. There are now impressive "qualifications frameworks" and corresponding programs for school principals. We also need formal and informal leadership development programs for all leaders. In the Ontario example, we are working with many change agents: school principals, superintendents, literacy and numeracy coaches and mentors, and student success leaders (high school teacher change agents). Once you proliferate a critical mass of change agent leaders focusing individually and collectively on capacity-building linked to results, you have a set of powerful change forces that in many ways has a life of its own.

In sum, several components are required for the development of a supportive infrastructure and leadership:

- Capacity development for each of the three levels: government, district, and school

- A degree of coordination and rapport across the three levels
- Leadership development for the change agents working in the infrastructure

Underlying Thinking

It is obvious that capacity-building will not develop on its own. It requires a refocused infrastructure whose main work is to build capacity with a link to results. Capacity-building represents an enormous and never-ending task. And if you do not refocus and refurbish the work of the infrastructure, it will continue to do whatever work it is cut out to do. Left alone, it specializes in bureaucracy—some of it necessary, but much of it unnecessary. Over the years, bureaucracy has become one of the main hazards to system reform. Bureaucratic distractors take us away from the core business of teaching and learning.

Managing the Distractors

In complex political systems, distractors are ubiquitous and inevitable. To minimize them, it helps to build up the positive side of the reform—a relentless focus on capacity-building—but you have to be equally explicit and aware of addressing distractors by preempting some, and dealing with others as they come in a way that does not divert and sap energy.

A main distractor to address is collective bargaining. It is not always possible, but more and more provinces in Canada, for example, are seeking and achieving 4-year collective agreements that usher in a period of relative peace and stability. Other potential distractors are managerial tasks such as paperwork, finances, building issues, safety, personnel, and so on. In *What's Worth Fighting for in the Principalship* (Fullan, 2008b), I give specific recommendations for both principals and system leaders for dealing with these types of distractors.

It is clear that effective schools and effective districts are better at addressing distractors and maintaining focus, and we must work at spreading those crucial habits. Guiding coalitions and other leaders at all levels of effective schools train themselves to make teaching and learning the core preoccupation and find ways to reduce the debilitating impact of distractors.

Underlying Thinking

We all complain about distractors inhibiting our ability to get the main work done. The difference in our TASC framework is that the concept of distractors becomes an item for analysis and action. People discover small and big ways to make distractors less consuming. Every hour saved is an hour gained for improvement work because every frustration experienced from negative diversions drains energy at the expense of learning priorities. Since time and energy are of the essence in school improvement, harnessing the resources to effectively reduce distractors produces substantial benefits.

Continuous Evaluation and Inquiry

A theory, in essence, is a set of tested hypotheses about reality. It is never assumed to be valid once and for all. Rather, the assumption is that a theory must always be subject to assessment in relation to today's realities and future realities. It is for this reason that constant evaluation and inquiry must be built into the mindset of the reform and the actions of the center and those in the field as the reform progresses. Leaders at all levels are expected to have an inquiring disposition: Are we implementing the strategy effectively? Is it working? Are there any surprises? What are we learning? And so on.

In addition, any theory of change worth its salt must continuously search for and spread effective practices for the task at hand, whether these are found in the system or in the worldwide literature. And assessment of implementation is a must to determine what is working and where, as well as what is not working and why.

For example, in the third year of Ontario's Literacy and Numeracy Strategy, the Secretariat identified and conducted case studies of 8 of the 72 school districts that seemed to have sound strategies in place and were getting results. These case studies were fed back to the districts in question and made available to the system as a whole, prompting numerous site visits to learn about the specific strategies being employed.

Theories of action should also employ third-party evaluators to provide critical feedback on the strengths, weaknesses, and impact of the strategies being employed. And systems should disseminate their theories and findings on a larger international level to contribute to the thinking of others and to be subjected to external scrutiny and critique. This chapter in *Change Wars* is a case in point. Further, systems should benchmark their efforts against the increasingly sophisticated and detailed international assessments of student achievement conducted by the Organisation for Economic Co-operation and Development (OECD) in its Programme for International Student Assessment (PISA) and by other international agencies.

Underlying Thinking

You have to practice what you preach. Modeling ongoing inquiry sends a powerful message, and you learn things essential to improvement. You are always testing and refining your theory of action. You learn to get better by gaining strategic insights of the kind that Duggan (2007) discusses. He says that such purposeful work builds on "intelligent memory" (what you have been experiencing) in a way that sparks new insights leading to more effective action. Such "flashes of insight" do not occur every day, but they are bound to emerge if you are immersed in implementing the kind of theory described in this chapter.

Two-Way Communication

If you do not have a sound theory of action, if your vision is mostly rhetoric, or if the vision espouses goals but is relatively silent on strategy, no amount of communication will get you anywhere. But if the strategy is solid, communication is of the utmost importance.

The first step to effective two-way communication within the education sector is taking every opportunity to state the reform strategy. This will help clarify it in the mind of the communicator, it will help clarify it for others, and it will provide ample opportunity for feedback and refinement. This is an exercise in giving and receiving information. Further, because this communication is coupled with action (for example, capacity-building experiences), the meaning becomes increasingly ingrained in the minds of educators. Leaders at all three levels—school, district, and state—should be able to articulate the strategy with a high degree of consistency and agreement, which also supports greater commitment by all.

The communication component of TASC is very much a two-way street: speaking and listening go hand in hand. Feedback from two-way communication provides ideas for reshaping or refining a strategy, and problems with implementation are often revealed and can then be acted upon. People know that leaders are not perfect, so being open about problems is necessary, and it can be seen as a sign of strength in a leader as problems are addressed.

Communication with the broader public is more complex. One of the most fundamental goals of system improvement, which should be stated and restated publicly, is to increase the public's confidence in the public education system. Since this is a goal and since transparency is part of our theory, evidence has to be constantly communicated to parents and the community. It is equally critical to situate the public school system in relation to societal improvement. The ultimate goals of system reform—literate and numerate citizens, social cohesion along with diversity, the development of positive character traits, low poverty, economic prosperity, and the general well-being and happiness of the population—all figure into the reform, not through the education system alone, but as a vital part of the larger community. We are, after all, talking about *societal* improvement.

Communication should be both small and big. Sometimes it is about individual school success, about parent engagement at both the local and school levels, and other times it is about the health of the society as a whole. In short, communication is an opportunity to disseminate and receive feedback, especially when communication is about vision and strategy. It is highly meaningful and commitment-generating when it is grounded in capacity-building, based in evidence, and related to solving and identifying problems. The outcome of good communication is prosperity and society's positive well-being.

Underlying Thinking

Change strategies in large systems are complex. It seems that a perennial complaint is that people do not see the big picture. Maybe the problem is that system leaders do not, in fact, have a clear policy, especially with respect to implementing the change. Or maybe people interpret the same policy differently. How many leaders have complained that their policies are crystal clear but practitioners seem to misunderstand or misinterpret them?

Policies and strategies require many more times the communication than you might rationally feel is sufficient. And when you articulate strategies along with progress or lack thereof, you become more clear, you monitor and spur implementation, and you continually link to people's ongoing new experiences. Communicate often, but be sure you have something specific to communicate about.

Bringing New Ideas to the Surface

This six-part theory of action for system improvement is grounded in intensive action of more than 10 years, and it holds up well when compared to evidence in the wider literature. Using TASC in Ontario, for example, has increased literacy and numeracy within 4 years, reduced (but by no means eliminated) the achievement gap, cut teacher attrition in the first 3 years of teaching by more than two thirds, and increased the morale of all (McIntyre, 2006; Ontario Ministry of Education, 2008). We continue to expand what we consider to be desirable education outcomes, such as the well-being of the whole child; the relationship between literacy, numeracy, and the arts; greater parent engagement; and so on. And these broader outcomes redound on the action theory itself and its components, resulting in continuous improvement of the theory.

There is still much work to be done in Ontario and in other jurisdictions that are showing strong interest in the ideas implemented there. You may ask, "What if the leaders of my government, district, or school are not interested in a theory of action that I know has great promise?" Well, one of the reasons we put new theories of action into place and then report on them is to provide people with ideas that they can promulgate and use. But in the final analysis, you have to do what you can in the situation in which you find yourself. At a minimum, you should influence your immediate sphere of relationships by advocating and supporting the actions embedded in our theory of action.

Finally, the theory of action presented here is just one theory; it is open to critique. It is this critical analysis that brings new ideas to the surface. Remember the criteria for an effective theory of action presented in the beginning of the chapter: It must promote system change, movement toward improvement, and motivation. Critique of existing strategies brings system reform to ever-higher levels as long as it is done with sound reasoning, evidence, and alternative recommendations. This is what "change wars" are all about—debating and sorting out promising theories of action. I maintain that the theory outlined in this chapter stands up well to empirical scrutiny. Good theories of action have another advantage—they "travel well" to other problems and jurisdictions, as I have shown in the six secrets of change (Fullan, 2008a). Give me a good theory of action over a strategic plan any day of the week.

References

Childress, S., Elmore, R., Grossman, A., & Johnson, S. M. (2007). *Managing school districts for high performance: Cases in public education leadership.* Cambridge, MA: Harvard Education Press.

Duggan, W. (2007). *Strategic intuition: The creative spark in human achievement.* New York: Columbia Business School.

Fullan, M. (2008a). *The six secrets of change: What the best leaders do to help their organizations survive and thrive.* San Francisco: Jossey-Bass.

Fullan, M. (2008b). *What's worth fighting for in the principalship* (2nd ed.). New York: Teachers College Press; Toronto: Ontario Principals' Council.

Fullan, M., Hill, P., & Crévola, C. (2006). *Breakthrough.* Thousand Oaks, CA: Corwin Press.

Gawande, A. (2007). *Better: A surgeon's note on performance.* New York: Metropolitan Books.

McIntyre, F. (2006). *New teachers thriving by third year. A report from the Ontario College of Teachers.* Toronto: Ontario College of Teachers.

Ontario Ministry of Education. (2008). *Energizing Ontario education: Reach every student.* Toronto: Author.

Make the Most of Your
Professional Development Investment

Let Solution Tree schedule time for you and your staff with leading practitioners in the areas of:

- **Professional Learning Communities** with Richard DuFour, Robert Eaker, Rebecca DuFour, and associates
- **Effective Schools** with associates of Larry Lezotte
- **Assessment *for* Learning** with Rick Stiggins and associates
- **Crisis Management and Response** with Cheri Lovre
- **Classroom Management** with Lee Canter and associates
- **Discipline With Dignity** with Richard Curwin and Allen Mendler
- **PASSport to Success** (parental involvement) with Vickie Burt
- **Peacemakers** (violence prevention) with Jeremy Shapiro

Additional presentations are available in the following areas:

- At-Risk Youth Issues
- Bullying Prevention/Teasing and Harassment
- Team Building and Collaborative Teams
- Data Collection and Analysis
- Embracing Diversity
- Literacy Development
- Motivating Techniques for Staff and Students

Solution Tree

555 North Morton Street
Bloomington, IN 47404
(812) 336-7700 • (800) 733-6786 (toll free)
FAX (812) 336-7790
email: info@solution-tree.com
www.solution-tree.com

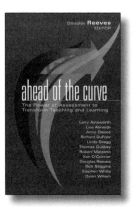

On Common Ground: The Power of Professional Learning Communities
Edited by Richard DuFour, Robert Eaker, and Rebecca DuFour
Examine a colorful cross-section of educators' experiences with PLC. This collection of insights from practitioners throughout North America highlights the benefits of PLC. **BKF180**

Ahead of the Curve: The Power of Assessment to Transform Teaching and Learning
Edited by Douglas Reeves
Leaders in education contribute their perspectives of effective assessment design and implementation, sending out a call for redirecting assessment to improve student achievement and inform instruction. **BKF232**

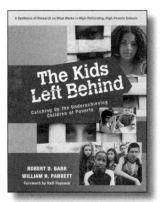

Revisiting Professional Learning Communities at Work™: New Insights for Improving Schools
Richard DuFour, Rebecca DuFour, and Robert Eaker
This 10th-anniversary sequel to Professional Learning Communities at Work™ offers advanced insights on deep implementation, the commitment/consensus issue, and the human side of PLC. **BKF252**

The Kids Left Behind: Catching Up the Underachieving Children of Poverty
Robert D. Barr and William H. Parrett
Successfully reach and teach the underachieving children of poverty with the help of this comprehensive resource. **BKF216**